BUSINESS, POLITICS, AND THE PRACTICE OF GOVERNMENT RELATIONS

Charles S. Mack

Foreword by F. Christopher Arterton

D0209905

Quorum Books
Westport, Connecticut • London

Library of Congress Cataloging-in-Publication Data

Mack, Charles S.
   Business, politics, and the practice of government relations /
   Charles S. Mack ; foreword by F. Christopher Arterton.
      p.   cm.
   Includes bibliographical references and index.
   ISBN 1-56720-057-5 (alk. paper)
   1. Lobbying—United States.   2. Business and politics—United
States.   3. Pressure groups—United States.   4. Associations,
institutions, etc.—United States—Political activity.   5. Lobbying—
United States—States.   6. Business and politics—United States—
States.   7. Pressure groups—United States—States.
8. Associations, institutions, etc.—United States—States—
Political activity.   I. Title.
JK1118.M276   1997
322′.3′0973—dc21   97-19230

British Library Cataloguing in Publication Data is available.

Library of Congress Catalog Card Number: 97-19230
ISBN: 1-56720-057-5

First published in 1997

Quorum Books, 88 Post Road West, Westport, CT 06881
An imprint of Greenwood Publishing Group, Inc.

Printed in the United States of America

The paper used in this book complies with the
Permanent Paper Standard issued by the National
Information Standards Organization (Z39.48–1984).

10 9 8 7 6 5 4 3 2 1

To Alice
Still the bringer of joy

Contents

Foreword

One rarely comes across a foreword that picks a fight with the book it introduces. There are good reasons for this: Not only is such behavior bad manners from an invited guest, but also the book's author has the option of adjusting the manuscript to those critiques with which he agrees or omitting the offending foreword entirely if the criticism seems inappropriate. Nonetheless, I believe this is that rare moment, even though I know that Charley Mack will agree with much of what I have to say.

Mack's task is to describe and advocate the techniques of effective lobbying. As the reader will quickly learn, he does so with remarkable success, providing a rich arsenal for those who would affect government policy making. He is a true believer in the correctness and indeed righteousness of the lobbying profession. Though he provides a brief defense of the craft of lobbying against its critics, his instincts are—quite naturally—to get on with the task at hand rather than to mount an extensive theoretical argument on behalf of the profession. But, in introducing a book on lobbying, I think it imperative to advance an affirmative argument that lobbying is not merely an inevitable ingredient of politics but serves, in fact, as an essential and positive requisite of American democracy.

As everybody who opens a book on this topic surely knows, the profession of lobbying is, to say the least, controversial. Why? As Mack correctly points out, these political rights of assembly and petition stem directly from the thought of our Founders and are expressed clearly and definitively in the First Amendment. Lobbying enjoys the same protections and the same legitimate standing as freedom of speech and a free press. Why should this activity not engender the same respect? Why should lobbying provoke such visceral criticism?

Consider, first of all, the possibility that the complaints themselves are politically motivated, that they emerge from one political or philosophical perspective that doesn't like the results. But even though every policy dispute is likely to generate complaints from the disappointed that somehow the process was "unfair," it cannot simply be that the critics disagree with the policy directions that emerge from the government institutions that are lobbied. Any fair reading of the policy directions of the American government over the past three decades—the years in which professional lobbying has come into its own—would surely conclude that policy has been as heavily influenced from the left as from the right.

Rather, the core of the argument attacking the craft of lobbying is that, as a result of its consequences, well-financed "special interests" distort the policy process to their own benefit and to the detriment of the general interests of society. All four of the elements of this argument—narrow interests, unequal resources, effective influence, and perversion of the common interest—are essential to the indictment. While each element is open to debate, the whole is more powerful than the sum of its parts because, by aggregating these components, critics surround their lament with the insinuation that lobbying is inherently undemocratic. In effect, the exercise of influence in the political process, a First Amendment right, is cast as an undemocratic practice.

In *The Electronic Commonwealth*, my coauthors and I described three separate models of democracy—three different theories, each with different institutional projections into the real world of American politics—which have traditionally characterized American politics. One certainly is the impulse to majoritarian rule, institutionalized in the electoral system, undergirded by populist sentiment of both the left and right, and giving expression to our general will as a nation and society. But that model cannot be the "be all and end all" of the democratic instinct in America. As Bernard Crick points out in *In Defense of Politics*, majoritarian democracy can become highly autocratic and dictatorial. He quotes Tocqueville, "If ever the free institutions of America are destroyed, that event may be attributed to the omnipotence of the majority."

The affirmative value of lobbying draws its justification from a second model of democratic practice, the pluralist conception of politics. Here expressions of the collective will of citizens come about through the formation of groups which represent their interests. Recognizing that the policy views and concerns of citizens in a diverse society would necessarily diverge and clash, the Founders deliberately sought to create institutions that would channel this inevitable conflict into the policy process. Where elections institutionalize responsiveness to majorities among citizens, the politics of pluralism become manifest through lobbying and representation within the processes of government policy making.

The mechanisms of responsiveness to the pressure of group conflict provide a critical safety valve for the pressures that inevitably emerge from majoritarian institutions, which, in theory, provide for equality among citizens (one person, one vote) and achieve political solutions by counting up numbers. But the raw counting of votes cannot embrace inequities in the intensity with which people hold preferences and calculate their stakes in the outcome of government. Therefore, all political conflict cannot be successfully resolved by recourse to a common interest or general will expressed through majoritarian politics. On this point, Charley Mack quotes Clausewitz's famous dictum that war is an extension of politics by other means. As Mack also notes, the inverse applies as well: If the mechanisms of resolving group conflict peacefully are choked off, social violence will inevitably result.

The third model of democracy evident in American intellectual history and political institutions—communitarian democracy—rests its claim upon efforts to advance common rather than private goals. Its proponents view democratic politics as a process of debate and discussion among citizens. Through active participation, members of a community come, by persuasion and accommodation, to share a common understanding of the policies, interests, and values that unite them and define their community and common interests. Traditionally, the New England town meetings and the jury system represent "real world" institutions that have sought to implement this vision of democracy. Numerous associations and organizations function under procedures which institutionalize these principles.

It would be a mistake to conclude that one model is preferable or more correct than another. Although these complex theories recognize important values, each also has its limitations and detriments. The headlong pursuit of one model to the exclusion of the others would undoubtedly lead to some conspicuous pathologies. In fact, the genius of American democracy results from preserving all three of these rationales for self-government. In order to solve social problems without violence and coercion, we need to maintain a balance in which articulations of community values, assertions of private interests, and expressions of the majority will all have an opportunity to offset and counterbalance each other.

Those who castigate lobbying as a process depriving the nation of its capacity to advance common concerns may have a legitimate point—to the extent they are addressing the relative balance of institutional power. But they cross over the line if they do not, at the same time, grant a fundamental legitimacy to this type of politics. Well meaning though their argument may be, to the extent these critics propose eliminating the pursuit of private interests through pressure on government policy making, they are advocating the destruction of a major component of American democracy.

Within the last three decades, the prospects of maintaining a symmetry of effective power among our political institutions—so as to give expression to these different values—have proven increasingly difficult. Two trends, professionalization and technology, are pushing us toward greater reliance on the politics of majoritarianism. On the one hand, as argued in *The Electronic Commonwealth*, the emerging communications media promote the use of plebiscites to implement majoritarian democracy. Since Charley Mack's instruction in the techniques of lobbying serves to champion professionalization, however, we should pay more attention here to the ways in which that trend—though it would, on its face, seem to be advancing pluralism—might actually be working to tip the balance toward majoritarianism.

Over the past two decades, the dominant strategy for mobilizing political power in both the electoral and lobbying domains has shifted from organizing to marketing. As a result, our politics are becoming increasingly depersonalized. Modern political professionals, more detached than their predecessors, have contributed to this trend. In the pre-existing system, strong party leaders relied on networks of personal contacts as critical to their power. Precinct leaders who knew voters personally were themselves distinct individuals to the bosses up the line. In legislative politics, the image of the backslapping lobbyist buttonholing legislators in the corridors of power is one in which personal connections constituted the base coinage of influence.

Those who learn from Charley Mack will follow a very different strategy, one essentially grounded in the techniques of marketing. The evolution is easier to observe in electoral politics. Modern campaigns attract voters probabilistically rather than personally. Based on their research findings, professional political managers reason that if they send out this mailing or run that television ad they will (they hope) achieve certain results. They no longer endeavor to enlist a cadre of individual persons in their cause. Instead, they labor to achieve a statistical response in which the actual individuals who exhibit that response are more or less interchangeable. Similarly, effective interest-group activity has shifted away from membership associations to organizations that derive their power through responses to direct mail. Membership becomes synonymous with contributing financial support from afar rather than participation in face-to-face meetings in which views can be exchanged. Corporate grassroots lobbying, which seeks to mobilize various stakeholders, can be conducted very much in this way. And so on through a list of examples in which, as our public life has become more complex, the problems posed by sheer numbers and diversity have impelled political managers to employ marketing approaches to mobilizing political support.

The importance of this change, which is supported and amplified by media technologies from public opinion polling to C-SPAN, is that legislative politics have become more subject to a referendum mentality in which practitioners nurture and respond to majority sentiment. Legislative opinion and public opinion become linked more closely, as each community is better able to observe and monitor the other. For example, as polls on the whole panoply of policy issues before a legislature become more common, policy making responds more to sentiment in the public at large than it does to pressures internal to the legislative process. As a result, political institutions across the board are increasingly susceptible to majoritarian impulses.

This issue may well be part of a larger problem that shapes contemporary politics. Political leadership—and those who undertake to lobby government institutions should certainly think of themselves as political leaders—requires a difficult balancing act between responsiveness and initiative. If they are to accomplish anything, leaders must be simultaneously empathic and manipulative. But as the activities of those in public affairs have become more observable to the public, the manipulative aspects of leadership—particularly when practiced as an exercise in marketing—have become all too apparent to the citizenry. The resulting cynicism toward politics and politicians that has become so evident in large segments of American society suggests that we must find the means of restoring a capacity for responsiveness to the leadership equation. Otherwise, professional political managers will find their marketing techniques losing power to evoke appropriate responses from citizens.

For the lobbyist, this problem poses a special difficulty. Paradoxically, as lobbyists apply the techniques of marketing to their endeavors, they may be weakening the very intellectual framework upon which their craft is based. Far from acknowledging the inherent legitimacy of private interests, practitioners of majoritarian politics tend to depreciate "special interest" factions in favor of the general will or common cause, however inchoate and ill defined those terms may be in any given situation.

Though it may sound simplistic, perhaps even banal, an answer can be found in remembering that in advancing political interests, lobbyists represent real people. The legitimacy of their cause—in fact of the profession as a whole—derives from relationships in which those people, those citizens, play a genuine part. No less than the elected public official, those who represent interests must recognize that their interactions with citizens obligate them to responsiveness as well as initiative.

F. Christopher Arterton
Dean, The Graduate School of Political Management
The George Washington University

Preface

Government is the largest single expense of doing business—for any company, in any industry. The business community has learned that it must manage its relationships with government effectively, regardless of which party controls the White House or Congress. Other interest groups, many of them adversaries to business, have increased the scope and sophistication of their efforts to affect public policy. The capability of business enterprises and associations to protect and advance their own interests through effective government relations therefore assumes ever-growing importance and complexity.

The tactics and tools of government relations have expanded accordingly. When I wrote *Lobbying and Government Relations* almost a decade ago, the field included direct and grassroots lobbying, political action, leverage through associations and coalitions, and the like. These techniques have become even more sophisticated in the '90s and will continue to do so for the foreseeable future. Computer and communications technologies are dramatically changing almost every aspect of government relations. Companies, business associations, and other interest groups are becoming involved in politics in ways that were not legally permitted just a few years ago. International government relations has become a major arena, supplementing activities at the federal and state levels that have themselves altered significantly.

Although this book started out to be a new edition of the 1989 work, most of its content is wholly new or substantially revised. For example, the chapters on international lobbying and interest groups are completely new. Other chapters have been updated and expanded to incorporate material on technological applications, new management techniques such as benchmarking, changes in lobbying regulation, new forms of political participation, and much else. Data from 1996 surveys of corporate management of government relations have also been incorporated.

No book of this kind can be prepared without the generous assistance of others, and I had more than my share—particularly from Christa Jones who was my indispensable research assistant. Her skill at unearthing information and source materials contributed significantly to the book. Aimee Malenfant assisted in the preparation of the appendix and in other helpful ways.

I am grateful to F. Christopher Arterton, dean of The Graduate School of Political Management at The George Washington University, not only for the thoughtful foreword he contributed to this book but also for his persistence in recruiting me to teach at the school. I continue to find it a stimulating experience.

Raymond L. Hoewing, the recently retired president of the Public Affairs Council, scrutinized many of the chapters and suggested a number of improvements. If this book has flaws, they are not for lack of my old friend's constructive criticisms.

Leslie Swift-Rosenzweig, executive director of the Council's Foundation for Public Affairs, reviewed the chapter on grassroots. I am also indebted to her for her impressive knowledge of source materials and unfailing graciousness in providing me with access to them.

Dr. Steven Billet, Director of Federal Government Affairs for AT&T, who represented his company in Brussels for several years, provided a number of thoughtful comments that improved Chapter 10.

Bernadette A. Budde and Carol A. Farquhar, colleagues on the staff of the Business–Industry Political Action Committee and the two best political analysts in the field, evaluated Chapters 13 and 14. I particularly want to thank them and my other friends and colleagues on the BIPAC staff who contributed significantly to this book in many ways, most of which they are unaware. Hardly a day goes by during which they have not broadened my knowledge and understanding of politics and its relationship to government affairs.

The late Richard A. Edwards, former senior vice president of the Metropolitan Life Insurance Company and, later, Kappel Professor of Business–Government Relations at the University of Minnesota, was unstintingly generous in his suggestions and support for the 1989 book. He is deeply missed by his fellow professionals in government relations and especially by his friends, among whom I was privileged to count myself.

Another departed friend, Don R. Kendall, taught me a vast amount about politics and the legislative process. Although he did not live to see the preparation of this book, it could never have been written without the knowledge and wisdom Don and his wife Barbara shared with me over three decades. His former colleagues at BIPAC mourn him every day.

My wife, Alice Barrett Mack, has been a constant source of loving encouragement and editorial advice. None of my books could have been written, or much else in life accomplished, without her support.

Others, regrettably far too numerous to mention by name, provided substantial information and advice on various subjects, for which I am most grateful. Of course, I alone bear the responsibility for any errors of fact or judgment the book may contain.

We are all creatures of our experiences. Mine are the product of a career spent in political activity and the service of business organizations. Those experiences and the points of view they produced are reflected in these pages. This book is not about policy or philosophy, however, but about process.

The government relations techniques used by business are also available to the vast number of other interest groups striving within this American republic. This book is offered to each of them in the conviction that the competition among them enhances democracy and the public interest in these United States.

Chapter 1

What Is Government Relations?

Congress shall make no law respecting establishment of religion, or pro-
hibiting the free exercise thereof; or abridging the freedom of speech, or
of the press, or the right of the people peaceably to assemble, and to
petition the Government for a redress of grievances.
　　　　—The First Amendment to the Constitution of the United States

The creation of laws, and government to enforce them, dates back at least to
the development of the tribe. Politics surely arose at the same time ("If you
select me as our tribal chieftain . . . "). And the process of lobbying must have
been invented moments later ("Chief, let me offer a suggestion about a couple
of our customs.").

We associate the concept of lobbying with government, as this book does.
But, in truth, all of us lobby every day:

"Dad, would you talk to mom about a bigger allowance?"

"If you'll take us to Europe for that vacation, dear, I'll buy you that arm-
chair you've wanted."

"Boss, about that raise . . . "

"Dear God, please answer my prayers."

Lobbying in its broadest sense is persuasion, requests, pleas, and any other
form of communication intended to get others to do what we want. We are all
lobbyists.

But lobbying as the term is most commonly used is inextricably intertwined
with government, just as politics is.

THE ORIGINS OF LOBBYING

The interaction between government and the governed has been the subject
of continuing analysis and controversy since the invention of government it-

self. The Greek philosophers spent considerable time discussing the nature of humanity and its government. Much of both the Old and the New Testaments of the Bible is devoted to the subject: The flight from Egypt was an escape from a tyrannical ruler; the crucifixion was the result of a Roman bureaucrat's decision to rid himself of a troublesome preacher.

Our preoccupation with law and governance is, perhaps, the second most popular topic of human discourse. Virtually all of what we consider news relates, one way or another, to the subject. And where there is government, undoubtedly there are politics and lobbying. These three processes—government, politics, and lobbying—are so interrelated that it is not always easy to distinguish among them:

Government is the exercise of sovereign authority in ruling a society or nation.

Politics is the pursuit of governmental power.

Lobbying is the process of influencing public and governmental policy.

Lobbying involves the advocacy, either by individuals or by groups, of a point of view—the expression of an interest that is affected, actually or potentially, by the affairs of government. *Issues* are public policy proposals; the word implies a topic of contention, and indeed lobbying commonly involves an adversarial and competitive process between different interests. *Interest groups* are organizations comprised of individuals or enterprises with shared points of view on issues. The proliferation of organized interest groups has typified American democracy since the founding of the republic. (See Chapter 2.)

Government, politics, and lobbying will always exist in any human society. What distinguishes democratic societies is the relative freedom and openness accorded all three processes. It is not that politics and lobbying do not exist where freedom is restricted, but that where they cannot operate openly they will operate secretly, and sometimes violently.

For example, the civil rights, feminist, and gay rights movements have all been fights for acceptance by government, employers, and other segments of society. In other words, they seek to become legitimate interest groups. In democracies, acceptance and negotiation are typically nonviolent political processes. But violence occurs even in democracies when the process is protracted, as in the history of the American labor movement.

Revolutions and civil wars are fought to alter the politics and policies of the established government, if not to replace it so that other policies can be adopted. The Irish Republican Army pursues its goal of driving out the British and unifying the north and south of Ireland. Wars in Africa and the Balkans are fought to elevate the power of certain tribes and nationalities over others. Islamic fundamentalists seek to remake secular states like Algeria into theocracies like Iran. All such groups are restricted in various ways in their ability to advance their policies openly or peacefully, and all therefore utilize means that are often violent, but *always* political.

One need not necessarily sympathize with these causes to understand that each illustrates the dictum of the German military strategist, Karl von Clausewitz: "War is not merely a political act, but also a political instrument, a continuation of political relations, a carrying out of the same by other means." Another military strategist, Mao Tse-tung, echoed the concept a century later: "War cannot be divorced from politics for a single moment."

The American Revolution was just such "a political instrument" as were the secession of the South and the Civil War that resulted.

All successful revolutions produce political change. The transition to a multiracial government in South Africa was a revolution that occurred peacefully, but only after decades of violence. The disintegration of the Soviet Union at the end of the Cold War was revolutionary and largely nonviolent.

A movement that is impelled by strong beliefs about its cause but is prohibited from advancing it openly and legitimately will resort first to illegal protest and ultimately to violence. Whether such a movement is a political organization or an interest group is unimportant.

We have seen this principle at work even in modern day America. Decades afterward, Americans celebrate the success the civil rights movement achieved through nonviolent (though often illegal) protests. We prefer to forget the memory of soldiers patrolling the streets of the nation's capital and other cities in the wake of the rioting that swept across the country. The stability of the system was preserved because the country adjusted its official values and altered its laws (ultimately changing much of its people's behavior) to accommodate a political cause that had been unsuccessful through traditional lobbying in its efforts to change federal, state, and local laws. Had that accommodation not occurred, had that cause not been legitimatized, it would have been the riots in Watts and not the march on Selma that we remember today.

It is this openness and the ability to accommodate diverse needs that is fundamental to democracy. The freedom of groups to lobby, to attempt to reshape unwelcome public policies, is among the greatest strengths of the American political system.

LOBBYING AMONG GOVERNMENTS

Lobbying is not limited to the efforts of political or interest groups to affect government. The fact is that governments also lobby each other:

- New York City lobbies the state legislature for changes in mass transit laws.
- Wisconsin lobbies the Federal government for more financial aid.
- Canada has lobbied the U.S. Congress to change environmental policies, and American officials have lobbied the Canadian government for changes in foreign ownership laws.
- The states of central and eastern Europe lobby western European governments for admission to the European Union.

Indeed, between sovereign powers, diplomacy is often merely another form of lobbying.

Lobbying is also prevalent within governments. Perhaps the most active lobbyists of the U.S. Congress are officials of the White House and the departments and agencies of the Executive Branch.

Nor is intramural lobbying restricted to democracies. In a totalitarian or single-party state, the absence of competing electoral forces makes it all the more certain that economic and social interests will try to influence government policies through informal, personal approaches—that is, lobbying. In China, for example, a slowly emerging private sector is beginning to influence governmental policies, while the ministries and the Communist Party undoubtedly lobby prodigiously to affect each others' actions.

LOBBYING AND GOVERNMENT RELATIONS

The focus of this book is the government relations activities of private-sector interests.

To most Americans, the word *lobbying* is a more familiar term than *government relations*. Traditional lobbying is still the core activity of government relations, but only one of its components. What is lobbying? What is government relations? How do they differ?

Government relations is the application of one or more communications techniques by individuals or institutions to affect the decisions of government—at the local, state, national, or international levels, or some combination of them.

As used in this book, *lobbying* means the practice of the various forms of government relations that include

• Campaigns to mobilize constituents at the grassroots.
• Political fund-raising and contributions programs.
• A variety of communications technologies and techniques.
• Alliances with trade associations, and with other groups with their own agendas.

All these are the media of modern lobbying. The term, *direct lobbying*, is used in this book to describe the traditional form of personal persuasion and to distinguish it from the other techniques used today.

These tactics, taken together, comprise the art form called government relations. Explaining how each of these tools and tactics operates and meshes with the others, as part of a comprehensive government relations program, is the purpose of this book.

Many of the techniques of government relations have been adapted from innovations, first of marketing, and then of politics. Stimulated by intense competition to develop new products, by new approaches to market research, and by new avenues of persuasion, consumer marketers have blazed a trail that political marketers have since been applying to electoral competition. From there, it has been a simple step to adapt these approaches to legislative and regulatory advocacy.

Marketing, politics, and lobbying share a common characteristic, the need to persuade in order to sell. Whether the sale be that of a product or service, a candidate, or a public policy, each of the three fields has become ever more sophisticated in its sales approach. Marketing, spurred by economic incentive, generally has taken the lead in technical innovation. Politics and lobbying have borrowed many of these innovations freely.

Government relations applies marketing and political techniques to the objectives of lobbying, a set of skills typically utilized by the *private sector* to affect the policies and actions of the *public sector*.

THE IMAGE OF LOBBYING

Its importance and prevalence notwithstanding, government relations in America has never been the most popular form of human endeavor. To call someone an "influence peddler" is to damn him or her as one operating in the gray reaches of the law and business ethics. Nor are the connotations of the word, "lobbyist," significantly better. The Thomas Nast cartoons of the nineteenth century, showing overweight, cigar-smoking railroad lobbyists trading bags of money to legislators in return for their votes, are still part of the folklore of lobbying—often reproduced in history books for the edification of our youth.

The historic image has valid elements. Direct lobbying has had its excesses. Its coupling with political finance has often raised hackles among Americans, a people whose populist streak is part and parcel of our national character.

With such an image, many organizations shun the use of the word lobbying, preferring instead such euphemisms as *advocacy, policy representation, policy marketing, legislative communications, public affairs, government affairs*, and, of course, *government relations*. These terms all have different connotations, but each expresses the same essential idea—the organization of efforts to affect public policy. The exception is *public affairs* which, as used by most practitioners, covers not only government relations but also public relations, community relations, educational support, philanthropic programs, and the like.

WHY GROUPS LOBBY

Organizations (and individuals) lobby public officials for any of several reasons:

1. *To gain benefits or relief unavailable in the private sector.* The environmental movement turned to government for actions to regulate what it considered unacceptable behavior by business. Labor unions and civil rights groups sought from government what they could not win in the private sector, as gay and feminist activists do today. Companies and their trade associations sometimes seek relief from unacceptable market conditions or onerous government regulations.

2. *To gain or retain an economic advantage.* Groups seek to obtain or hold onto a privilege bestowed by law. Farm groups seek to retain and sometimes expand agricultural subsidies. Veterans' organizations press for improved benefits. Retirees fight any changes that they feel might weaken their income and medical benefits. Companies press for the elimination of restraints that hamper their ability to penetrate new markets.

3. *To gain relief or advantage at one level of government that has been denied at another.* Civil rights groups turned to Washington when they could not win the legislation they sought at the state and local levels. Some industries seek federal legislation, pre-empting a diversity of state regulatory activities that they feel interferes with interstate marketing. Other industries prefer state regulation and oppose federal intervention. Consumer groups and some state and local officials argue for pre-emption that sets a floor but allows state and local governments to impose stricter standards above the floor.

4. *To create beneficial programs.* Educational institutions lobby for enactment of grant-in-aid programs for which they can then apply as new revenue sources. Defense contractors work to persuade legislators to support new weapons systems that they can then bid to supply. Labor unions back public works programs that then become sources of new jobs for their members. Business groups support economic policies that encourage capital formation and investment, but that also reduce their taxes. Liberal groups press for other kinds of tax changes in order to redistribute income through new government social programs.

5. *To resolve public problems only governments can handle.* Whether for reasons of law or practice, there are certain problems that only governments can resolve. Because AIDS is a public health problem, it requires government action. Environmental issues have ramifications that often involve governments internationally as well as domestically. On issues as varied as international trade, school prayer, abortion, educational standards, and police protection, government makes the key decisions and in some cases the only ones.

Some people may look at these varied motivations to lobby and see selfishness and greed. Others see enlightened self-interest or even the public interest—perceived, astoundingly often, as the same thing. Some may see government as the court of first resort, others the last.

Groups lobby governments because government, and frequently only government, has the power to give them what they want.

THE DEMOCRATIC FUNCTION OF LOBBYING

Government relations performs three functions essential to the proper functioning of government and democracy:

1. Providing means for the resolution of conflicts, essential to the perpetuation of a democratic and mutually tolerant society.

2. Funneling important information, analysis, and opinion to government leaders to facilitate informed and balanced decision making.

3. Creating a system of checks and balances, comparable to that within our government, by which competition among interest groups keeps any one of them from attaining permanent power.

These concepts merit elaboration.

Conflicting Interests

Sorting out adversarial interests and points of view is a major function of government and of elected legislators in particular. Boiled down to its essentials, government relations is really only the organized expression of those interests and views.

Interests are inherently neither good nor evil. A basic tenet of elementary sociology is that every human being has multiple interests: jobs, family, hobbies, religion, social causes, civic concerns, taxpayer stakes, and innumerable others.

Differences arise between and among those interests, thereby creating issues. Some of those issues move into the public arena because of the size or number of interests affected. Those interests may already be organized. If not, and if the impact of the issue is great enough, a new special interest may be formed and a new organization established.

As individuals, the same proposal may affect our personal interests in different, possibly conflicting, ways. Consider the following example:

Let us say that the county is considering a program to expand an airport near my home. I travel considerably, and the airport now will be even more convenient since I can fly to more destinations on more airlines. New companies may be attracted to the area, and this will increase the value of my home and perhaps provide new opportunities for my business. New jobs will be created, which is good because my son is always looking for one.

However, the planes take off right over my home and the roar is very annoying. Sometimes the noise is so bad that it gets on my wife's nerves, and then our medical costs go up. It also disrupts rehearsals of a string quartet in which I play. Local taxes will rise to fund the costs of airport expansion and road construction to get the additional passengers to the airport. All this construction will jeopardize the flop-eared jacknape, an endangered species I am committed to preserving.

As individual citizens, we sort out our own conflicting personal pressures all the time. But the personal conflicts pale into insignificance compared to the problems of the government officials who must somehow resolve the competing interests of local citizens, homeowners, and taxpayers . . . environmental groups . . . airlines now serving the airport that would like to keep out competing airlines wanting to come in . . . labor unions, the construction industry, and local merchants who want to see new jobs created . . . the state and federal agencies that regulate airports, to say nothing of local governments of the neighboring communities . . . and, of course, my quartet, my son, my wife, and her physician.

All these interests will have something important to say on this issue—and they have every right to say it in every legitimate medium they can find and afford—to the legislators who must make the ultimate decision.

It is the job of the legislator to sort out all those competing, conflicting interests and decide what the public interest really is on this issue.

Information and Diversity

The public also tolerates lobbying because the system benefits from the expression of diverse views. No legislator nor government agency can possibly have all the information needed to make sound public policy decisions. But the affected interests do.

The late Richard A. Edwards, who was a top government relations executive for many years before joining the academic world, offered this perspective:

Lobbyists serve essentially the same role in the legislative arenas that lawyers do in the judicial branch. Every point of view, on all public policy issues, is or can be provided by lobbyists to those responsible for the formulation of public policy, national and state. The reason is clear: Lobbyists have access to the information needed for the creation of regulatory and tax policy that is founded upon actuality rather than assumption. The conflict of opinion among lobbyists provides the legislators with a comprehensive spectrum of decisional options, a rationale in support of or opposition to each, and relevant factual data.[1]

In marshaling their arguments, interest group advocates add value to the legislative process by bringing forth data, analyses, insights, and points of view that policymakers must have in order to make rational and fair decisions on the issues. Indeed, legislators frequently solicit information from interest groups and their representatives.

Because interest groups and their lobbyists generally play adversarial roles on particular issues, they tend to act as a rein on each other, preventing any single interest from getting too powerful for too long. Business groups contend with unions on various issues, but the contention may also be intramural. Company X favors certain tax changes that Company Y opposes. Union A fights tax benefits for industry; Union B supports them to the extent they create new jobs for its members. One environmental group opposes commercial nuclear power for safety reasons; another group favors it because it is the principal alternative to petro-power that may be damaging the ozone layer; both fight the efforts of some manufacturers to ease clean air and water regulations.

Thus, each group tends to check the others while elected lawmakers sort out the substantive and political factors involved in public policy decision-making. No one interest is allowed to dominate for very long. Cycles in public opinion, working through the political process, keep interest group alliances of either the left or the right from gaining permanent ascendancy.

Moreover, the very debate between competing interests and competing lobbies contributes, win or lose, to acceptance of the process, just as it does in both law and electoral politics. Knowing that at least it has had its day in court and that there are other opportunities and other issues, each interest group accepts the validity of the legislative process, often agreeing to compromises that make the final decision at least tolerable.

Thus, in our pluralistic society, it is the breadth, skill and comity of interest groups that allow democratic policymaking to occur.

This is no small asset in a society as heterogeneous as ours. Groups vie for their points of view, struggling to prevail totally if they can or at the very least to gain as much of their position as circumstances permit. Yet, in the end, the policymakers decide, and the decision is accepted—without recourse to the military strategies of Clausewitz—and rarely even to public protests.

Even in the advanced democracies of western Europe, unpopular legislative decisions have often led to huge demonstrations and even general strikes. In still other countries, usually far less socially diverse than the United States, unpopular governmental decisions have commonly produced riots, military coups, and violent revolutions. Though hardly unknown in America, violence tends to be rarer here.

Many factors work against violent refusals and protests in this country, but lobbying—the interaction of the legislative and lobbying processes that allows each point of view to be heard—surely ranks high on the list.

It is the ability of the lobbies to express and represent their rival interests that allows those interests to tolerate each other and for democracy to function—and perhaps even survive—in America's diverse and constantly quarrelsome society.

Which brings us back once again to the problem of defining what government relations in America is really all about.

Government relations encompasses all the means used by the people, operating through their interest groups, to keep their governments responsive to social and economic demands. Government relations, together with the processes of free elections, is the lubricant that allows competing social and economic forces to contend within the democratic framework. Indeed, government relations is the complex of instruments used by interest groups to hold government accountable between elections.

Examining those diverse instruments is what this book is all about.

NOTE

1. Richard A. Edwards, "The Ethics of Lobbying," *Ethics: Easier Said Than Done*, Spring/Summer 1988, p. 106.

Chapter 2

Interest Groups

> An association for political, commercial, or manufacturing purposes, or even for those of science and literature, is a powerful and enlightened member of the community, which cannot be disposed of at pleasure or oppressed without remonstrance, and which, by defending its own rights against the encroachment of the Government, saves the common liberties of the country.
> —Alexis de Tocqueville

Americans as individuals probably have no greater range of personal interests than the people of any other advanced society. Interest groups exist in every country, but nowhere else in the world is there a nation with the sheer number and diversity of organizations found in the United States.

Interest groups are organizations that are formed to advance and protect the common interests of their members. A simple directory of such associations runs into multiple volumes and grows with each new edition. About a thousand new associations are created annually. The diversity of these groups is astounding. There are organizations of barbed wire collectors, aardvark aficionados, prostitutes, flying chiropractors, and descendants of the illegitimate children of British monarchs. Hermits are perhaps the only people without their own association, and it would not be surprising to find that even they get together from time to time to discuss the fine points of living alone; in fact, with today's technology, they can communicate without ever actually meeting. The management of associations is a recognized profession, and of course, its practitioners have their own organization, the American Society of Association Executives, a large and active interest group.

THE NATURE OF INTEREST GROUPS

Interest groups, at least those with an economic concern, have their origin in the merchant and craft guilds that existed in ancient civilizations and that became a dominant institution in the middle ages, enduring in Japan and some European countries into the nineteenth century.

The rise of organized interest groups in America can be traced back to the early eighteenth century, and they have proliferated without limit to this day. The oldest business organization still active in this country is the New York Chamber of Commerce (1768); the second oldest is the New York Stock Exchange (1792).

Government relations is only one of the functions of interest groups, and there are undoubtedly many organizations that do not practice it. Many exist simply to provide a venue in which members can discuss the niceties of their common interest or to promote it. Others engage in a range of services that may include setting standards, buying discounts and affinity credit cards, offering insurance and education, issuing publications, advertising, and undertaking public relations. Virtually all hold meetings and conventions of varying frequency and duration. Is there a human being in this country over the age of six who has never attended a meeting of some organization?

Why do interest groups arise? Primarily to advance and defend the needs of their members and to differentiate themselves from others, especially in socially, economically, and (today perhaps) technologically complex societies. Complexity is not all of the story, however. The more homogeneous the society, the smaller the impulse for people to distinguish themselves by identifying a particular interest and creating an interest group to represent it; the more heterogeneous the society, the greater that impulse. Japan and European countries are complex societies, but they are still more homogeneous than the United States—which is a major reason that interest groups abound here.

In this country, interest groups have tended to grow in spurts. Some arose with the social and economic changes that followed the Civil War, notably because of the rise of rival interests. Unions, for instance, gained strength as labor increased its efforts to organize and gain power, and that in turn led to an increase in the number and strength of business associations to combat them. Associations also grew during the Depression and in response to war mobilization efforts in World Wars I and II. The greatest increase has occurred since 1945, with the rapid economic, social, and technological changes that have taken place. Interest groups have also grown in importance as that of the political parties has diminished, assuming to an extent some of the functions the parties formerly performed.

INTEREST GROUP THEORY

Interest groups have been widely studied and analyzed by observers, analysts, and political scientists, not all of whom see the role of interest groups as wholly beneficial. Some who have were Alexis de Tocqueville—the first serious student of the subject, who viewed them as one of America's great strengths—and David Truman. Truman argued that in our pluralistic society competition between groups results in public policies that at least approximate what the public wants and so that no single group will be predominant.[1]

Another point of view sees this analysis as idealistic. There are always organizations whose funding, membership size, single-mindedness, or political access are such that they consistently prevail over other interests lacking those resources. Examples include the National Rifle Association on gun control, tobacco companies on smoking issues, and the American Association of Retired Persons on Social Security reforms.

There is also the related argument that the power of interest groups produces stalemate and diminished accountability in government. Congress and succeeding administrations have never been able to develop a coherent energy policy, for instance, because of the power of competing interests: those who want to discourage dependence on oil imports and to develop energy sources not based on petroleum and coal versus others who oppose increased oil consumption taxes and the development of nuclear power. Potent interest groups often stalemate each other. Moreover, their self-protection efforts can diminish competition and economic performance and productivity—as some labor unions and industries have done in their resistance to competition from imports.

Interest group competition can also result in the application of public resources to conflicting objectives. The federal government famously spends considerable sums to discourage smoking while simultaneously paying subsidies to tobacco farmers.

Interest groups have grown so powerful in America, said another political scientist, Theodore Lowi, that government has ended up providing protection to almost every interest, some substantial, some symbolic. He called this phenomenon "interest-group liberalism," which, he said, provides "the system with stability by spreading a *sense* of representation at the expense of genuine flexibility, at the expense of democratic forms, and ultimately at the expense of legitimacy."[2] "Interest group liberalism is pluralism," added two other political analysts, "but it is *sponsored* pluralism, and the government is the chief sponsor."[3]

All of which leads into the running debate about what is in the "public interest," as contrasted with "special interests." There are several difficulties with these concepts. First, "special interests" is a term of opprobrium that is used to mean, "selfish groups that are opposed to mine and to my enlightened point of view." Second, there has never been agreement as to what constitutes "the public interest." Like Justice Potter Stewart's oft-quoted remark about obscenity, we can't define the public interest, but we know it when we see it (or think we do). The difficulty is that characterizations of the public interest are all in the eye of the beholder. Ralph Nader, the apostle of latter-day populism, defines the public interest as that of consumers, consciously excluding the interests of producers, sellers, and the economic "establishment" overall—even arrogating the term to title his satellite organizations "public interest groups."

The public interest—however defined—surely includes *all* interests, and not merely those we choose to drape in a mantle of nobility. The concept remains an important one, but the term has become so abused as to be vacuous.

PROFILES OF MAJOR INTEREST GROUPS

Because interest groups are the operators of government relations, it is worth examining several important organizations and interest group sectors. ("An 'interest group sector' is a set of organized groups that share broadly similar policy concerns, such as labor, business, or ideologically oriented groups.")[4]

Business Groups

The interest group sector that comprises the business community is perhaps the largest and most complex of all. Individual companies, especially larger ones, often behave like interest groups in their own right. Many have their own government relations offices in Washington and the state capitals. (See Chapters 8 and 9.) Also contained within this sector are such organizations as the following:

• Umbrella organizations, such as the U.S. Chamber of Commerce or the National Federation of Independent Business, that represent companies in any industry. Umbrella organizations exist at the state level, too—usually called state chambers of commerce or business councils. Local chambers of commerce also abound.

• Restricted umbrella groups, composed of companies in groups of industries. Examples are the National Association of Manufacturers and the National Retail Federation. Such groups are also found at the state level but seldom locally.

• Trade associations that represent companies in a specific industry or line of business. If the industry is quite large, in addition to organizations representing its interests as a whole, other groups may speak for significant segments.

• Professional societies, made up of individual practitioners in specific professions or occupations, some of them associated to some degree with the business community (e.g., accountants), but by no means all. Medical societies, especially the American Medical Association, have frequently been closely allied with the business community in the past, although they are not part of it.

• A wide range of specialized business organizations, some of which lobby and some of which do not. This category includes a large number of groups like the Business–Industry Political Action Committee and the Public Affairs Council, Better Business Bureaus, and business policy and research organizations, such as the Conference Board and the Committee for Economic Development.

No two of these types of organizations are structured or behave identically, but there are recurring patterns that can be illustrated by a look at the National Association of Manufacturers.[5]

Established in 1885, the NAM represents more than 12,000 companies that produce 85 percent of the nation's manufactured goods. Affiliated with it are about 150 national trade associations and state manufacturing associations which, together with the NAM's direct members, contribute to its grassroots lobbying capability.

The NAM's primary purpose is to lobby the federal government on behalf of the interests of U.S. manufacturers, including the development of a pro-growth economic agenda. Virtually all associations utilize a structure of specialized committees to establish their positions on current issues, and the NAM is typical in this regard. Its committees deal with labor relations, employee benefits, energy and natural resources, environmental quality, regulatory reform, federal fiscal policy, international trade and finance, public affairs, and so forth. Most committees are divided into several even more specialized sub-committees and task forces. Again, as in most associations, recommended issue positions go to the board of directors for approval. Theoretically, association boards coordinate potentially conflicting recommendations and assure consistency with past positions. In practice, this role is generally performed by the staff.

A problem for many large, heterogeneous associations is the role of their small business members. In many such organizations, smaller companies feel overwhelmed by large corporate members. In the NAM's case, 10,000 of its 12,000 members are companies with fewer than 500 employees. NAM deals with this problem through a special staff department and committee that organize conferences, promotional events, and publications dedicated to the interests of its smaller members. A substantial percentage of its board members are drawn from this membership segment.

The NAM's staff is quite large. There are more than sixty people at its Washington, D.C., headquarters, about three dozen of whom are issue specialists and lobbyists. NAM's lobbyists are regarded as among the best representing national business associations. In addition to advocating NAM's issue positions to Congress and various regulatory agencies, these specialists staff the various committees and organize its various issue conferences. Unlike many other associations, NAM does not have a single annual meeting, but instead holds conferences in subject areas that largely parallel committee jurisdictions.

Other staff members deal with law, communications, association affiliate liaison, administration, and membership services. Most of the latter focus on membership sales (primarily via telemarketing), with a smaller group distributed among ten regional offices that also provide informational services and liaison with larger members.

NAM's Public Affairs Steering Committee and its five-person staff, headed by a senior vice president with extensive political experience, guide the development of association policy on lobbying and campaign finance legislation. They also administer its political education and grassroots programs to inform and involve the membership and motivate them to communicate with their senators and representatives on current legislation.

As a matter of policy, NAM does not have a political action committee. Instead, it provides strong support for the Business–Industry Political Action Committee

(BIPAC), an independent organization that works to elect pro-business candidates for Congress but, unique among business PACs, does not adopt issue positions or lobby Congress. BIPAC has an extensive program of political research and analysis on congressional campaigns and candidates, and its publications and briefings are highly regarded in the business community. In addition to the individual contributors and business PACs that provide the funds for its candidate contributions, BIPAC's Business Institute for Political Analysis is supported financially by about a thousand companies and business associations. Among its major supporters are NAM, the U.S. Chamber of Commerce, and the Business Roundtable, along with a number of corporations.[6]

A persistent, if sporadic, problem for business has been a lack of lobbying coordination among companies and associations on particular issues. The most obvious cause has been a conflict of interests and therefore of positions. An industry that depends on imported components, for instance, will have a position on certain international trade issues diametrically opposed to another industry that makes the products with which the imports compete. Sometimes, there have been other causes—notably competition among trade associations that may agree on the issue but are reluctant to cooperate or share credit.

This has been a diminishing concern in recent years, as interest groups have learned, often the hard way, that it is better to share credit than to lose. As a result, a growing number of ad hoc issue coalitions have arisen to coordinate lobbying information and action. (See Chapter 12.)

Cooperation among business associations took a major advance in the 1996 campaign when a number of umbrella and trade associations agreed to form a *political* coalition to protect Republican majorities in Congress. The triggering events were, first, the AFL–CIO's announced campaign to defeat those majorities and return control of Congress to the Democrats (discussed later); and, second, an analysis by BIPAC that described a number of campaign techniques that federal court decisions had recently legitimized. The U.S. Chamber and the NAM, among other associations, then created a new political structure called simply, "The Coalition," which contributed significantly to the reelection of the Republican Congress. (More on this will be found in Chapter 14.)

The success of this political cooperation may contribute to expanded use of legislative coalitions in the future.

Labor

Union involvement in politics and lobbying was perceived as a dire necessity if the organized labor movement was to survive its formative years and achieve the objectives it was unable to win in direct dealings with management. Labor's fortunes have ebbed and flowed since its great legislative successes began in the Depression of the 1930s, but the high priority given its legislative and political activities has not been seriously debated within the labor movement in over half a century. Indeed, the fight for the presidency of the AFL–CIO in 1995 was not about whether labor should be involved but about its political effectiveness.

The history of the labor movement's commitment to government relations is a classic illustration of interest group theory. What unions could not win in negotiations with business they sought from government. The alliance with the Democratic Party and the administration of Franklin Roosevelt led to the enactment of a considerable body of legislation raising wages, changing working conditions and, most notably, legitimizing (in the Wagner Act of 1935) the right of unions to organize workers without employer coercion or interference. Government thereby became the statutory protector of labor unions.

Labor was the nation's politically most powerful interest group for more than thirty years. Its successes, however, contained within them the seeds of its own downfall. High labor costs drove manufacturers to relocate operations to lower-cost, often nonunion facilities in the south and, later, to sites in other countries. Union membership began to decline significantly. Labor's response was to adopt the self-defeating stance of protectionism. The obvious benefits of imports to consumers, and to industry through global competitive pressures were too much to resist, however. The unions lost all these battles, under both Democratic and Republican presidents.

Meanwhile, major changes were occurring within the labor movement itself. Union membership continued to decline in the private sector—from more than 17 million in 1970 to fewer than 10 million in 1997, but a great upsurge took place in unionization of government employees at all levels; public employees now constitute almost a quarter of the AFL–CIO's membership.[7] Union membership as a percentage of the labor force continues to drop (14.5 percent in 1996). The AFL–CIO has announced a major campaign to improve its public image and recruit women, particularly, to join its seventy-eight member unions.[8]

Three developments epitomized the weakness that beset the labor movement: a steady series of legislative defeats in Congress during the 1980s and 1990s; negotiations with employers that were characterized by labor "givebacks" rather than management concessions; and the Reagan administration's success in crushing a striking public employees union, the air controllers' organization.

The Republican Party's capture of Congress in the 1994 elections triggered a "now-or-never" attitude among many union leaders, including those heading the public employee unions. In a palace revolt, the longtime president of the AFL–CIO was forced out; his lieutenant was subsequently defeated in a hotly contested election. The new president, John Sweeney of the Service Employees International Union, pledged to revitalize union organizing and labor's political and government relations effectiveness. Sweeney announced a $35-million campaign to help reelect President Clinton in 1996 and, particularly, to win back control of Congress for the Democrats. Mr. Clinton was reelected, but the congressional campaign was a failure. The GOP retained its majority in the House of Representatives, losing only a handful of seats, and actually gained two seats in the Senate.

Part of labor's political problem is that it simply does not speak for a substantial portion of its membership although it uses their dues to finance its campaign activities. The Friday after the 1996 elections, the head of the AFL–CIO's political operations bragged on a C-SPAN program that "only" 35 percent of union members had voted Republican the previous Tuesday, according to exit polls. He was pleased, he said, because 40 percent had voted for GOP candidates in 1994.

Labor's failure and diminished stature were evidenced shortly after the 1996 election when President Clinton reorganized his cabinet for his second term. Spurning the unions' choice for secretary of labor, he named an innocuous second-tier White House aide to the post.

The AFL–CIO and most individual national unions maintain sophisticated political and legislative operations. Each union may have several lobbyists working Congress, advocating positions of special importance to the union but working on broad labor issues with colleagues representing other unions, coordinated by the AFL–CIO's legislative department. With millions of members, labor can mobilize an impressive and daunting grassroots response on its issues, even if only a fraction of unionists participate. In political campaigns, the unions participate actively and aggressively in both primaries and the general election. In many states, labor still can affect the nominating process to assure that candidates who support union positions receive the Democratic nomination. These candidates receive substantial, often massive, help in the fall campaign through union political action committee contributions, phone banks and precinct workers, strategic advice, polling services and other in-kind contributions, and now increasingly through the use of advocacy advertising. This kind of assistance is made available to favored candidates for state and local offices, as well as those running for Congress or the presidency.

Unquestionably, organized labor's financial resources, membership size, and aggressive political activities will maintain it as a significant interest group for many years to come. Its influence and effectiveness, though, are no more than a shadow of what they once were, brought low by economic and political forces that the unions themselves inadvertently helped bring about.

Minority Groups

Civil rights groups have a constituency that is mainly black (to some extent Hispanic); they have been deeply involved in government relations for reasons similar to those of organized labor, namely, their inability to achieve their objectives within the private sector. These organizations substantially broadened the government relations arena through extensive and largely successful use of the judiciary to alter public policy when legislative efforts stalled. Like labor, civil rights groups also successfully brought issues to Washington when they felt thwarted by state and local governments or the private sector, and they and their members enjoy the protection and the patronage of the federal government.

Black organizations often have been effective lobbying organizations, using most of the same techniques that other groups do. However, their political infrastructure is unique among interest groups in that it is primarily centered around black churches. Black ministers, of whom Martin Luther King, Jr., and Jesse Jackson have been among the best known, tend to be actively involved in politics and civil rights organizations. They frequently endorse candidates from the pulpit, endorsements that carry great weight with their congregations.

Blacks vote overwhelmingly for Democratic candidates on the whole, and this is the cause, ironically, of a serious problem for them, both politically and legislatively. Frequently, they find their leverage reduced because most Republican candidates know they will receive few black votes, and Democrats know that blacks will either vote for them or stay home on Election Day rather than vote for their opponents. This limits blacks' ability to negotiate on key issues. A major political factor in the passage of the 1996 welfare reform bill was the fact that the Republicans knew they had little to lose among black voters and much to gain among suburban whites.

The two fastest-growing minorities are Hispanics and Asians, Hispanics by total numbers and Asians by percentage growth. Hispanics will outnumber blacks early in the 2010s, according to Census Bureau projections. It is erroneous to think of Hispanics as a monolithic group because of their diversity of traditions and political behaviors. Hispanics are made up of three principal strains and several minor ones: Mexican-Americans in California, Texas, and the southwest; Puerto Ricans in New York, New Jersey, and the elsewhere in northeast; and Cuban Americans, residing primarily in Florida. Mexican-Americans and Puerto Ricans, who have had difficulty in rising economically, tend strongly to vote Democratic. Cuban-Americans as a group have risen much faster economically; powerful anti-Castro feelings have generally impelled them toward Republican candidates, although they gave their votes to Clinton in 1996 because of certain actions concerning Cuba taken by his administration, helping him carry Florida, the first Democratic presidential nominee to do so in several decades.

Hispanic interest groups have been regionally focused rather than national. Despite some rivalries, Puerto Rican organizations and, to a lesser extent, those of Mexican Americans have usually cooperated with black organizations. Cuban-American organizations seek to influence national policy primarily through Florida's congressional delegation.

Asian Americans are even more ethnically diverse, primarily comprising of immigrants and their descendants from China, Japan, the Philippines, Korea, and Vietnam. As a group, they have tended to have a high work ethic and to place a premium on education for their children, often moving into high middle- and upper-income levels within a single generation. Their votes have therefore often gone to Republicans, except on those occasions when Republicans gave them a reason to vote Democratic (as they did in 1996 on immigration-related issues, primarily in California).

Immigrants from Asian countries tend to head, at least initially, to the sunbelt cities of the south and west plus New York, Chicago, and Washington, D.C. However, there are localized aggregations of some groups—Vietnamese in Houston and Minneapolis–St. Paul, and Asian Indians in Chicago, for example.

Agricultural Interests

For American agricultural organizations, government relations has long been a high priority because of farmers' economic fragmentation and their dependence on government support to ease high susceptibility to great swings in weather and market conditions. Farm lobbying efforts have also often been fragmented, perhaps less than those of business, but more than labor's. The political power of agriculture has declined somewhat along with its relative economic importance in America but is still quite substantial—in large part because so many individual farmers are politically active and in frequent touch with legislators on their needs and issues. Agricultural groups are often exceptionally influential on price support policies for specific commodities, ranging from milk and peanuts to tobacco and cotton.

Competing agricultural interest groups have often taken contrary ideological views toward the role of government. Some have favored a high degree of government regulation of crop production and prices to minimize the boom-or-bust cycles that historically have beset agriculture. Others, such as the American Farm Bureau Federation, have preferred minimum controls to allow free competition and greater exports.

New legislation adopted by the 104th Congress (1995–1996) made major changes in commodity price supports and acreage controls, intended to enhance agricultural competition and, ultimately if not in the short run, to reduce federal expenditures for farm programs.

The Environmental Movement

Among newer interest groups, such as those concerned with the environment and consumers' interests, the need to be involved in lobbying has rarely been in question. The few debates that have occurred have largely taken place within older organizations like the Sierra Club that had longstanding programs that many members had feared would be lessened in importance if lobbying became a major priority, as it indeed now has. Most of the environmental and consumer groups that arose during the 1960s and thereafter—such as the Consumer Federation of America and the Natural Resources Defense Council—were created for the express purpose of influencing governmental policies, and this remains an overriding objective for virtually all these groups. Indeed, the most recent controversies have centered on the question of whether these groups are *too* partisan politically, as one author suggested in 1988.[9] Since then, the question has been largely resolved in favor of increased partisanship and aggressive lobbying. Consumer interest groups (some of them founded and funded by the AFL–CIO) have been moderately active lobbyists but largely uninvolved politically.

Environmental organizations, however, have become exceptionally active in politics in recent years. Although these interest groups have given some aid to a small number of moderate Republicans, the principal beneficiaries of their political support have been Democrats. The League of Conservation Voters periodically publishes its "Dirty Dozen" list of members of Congress whose voting records the League finds most objectionable. Its 1996 list included one Democrat and eleven Republicans, one of whom was at that point not even an incumbent.

The environmental interest group sector includes a number of organizations with essentially similar objectives—the Sierra Club, the League of Conservation Voters, the Environmental Defense Fund, Environmental Action, the Natural Resources Defense Council, the Wilderness Society, the Friends of the Earth, the Audubon Society, Greenpeace USA, the National Wildlife Federation, the Defenders of Wildlife, the World Wildlife Fund, and the Nature Conservancy, among others.

In terms of membership, the largest of them range in size from Greenpeace (nearly two million), the National Wildlife Federation, and the World Wildlife Fund (both nearly one million), down to groups in the low five figures. Financially some, like the Nature Conservancy, have huge budgets, while others barely top $1 million.[10]

Although all these interest groups could no doubt make a vigorous case for the need for each to exist, they compete for members and other funding sources. They are in broad, if not complete, agreement on at least core environmental issues, if not always on peripheral ones like the 1993 North American Free Trade Agreement.

On the other hand, there are shades of green. Groups like the Environmental Defense Fund are willing to consider that free-market incentives are a way to tackle environmental problems. Others, like Greenpeace and the Sierra Club, have a deep-seated hostility to business and capitalism.

Some (though certainly not all) environmental organizations rely on scare tactics and extreme language to solicit membership and funds. An October 1996 solicitation for the Sierra Club's Legal Defense Fund contains words and phrases like, "fouled . . . corrupted . . . exterminated . . . wholesale destruction . . . degradation and ruin . . . annihilating . . . atrocities . . . greedy polluters and exploiters with unlimited resources." Nor is this kind of language limited to fund-raising. One congressman who opposed the Sierra Club on an issue was described in a statement as an "eco-thug."

Many environmental organizations stagnated financially or suffered losses in the early and mid-1990s and consequently reduced staff, closed offices, and cut some operations. Interest groups like these thrive on adverse political conditions, however; and it would not be surprising to learn that membership and revenues improved after control of Congress passed to Republicans, many of whom oppose further environmental regulation.

Unlike many other liberal activist interest groups, however, the environmentalists had some success in resisting conservative encroachments on their earlier gains. Public opinion polls show that the voters have considerable sympathy for the environmental movement. Because of that, environmental groups were able to assemble legislative coalitions of Democrats and moderate Republicans that, for the most part, kept the conservatives at bay. As a result, congressional conservatives have more recently eased some of their more extreme positions.

Nonetheless, environmental groups joined with labor unions and other elements of the liberal coalition to mount a major effort to defeat congressional Republicans in 1996. Their first success occurred in January of that year in an Oregon election to fill a vacancy in the Senate. Groups such as the Sierra Club and the League of Conservation Voters utilized political action committee contributions, independent expenditures, direct mail, and door-to-door canvassing to mobilize support for the Democratic candidate, Ron Wyden. Wyden narrowly defeated Republican Gordon Smith. (Smith ran again in the November election for Oregon's other Senate seat and won, despite renewed environmentalist opposition.)

The political efforts of the environmentalists met with some success in the 1996 general election; among the League's "Dirty Dozen," seven were defeated, the sole Democrat and two Republicans were reelected, and two GOP Representatives were elected to the Senate.

Ideological movements like environmentalism often do best when there is a group or individual whom they can satanize. As long as conservative Republicans control Congress, environmental causes will embrace their enemy with joy.

Senior Citizens

Debates over the future of Social Security and Medicare are not only about finances. They have at their root hard demographic projections: America is getting grayer, with the median age steadily rising. At mid-decade, the number of people over 65 is half that of children under 18; in thirty or thirty-five years, both population cohorts will be equal. People over 85 are the fastest growing age group. As recently as 1950, the working age population was sixteen times the number of people on retirement. Today, there are 4.5 working Americans for each retired person. By the 2030s, demographers project only two workers per retiree—which means that the working-age population will bear a steadily increasing share of the aged's social and economic costs. Without major reforms, Social Security and Medicare taxes may consume one-third to half of workers' paychecks in that decade, *before* deducting federal and state income taxes.

Such statistics imply that ideological conflict in the twenty-first century may be not so much right versus left as young versus old. Generational issues inevitably will dominate the politics of the next century.

The interest group that will be at the heart of these debates is the American Association of Retired Persons. AARP, with 33 million members over the age of fifty, is the second largest interest group in America. The only one larger is the Roman Catholic Church. AARP's membership is three times that of all labor unions combined.

In eight years, AARP's membership has grown by close to half, and its revenues have increased by more than 40 percent. Its dues are minuscule ($8 a year); the bulk of its income comes from commissions on the sale to its members of mutual funds, insurance, prescription drugs, travel discounts, automobile club memberships, credit cards, and the like—and from federal grants, a subject of congressional criticism and IRS investigation.

AARP has become possibly the most feared interest group lobbying the nation's elected officials. Even if most of its members join for the buying discounts and only relatively few respond to its grassroots appeals for help on legislation, a small percentage of 33 million is still a very substantial number of letters and telephone calls to congressional and state legislative offices. Retirees have more discretionary time than the working population and have repeatedly shown their willingness to use it to lobby their legislators on issues affecting them personally. Moreover, people over 65 are more likely to register and vote than young people.

Grassroots clout of that magnitude, plus a lobbying budget that approaches $7 million annually, obviate any necessity for a political action program or other forms of political activity. The only threat to AARP's continued legislative influence is the growth of rival interest groups, such as the Gray Panthers, the 60/Plus Association, the Seniors Coalition, and the United Seniors Association. At least in part because of the rise of other senior citizen organizations, AARP's "market penetration, as a percentage of the over-50 population, has slipped four percentage points since 1990 to 48 percent. Without new growth in membership, market share will drop to 44 percent by the year 2000."[11]

AARP's lobbyists have sometimes shown a willingness to negotiate on issues affecting the aged, but the organization also supports broad liberal positions, not merely increased federal spending for social programs benefiting the elderly but also public housing, minimum wage increases, rent control, tax increases, and President Clinton's ill-fated 1993 health care proposals.

In 1988, AARP discharged its executive director after less than four months on the job; the organization's board reportedly concluded that his philosophic preference for private-sector remedies to address the needs of the aging was incompatible with AARP's longstanding commitment to governmental action.

That commitment continues to dominate its legislative positions. Whether AARP modifies its traditional positions to participate constructively in the coming national debates over Social Security and Medicare reforms, or chooses to stonewall on behalf of its members, will be an absorbing study in interest group politics.

Cause Groups

Cause groups have an interest that is essentially ideological or social rather than economic. Among the earlier cause groups in recent decades are those founded by or affiliated with Ralph Nader; active on diverse agendas, they share a common aim of demolishing corporate interests wherever they can find them. Many environmental and some consumer organizations behave like subspecies of cause groups.

Cause groups span the ideological spectrum from left to right, as illustrated by the abortion issue; both pro-life and pro-choice organizations are cause groups. Some cause groups confine themselves to direct lobbying and grass-roots advocacy. Others not only have comprehensive government relations programs but immerse themselves in politics as well.

The Christian Coalition is one of the most potent of the latter. Made up of essentially social conservatives, the organization is closely allied with the Republican Party. It lobbies at all levels of government on behalf of its issues—a pro-life stance on abortion, support for school prayers, opposition to sexual content in the mass media, and so forth. The coalition has utilized rather sophisticated techniques to advance its agenda. For instance, it cooperated closely with the Republican leadership in the 104th Congress in pursuit of various economic and budgetary measures to build good will for later action on its social issues. It employs the full range of government relations techniques from direct lobbying to political action, from grassroots to issues advocacy. The Christian Coalition has also borrowed a tactic from black groups, employing Protestant churches to get out its Election Day message. Rather than relying on overt endorsements from the pulpit, however, the coalition hands out millions of leaflets comparing the views of competing candidates on its issues; the effect is probably the same, but the coalition has managed to avoid challenges to its tax status. However, it is being sued by the Federal Election Commission, which claims the coalition's political activities have crossed the line into activities of a political committee and wants it punished for not registering as such.

Think Tanks

Think tanks—no one calls them policy research organizations anymore—have become a ubiquitous adjunct to the public policy process. Often fugitives from the ivied halls of academe, their staff personnel tend to be highly educated researchers and analysts—often former government officials who want to make a significant impact on public policy. Think tanks generally have an ideological point of view and fall somewhere between pure research organizations and interest groups. The Brookings Institution at one time had so many alumni of Democratic administrations on its roster that it was called the government in exile during Republican presidencies. The American Enterprise Institute for Public Policy Research (AEI) filled a similar niche for Republicans.

There may be as many as two thousand think tanks today. They range from the Alexis de Tocqueville Institution, an organization of libertarian bent that has focused on immigration issues, to the Worldwatch Institute that periodically issues well-publicized forecasts of global doom on environmental and population issues. Most have more immediate, and political, agendas than proclaiming the falling of the sky, however.

Funded by combinations of foundation grants and business and individual contributions, think tanks have proliferated in recent years, with most of the newer ones oriented toward conservative agendas. (One that is not is the Progressive Policy Institute, affiliated with the centrist Democratic Leadership Council.) Organizations like the Heritage Foundation, the Cato Institute, Citizens for a Sound Economy, the Competitive Enterprise Institute, the Progress and Freedom Foundation, the Free Congress Foundation, and the Hudson Institute operate essentially as policy research arms of the Republican congressional majority. Those that are old enough (not a very large number) played a similar role with the Reagan and Bush administrations. The newer think tanks "have abandoned the tradition of detached scholarship, choosing instead an activist approach that fuzzes the line between research and advocacy. Many employ a younger generation of policy specialists who have forsaken the academic career ladder to flit back and forth to jobs on Capitol Hill. Instead of targeting an audience of scholars, they churn out policy analyses closely attuned to the agendas of their favorite politicians."[12]

A few, most notably Citizens for a Sound Economy, have overtly crossed the line from mere policy advocacy into direct legislative action. CSE has developed its own grassroots network of over 200,000 members and engaged in advocacy advertising on particular causes.

Increasingly, therefore, many think tanks are beginning to resemble ideological cause groups.

Intergovernmental Interest Groups

Governments lobby each other. A number of organizations of state and local governments and their officials exist to persuade the federal government to pay more attention to their needs and, indeed, to pay more to them—which is to say, more federal funding and more support for state and local programs.

Although lobbying is an important activity for these organizations, they do more than advocate the interests of their members. They also engage in policy analysis, collect and disseminate information, and facilitate communication and cooperation among governments and with some private-sector organizations. (See Chapter 9.)

The broadest of these groups is the Council of State Governments. CSG's members are the state and territorial governments, and it compiles from and for them a wide variety of comparative information and data. It also provides staff for a number of specialized groups, such as the National Association of Lieutenant Governors. CSG does not lobby.

Two intergovernmental organizations that do lobby are the National Governors Association and the National Conference of State Legislators. A few years after NCSL was formed through the merger of two other groups of state lawmakers, it suffered a secession when a group of conservative legislators left to create their own organization. The members of the new group, the American Legislative Exchange Council (ALEC), constitute more than a third of all state legislators. ALEC has a relationship with a conservative think tank, the Heritage Foundation, with which its headquarters are housed.

Other intergovernmental groups include the National League of Cities, the United States Conference of Mayors, the National Association of Counties, and the International City/County Management Association. All but the last lobby. There is also a large number of more specialized intergovernmental organizations.

Most of these groups are either headquartered in Washington or have offices there, many of them housed in an office building near Capitol Hill called, rather grandly, the Hall of the States.

NOTES

1. David B. Truman, *The Governmental Process* (New York: Alfred A. Knopf, 1964).

2. Theodore J. Lowi, *The End of Liberalism*, 2nd ed. (New York: Norton, 1979), 62.

3. Allan J. Cigler and Burdett A. Loomis, eds., *Interest Group Politics*, 4th ed. (Washington, D.C.: Congressional Quarterly Press, 1995), 5.

4. Beverly A. Ciglar, "Not Just Another Special Interest: Intergovernmental Representation," in *Interest Group Politics*, 4th ed., ed. Allan J. Cigler and Burdett A. Loomis (Washington, D.C.: Congressional Quarterly Press, 1995), 132.

5. For a more complete analysis, see Charles S. Mack, *The Executive's Handbook of Trade and Business Associations* (Westport, Conn.: Quorum Books, 1991).

6. In this era of full disclosure, it is incumbent on the author to reveal to the unwary that he is BIPAC's president and CEO.

7. Leo Troy, cited in *The Wall Street Journal*, February 18, 1997, p. A-24.

8. Ibid.

9. Douglas P. Wheeler, "A Political Handbook for the Environmental Movement," *The Washington Post National Weekly Edition*, September 19–25, 1988.

10. Christopher J. Bosso, "The Color of Money: Environmental Groups and the Pathologies of Fund Raising," in *Interest Group Politics*, 4th ed., ed. Allan J. Cigler and Burdett A. Loomis (Washington, D.C.: Congressional Quarterly Press, 1995), Chapter 5.

11. John Lombardo and Fred Williams, "AARP Feeling Its Age?" *Washington Business Journal*, February 2–8, 1996. See also Thomas J. DiLorenzo, "Who Really Speaks for the Elderly?" *Consumers' Research Magazine*, September 1996; Laura Muha, "Retiring? Hardly," *Newsday*, June 12, 1995; John L. Hess, "The AARP: America's Most Powerful Lobby and the Clash of Generations," *The Nation*, August 26, 1996; Marilyn Werber Serafini, "Senior Schism," *National Journal*, May 6, 1995.

12. Louis Jacobson, "Tanks on the Roll," *National Journal*, July 8, 1995.

Chapter 3

Issues Research and Issues Management

> Facts are stubborn things; and whatever may be our wishes, our inclinations, or the dictates of our passions, they cannot alter the state of facts and evidence.
>
> —John Adams

Issues research is important in order to develop sound positions and action plans, whether the issues be offensive or defensive, current or emerging. As in any other kind of managed activity, it is better to aim before firing. The aiming process in government relations means learning what is happening and why, what the impact is internally (on the company or among the organization's members), and also the significance externally—on friends, foes, and potential allies.

Researching issues involves three basic elements: (1) formulating the questions to get the necessary information, (2) knowing how and where to get the answers, and (3) analyzing and interpreting the results in the light of the organization's needs. The first two elements are discussed in this chapter; the third is the subject of Chapter 4.

Time frame is the critical first consideration. If the issue is current, the kinds of information needed and the actions to be considered are wholly different from those required if the issue is still emerging or long term.

RESEARCHING AND TRACKING CURRENT ISSUES

To develop sound intelligence on current issues, the government relations researcher will seek out answers to such questions as these:

- What is this issue all about? What are the key bills or regulatory proposals? What are their provisions? What is their significance?
- How, precisely, will it affect us?

- Who are its governmental sponsors? What interest groups are their backers and allies, both actual and potential?
- What is the rationale underlying the proposal, and what are the motivations of its supporters?
- Who are the issue's opponents, both real and potential?
- What are the rationales and motivations of opponents?
- Are there relevant government reports, academic studies, or other pertinent documentation on this issue?
- What are the issue's prospects? Is it going anywhere?
- What are the political implications of this issue? Is it part of some larger effort or movement? Does it relate to the fortunes of important interest groups, political leaders, or candidates?
- What is the likely timetable for action—immediate, near future, or down the road? What is the issue's probable lifespan if action does not occur in the near term?
- Will hearings be held? When? Who will testify? What are they likely to say?
- As the issue moves along, what is its status at any given time? Are amendments being offered? What is their significance?
- What are the long-term and strategic implications of this issue for our company or organization?
- Are there timely steps that could be taken either to promote or forestall action on the issue?

The issues researcher must develop answers to these questions that are both accurate and actionable. Information and intelligence should be verified to the extent possible (not always feasible, though, particularly on political matters). Research also needs to be kept completely up to date. Once issues start to move, they can progress with speed. The political, legislative, or regulatory environments can shift quickly.

Researchers get their information on issues from a large array of information sources—some published, some public though unpublished, and some private. Information from private, or "back-channel," sources is usually political intelligence about issues and their background and prospects. It is gathered on a confidential basis by lobbyists in the course of their activities and is critical to the effectiveness of direct lobbying on specific issues. (See Chapter 7.)

Issues research is being transformed by technology, enabling it to become increasingly sophisticated in a variety of ways. In part, this is because of the steady growth in availability of new data bases and tracking tools, in part because of new ways to correlate information and in part because of increases in personal imagination and creativity that these techniques stimulate. The researcher who thinks, "I wonder if I can find something on subject X," no longer needs to set the idea aside because it would take too long to look up. Tools like the Internet and on-line services not only make it possible to get the information in minutes but also to integrate or correlate it with other forms of data, producing analyses that were impossible or impractical not very many years ago. (Technology in government relations is discussed in further detail in Chapter 5.)

Public Information Sources

Most of the information about issues is in the public domain—somewhere. However, information that is *public* is not at all the same as information that is *published*. Many of the essential facts about any issue are readily available, but a great many are not. The latter are almost always available, though, to researchers who know how to go about getting them. (The most valuable trait in an issues researcher is not so much in knowing the answers to questions as in knowing how to find them.)

Networking

Apart from published information sources, there are vast networks of individuals who can provide much of the information needed to understand an issue. These include

- Issue experts in the Congressional Research Service of the Library of Congress and their counterparts in state legislative information services.
- Staffs of individual legislators and legislative committees.
- Personnel in executive and regulatory agencies.
- Government relations personnel and issue experts in other companies and organizations.
- Trade and professional associations' staffs, particularly including issue experts with such umbrella business groups as the U.S. Chamber of Commerce, the National Association of Manufacturers, the Business Roundtable, and the National Federation of Independent Business—as well as state and local business councils, chambers of commerce, and other trade and business associations.
- Researchers with think tanks, other policy research organizations, and academic institutions—and those with state government resource groups.
- Political and public affairs organizations, such as the Business–Industry Political Action Committee (and its state counterparts) and the Public Affairs Council.
- Research staffs of national, state, and local Republican and Democratic committees.
- The Conference Board and other business research groups.
- Staffs of such non-business interest groups as labor unions (particularly the AFL–CIO at both national and state levels), environmental groups, consumer organizations, and cause groups.

Every government relations and public affairs professional has a network of such sources, often cultivated and maintained over the years. Researchers, even those of competing organizations, often maintain relationships to trade data.

Published Sources

The firms and organizations that specialize in publishing information on government policymaking have grown into a major American industry. There is an enormous wealth of published information on both governmental and political developments, as well as specific current legislative and agency issues. Directories, published annually and sometimes more frequently, list legislators, their staffs, and executive and regulatory officials at federal and state levels, and occasionally for local governments. Other directories enumerate lobbyists, trade association personnel, and the like. The researcher's problem is less in obtaining data than in winnowing it to manageable proportions for useful analysis.

Every day, more and more of this information can be found on the World Wide Web or through specialized on-line services, usually at little or no cost. Although there are wide variations in the amount and quality of data supplied, virtually every significant government agency and private-sector organization now has its own homepage on the web, updated frequently. (See the Appendix, "Sources and Resources," for information on where to obtain specific information.)

Legislative Reporting Services Proceedings and documents of Congress, the state legislatures, and the larger local governments are often published by government publications offices or sometimes by commercial firms. These include texts of bills, amendments and revisions; current status and legislative histories (i.e., chronology of actions taken on particular bills); hearing transcripts; committee studies, votes and reports (including minority reports); texts or abstracts of floor debates; recorded floor votes, and similar material. For the national legislature, most of this information is published in *The Congressional Record*, except for committee documents that must be obtained from the particular Senate or House committee. Much of this information is also available on-line.

Specialized commercial publications and on-line subscription services offer information on regulatory developments as well, indexing or abstracting by topic *The Federal Register* (the official record of departmental and agency procedures, rules, regulations, and announcements) and its state and local counterparts.

On-line data is almost always more current than printed materials, and allows users to import information into their own computers, perhaps combine it with materials from other sources, and manipulate in any of a variety of ways—for instance, cross-tabulating the legislative sponsors of a bill by their political contributors. The principal disadvantage of on-line services relative to their printed counterparts is cost: Frequent usage of on-line services (especially commercial ones) can quickly become expensive.

The Press National and regional newspapers offer important coverage of issues at all stages, though rarely in vast detail. Some, like those listed in the Appendix, are "must" daily reading for certain kinds of issues, and versions are often available on-line. Others can be covered by subscription to a clipping service that will provide copies of stories covering particular topics or names (both individual and organizational).

Television and radio monitoring services provide transcripts to clients on broadcast coverage of particular problems, issues, or organizations. The electronic media are sources of news and comment but rarely of in-depth data. It is important, however, to know what the public is being told about relevant issues and developments.

Commissioned Data Market surveys, public opinion polls, and sociopolitical analyses can be commissioned from specialized firms to help ascertain the state of the public and business environment with respect to particular problems and issues. A large variety of commercial and academic resources offer services in these areas. Indeed, existing data of this kind may well be available through networking or other resources.

Government Publications Federal, state, and local departments, agencies, and commissions are generally invaluable sources of specialized studies, analyses, and compendia of information. For the federal government, the catalogs of the U.S. Government Printing Office are a good place to start.

Trade Associations and Other Interest Groups Virtually all organizations involved in the legislative process publish bulletins and other publications to update members on government and political developments affecting the industry within their geographic purviews. Many of these publications (and, increasingly, on-line services) provide the most authoritative information available from any source in their subject areas.

Trade Journals and Newsletters In many industries, privately published newsletters report in greater or lesser depth on governmental developments. Some are four-page monthly newsletters. Others appear daily, may run to nearly 100 pages, and include full texts of important documents.

Trade newspapers and magazines, typically published weekly or monthly, also cover legislation and regulatory developments affecting the industry—though typically in less depth than specialized newsletters or trade association publications.

Researching Federal Issues

Of the sources of information about the federal government, there is no end. New directories, almanacs, newsletters, tracking systems, on-line reporting, and data bases appear—and sometimes disappear—with dizzying frequency. Indeed, information about the structure, personnel, and doings of Congress and the executive and regulatory agencies has become so plentiful that the user's problem is how to sort through it all.

Virtually every industry and issues group is served by specialized issue-tracking services, mostly in the form of newsletters or other periodicals. Some of these are published commercially, others by trade associations and similar interest groups. There are also numerous broad-spectrum tracking and information services covering the federal policymaking structure. Among these, *Congressional Quarterly Weekly Report* and *National Journal* are indispensable. Other publications and media are listed in the Appendix.

Researching State and Local Issues

Obtaining sound information has always been more of a problem for those who lobby in the states (and even more so for local lobbyists) than for their Washington counterparts. This is a shrinking problem as computerized information grows, but there is often still little advance warning of planned actions, particularly at the regulatory level and in the smaller states and localities. On the whole, though, there is much more information available now and it is available on a more timely (though sometimes more expensive) basis. But timeliness does not always mean immediacy; even some of the on-line computer services may be several days late in reporting events and developments. There are far fewer occurrences than there once were of bills introduced and enacted before the information can become widely known, but the problem still exists here and there.

Interest Group Ratings

Many interest groups compile ratings of legislative voting records, particularly for members of Congress. (State legislative vote ratings are less common.) Such voting record indexes are popular because they provide a shorthand evaluation of the positions of individual legislators on issues of concern to the interest group and its members.

These ratings should be treated with caution. For one thing, the criteria (and sometimes the issues) are chosen more or less arbitrarily. For another, the votes selected are usually recorded floor votes, and not all votes are on the record (for example, voice votes cannot be recorded). Moreover, the particular vote included in the rating may or may not always be the most significant one on a particular issue; for example, a vote on a key amendment or a vote to table a bill may be more important than the vote on final passage. It is therefore possible to make any legislator look good or look bad, depending on which votes are selected for the ratings. Some groups are also much more careful than others in using objective criteria and language to describe the issue and its relevance to the interest group. Finally, a legislator's actions in committee (not usually rated) may be more significant in some cases than floor votes.

Ratings are also vulnerable to political manipulation. One interest group's ratings were publicly discredited some years ago when it revised them in response to complaints from some legislators and altered the issues to give those lawmakers higher scores.

In any event, a company or group with relatively few priority issues is likely to be more concerned with a lawmaker's actions on those bills than with how he or she scores on a broad, often ideologically selected index of issues.

It is not difficult to develop one's own analysis or index on issues. All that is required is to pick the key votes on priority issues, tally each lawmaker's vote on those issues, and run a percentage of the total. (Some groups consider an absence or other failure to vote the equivalent of a negative vote, which is quite unfair.) If the index is to be disseminated, the description of each vote included should be set forth as objectively as possible.

ANALYZING TOMORROW'S ISSUES

Issues never arrive unannounced. They arise out of developments and potentialities that emit signals in advance of their advent. But analyzing emerging issues is something like consulting the Oracle of Delphi. The clues to the future are all there, if only they can be read; with the acuity of hindsight, they are always perfectly clear.

The dilemma lies in being able to discern which of the vast number of possible issues are actually likely to materialize and do so in ways that will materially affect the company or organization. Thus, assessing both timing and the probability of impact is critical.

Books, articles, and papers in specialized, often obscure magazines and journals, publications of the so-called "public interest groups," the rise of particular bulletin boards and chat rooms on the Internet, a scientific study here, a speech there—all may be symptoms of the rise of a potential issue.

The development and growth of the environmental movement, for example, was telegraphed long in advance by Rachel Carson and other writers. As the literature on environmental concerns and problems expanded, longstanding conservation groups adopted environmental agendas and new activist groups began to spring up. After a time, the likelihood that the public agenda would shortly include environmental issues became predictable. But which issues? Around 1970, it might have been reasonable to conclude that air and water quality, solid and toxic wastes, would all be major candidates. Air and water turned out to be, of course. But toxic waste problems did not become truly major governmental issues until the 1980s, and the 1990s have largely been a decade of environmental fine-tuning and reform. Emerging issues analyses forecasting a national public policy crisis in solid waste disposal would have missed the mark, although there have been local problems here and there.

While forecasting which issues will affect any single enterprise is difficult, it becomes easier the nearer one gets to the event. On the other hand, the closer one comes to the explosive "critical mass" of the issue, the more difficult and expensive it becomes for individual companies to cope with it—and therefore the more reluctant they become to act pro-actively and the more fiercely they resist mandatory government remedies.

This is the dilemma for many business executives: Emerging issues are often too diffuse, too distant, and too hard to filter into the reality of the present to gain high corporate attention—even though they are far easier to cope with than they will be once they become current issues. Once tomorrow's issues become today's, the company knows what it is confronting, but by then the economic, social, and political costs of addressing them may well be vast.

There is often a psychological obstacle to recognition of an emerging trend. Many executives treat the unpleasantness such an issue would create by dismissing the issue as unimportant and its advocates as troublemakers. Being able to put aside such blinders and evaluate trends and issues objectively is not as common a trait among executives as might be wished. Nevertheless, objectivity is critical in evaluating the significance of emerging issues (and, for that matter, current ones).

Business executives are by no means the only group that finds future signals hard to discern. For example, few union leaders perceived that labor's political influence would decrease sharply in the 1980s and 1990s as a result of the decline in the nation's "rustbelt" industries, the pressures of overseas competition, the stabilizing of both inflation and unemployment at low levels, and the conservative political trend that swept the country.

The advantage of spotting issues early is that something can often be done at an early stage to mitigate the worst effects of the issue on a company or organization, if indeed not to forestall it altogether. There are two drawbacks, however, to recognizing emerging issues.

First, out of the many trends that can be identified at any given time, it is extraordinarily difficult to know which few will mature into major issues with great impact on the organization—not impossible, but very hard.

Second, even when this has been done and steps have been taken to alleviate the potential worst effects, it is rarely possible to state with assurance that the issue would not have died without help anyhow, as most such public trends and concerns do. This problem is complicated by fears among many government relations and public affairs professionals that their managements will mistake effective fire prevention programs to mean that the risk of fires has now died out and the organization no longer needs firemen.

Notwithstanding these difficulties, a clear understanding of the value inherent in emerging issues identification can significantly alter the public issues agenda for many interest groups. Especially for businesses, so frequently on the defensive in issues debates, programs to identify and manage such issues can enhance opportunities to utilize the techniques of government relations and public affairs to open the public agenda for beneficial objectives.

The Evolution of Issues

The Path of Emerging Issues
Concerns > Problems > Trends > Issues > Laws > Regulations

Issues first originate as concerns of an interest group or some other segment of the public. If that concern increases sufficiently, it will escalate into a need of that group, and pressures for change will begin to be felt. As the problem evolves, it will acquire a name, a very critical point in the evolution of issues for several reasons: First, a thing does not exist psychologically until it has been named; to label a concept is to give it life. Second, naming that concept also defines it; certain characteristics are defined in, others are implicitly defined out. Third, the name itself can empower the concept and turn it into an issue of public concern and debate. For instance, the concept that the public should have increased access to certain data in government files generated only modest public interest until naming it "Freedom of Information" turned it into an issue with vitality and excitement.

Max Meng has identified five stages in the life cycles of issues.[1]

Stage 1 is the potential issue: Isolated events may begin to develop into a pattern and then into a trend. Or a historical pattern may begin to increase in frequency or magnitude. The general public's attention has not yet been captured, but certain experts or interest groups adopt the problem as a cause.

In Stage 2, the issue is clearly emerging. A public crisis of some sort, an attention-getting book, or a court decision all can be crystallizing agents that begin to generate media attention and move the issue toward the critical mass necessary for legislative or regulatory action.

As the issue develops, the interest group that "owns" it seeks to broaden its support base. Other groups may begin to take an interest in the issue. It may become the subject of articles, first in specialized or even obscure publications, but then in the general media, electronic as well as print. Once an issue has reached this stage, it becomes possible to begin tracking it—to identify patterns and trends in its development.

This is also the stage in which the institution, industry, or other target of the issue can take proactive steps to neutralize or co-opt the trend. This may well be the target's last best chance to adopt a voluntary course that preempts governmental action.

In Stage 3, the issue has become current. Political figures become aware of it, perhaps because of a constituency interest. Friendly interest groups may bring it to the attention of lawmakers or candidates and urge them to become involved. These politicians may see the issue as a cause consistent with their personal beliefs or as an opportunity to "ride" it to more personal visibility and political influence. Any or all of these can be critical factors in building support for public policy action—legislative, executive, or regulatory. The target is now clearly in a defensive posture.

In Stage 4, the issue is at the crisis stage. Various policy alternatives compete, and one will survive the process of policy consideration and be enacted or adopted. The target has no option but to comply by altering its behavior.

Stage 5 is dormancy. Now metamorphosed into a law, the issue moves into the hands of the regulators where, as a government mandate or program, it will continue to evolve through regulatory and perhaps judicial case law. What was once an emerging issue is now a public norm, and even the target now proclaims its support for it. Dormancy is not death, however. Action or behavior that violates the new public norm may well resurrect the issue and give rise to even more stringent public policy.

When the issue, or rather the problem or concept underlying it, first began there were of a number of courses it might follow as it evolved. But at each of the phases in the issue's development, options disappeared. At some points, the issue might have been completely dissipated if certain private-sector actions had, or had not, taken place. At other points, resolution of the issue might have been possible prior to governmental action. At still later points, one governmental strategy might have been substituted for another, perhaps weakening it, perhaps strengthening it.

This pattern of issues evolution is essentially pyramidal: At the beginning, there are almost an infinite number of courses along which the issue might develop, but these become fewer and fewer as the issue evolves until finally there are only a few possibilities open; and then, at the end, there is only one.

Issues development is pyramidal in another sense too. The vast majority of potential issues are culled and winnowed at each progressive stage. Only a tiny fraction ever make it from one phase to the next. It is as if, millions of years ago, an observer were watching a number of unicellular species and trying to determine which ones would stabilize, which would become extinct, and which would someday evolve into intelligent beings.

This is the dilemma of emerging issues analysis. Clearly, the earlier the stage of an issue's development, the easier it is for an interest group to influence or transform it. But how is one to know which issues will eventually become full-blown, and which will fall away? Careful tracking, research, and analysis can provide valuable clues.

Emerging Issues: Leading Indicators

By the time issues reach the fourth stage, legislative or other policy action, they are well advanced in their evolutionary cycle. The introduction of a bill is a *lagging indicator*, a strong signal that an issue already has developed fairly extensively. Spotting the *leading indicators* is what emerging-issues analysis tries to do. The process of analyzing emerging issues utilizes a number of techniques that are part of a process called "issues management" (a misnomer since it is not the issue that is being managed as much as the organization's analysis and response to it. Issues management also includes action planning and implementation phases.)

Scanning and Tracking

Once someone has identified a potential problem, articles and papers about it begin to show up in periodicals. Research about scientific and technical problems is reported in professional journals; then in specialized magazines, newsletters, and reports; and then often in major newspapers. Social and economic developments are similarly analyzed and reported.

Content analysis data bases and services are available that report to clients on the trends in media coverage of current and potential issues. Other data bases and services track changes in the focus and concerns of particular stakeholder and interest groups.

Futurism is a specialized field of several research and consulting organizations that forecast trends, conditions, and potential issues. Some of these develop scenarios of possible events that could lead to significant social, economic, technological, or political developments. Others use different forecasting techniques, such as Delphic surveys, model-building, or matrices that analyze the impact of a variety of socioeconomic and technological variables on each other.

Several states are often *pacesetters* whose innovations others (sometimes including the federal government) tend to follow. The list of such states (and a few local governments) changes over time and according to the subject matter, but there are always some that others seem to follow. Oregon, for instance, has utilized voting by mail in some recent elections. Perhaps this is the start of a trend among the states, perhaps not. It is a signal worth watching.

Coverage, analysis, and public interest increase, of course, as issue indicators move from leading to lagging, or at least to immediate. *Public opinion surveys* are a principal signal of trends among major demographic groups or in the public at large. Surveys can be commissioned by individual clients on particular topics, but several survey research organizations offer subscription services to groups of clients in which they regularly report on public opinion trends and developments.

Less systematic, but nonetheless potentially valuable, can be "brainstorming" seminars with academic and issue experts. Dialogues with leaders of activist groups, so often the issue makers, can also point up concerns that may develop into future issues.

Screening and Evaluation

Hundreds of potential issues will surface through the tracking and scanning processes. These must now be screened and culled to produce a list meaningful and relevant to the company or organization. While specialized consultants can help in the winnowing and evaluation process, it is also possible to use an internal committee or task force for the same purpose.

Such a task force will be engaged in work that may be speculative in its process and sensitive in the implications of its findings. For that reason, it should not be attempted without the strong backing and participation of the highest levels of management. In the case of membership organizations, support must also come from the board of directors where the political power usually lies.

Members of the task force should be talented and imaginative individuals with a variety of skills, training, and expertise. While some of these will be staff experts, it is important also to include line personnel from operating units. They will not only add different and valuable insights and viewpoints, but also give the study group a credibility within the organization that avoids the taint of "another report from the ivory tower."

In a company, the mission of such a group is to assess the possible or likely impact of each potential issue on the company's existing or planned lines of business, markets, products, or services. In trade associations and other membership groups, the impact analysis will necessarily be somewhat broader, examining the industry's future development or current or planned programs.

To the maximum extent possible, these impacts should be quantified so that they can be compared and prioritized. The probability that events will materialize should also be estimated on a time scale. The interrelationship of impacts and probability can be charted as a guide to prioritizing issues for action planning. (See Figure 3.1.)

Dissemination

To be useful, the products of emerging issues analyses must be communicated to decision-makers as inputs to the strategic and business planning process. This might occur through distribution of an annual or semiannual issues inventory to corporate and operating managements or to association boards of directors and members. As an alternative, a periodic emerging-issues newsletter could be developed to disseminate research findings and analyses. Special reports are still another approach to communication. A corporate planning committee is a way to connect issue researchers and operating executives.

Whatever the medium, it should provide the following information:

- Name and brief description of the emerging problem, concern, or issue.
- Its background, history and origins, sponsoring or opposing interests, causes and symptoms of its development.
- Assessment of the time frame of its potential emergence and its potential *internal* impact on the organization—along with an evaluation of its possible beneficial or adverse *external* consequences. This assessment should also rate the issue's priority, based on the cross-evaluation of impact against probable emergence.
- The relationship of the issue to other existing or potential situations, problems, or information, including recommended positions and strategies.

Plans and Action

Some emerging issues will be potential threats. Others will present marketing or other kinds of opportunities. Many will have mixed or unclear significance. But all should be assessed with an eye to the possibilities of influencing their course to the organization's advantage. That, after all, is the purpose of an emerging-issues analysis.

Figure 3.1
Issue Impacts and Probability Chart

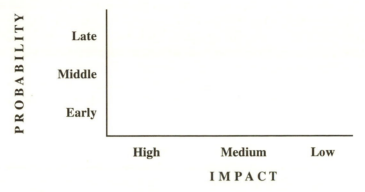

Issues that cluster at the lower left corner of the graph clearly demand priority attention; their impact will be great and they are very close to being current. That is not to say, however, that other issues should be ignored. Issues are fluid creatures; those of medium and low impact should continue to be monitored to be sure that they are not reshaped by someone else in ways that could be injurious. Conversely, it may be possible to take actions that would increase their potential for beneficial impact on the organization.

The most effective time to neutralize a potentially adverse issue is before it has become politically polarized. Once positions harden, interest groups and lawmakers become publicly committed, and emotions start to ride high. Issues become much more difficult to resolve amicably than they were before they became adversarial.

Action plans are imperative for high-impact issues although the nature of the action will depend on where the issue falls on the probability axis. Early issues, close to being current, should probably be treated tactically as such, utilizing as appropriate the various techniques of government relations. Longer-range issues, however, are susceptible to broader planning.

Those plans may call for action that is external, internal, or both. An issue may warrant a publicity drive, a series of speeches or publications, advocacy advertising, an effort to reach out to thought leaders or public interest groups, or some other communications program. Possibly it could be defused if some internal actions are taken. This is not always easy unless the company or group has a mindset that is open to potentially unpleasant information and a willingness to act on it. For instance, it may be difficult to accept the implications of an issue if it means scrapping or drastically modifying a line of business, withdrawing from major geographic markets or expanding into sensitive new ones, or the need to develop wholly new and expensive alternative technologies. Such situations underscore the necessity for the active support and involvement of both top management and line executives in the emerging issues process to maintain internal credibility.

Preemptive voluntary action may be an effective strategy for some organizations in some sets of circumstances. In other situations, companies sometimes actually prefer regulatory action to avoid taking steps that would raise costs and thereby give competitors a possible cost advantage. This regulatory strategy ensures that all competitors are given equal treatment in terms of economic costs, although perhaps at a sacrifice of political or public relations benefit.

Each of these strategies may have merit strategically if it is the result of careful analysis and planning of an emerging problem area. Too frequently, though, action may be postponed because of management reluctance to accept unpleasant information and its consequences. This can prove enormously expensive in the long run.

On the other hand, it can be equally risky to act precipitously. Careful action planning has to assess the merits and implications of all significant inputs, not merely the comfortable ones. Tobacco companies decided decades ago on a complex three-part strategy: (1) stonewalling domestically on health challenges in the United States; (2) rapid expansion into overseas markets where health and safety concerns have lower public priority; and (3) diversification into nontobacco markets. Endgame negotiations with opponents are quite recent. Public relations aspects aside, companies like Philip Morris and RJR have been among the most successful and profitable businesses anywhere.

Action planning cannot be a static process. By their very nature, emerging issues are in a state of constant movement. This means that monitoring, analysis, evaluation, and review of the issue have to be continuous, and that both internal and external strategic action planning must be flexible to accommodate new developments, pressures, and insights.

We are surrounded by an ever-shifting flux of indicators of tomorrow's issues and possibly even historic trends. What is the future role of currency in an economy dominated by credit cards for consumer transactions and by electronics and satellites for institutional ones? How will computerized commerce be regulated and taxed in the future? In a global economy that knows no borders, what will be the role of the nation-state? Public value systems change every couple of decades; what new ones will impact public policy as, for instance, the environmental movement and the sexual revolution have done? What new technologies and inventions will alter our world as dramatically as transistors and "the pill"?

It takes minds that are analytical, imaginative, visionary, and highly intuitive to spot the events, trends, and patterns that will shape the future. The organizations and institutions that will thrive in tomorrow's world are those that know how to utilize such minds and that are open to the kinds of change their analyses suggest.

NOTE

1. Max Meng, "Early Identification Aids Issues Management," *Public Relations Journal*, March 1992.

Chapter 4

Needs, Plans, and Strategies

> O! that a man might know the end of this day's business, ere it come.
> —Shakespeare, *Julius Caesar*

Some years ago, the comptroller of a large corporation was told by his company's public affairs officer about a new tax proposal being considered by a congressional committee. His immediate response: "Look, you better get yourself on the next plane to Washington and tell those damn politicians to kill that bill. It would cost us a fortune."

The financial executive's reaction was intuitive and emotional. He understood immediately that his company would be adversely affected if the tax proposal became law, and his reaction was also colored by his lack of affection for government. The political considerations were as irrelevant to him as his personal opinion would have been to the legislators; overlooked was the small fact that they, not he, had the power to decide the issue.

He also neglected to ask what the bill was really all about. What was its justification? Who would benefit from it, and how?

Too often in many organizations, there is a strong reflex to act immediately on defensive issues without taking time to understand what may be really involved or at stake—substantively or politically.

It is important to analyze issues in terms of both their impact on organizational needs and the dynamics of the public policy process: The needs of an interest group may produce a desire for change. This leads to the development first of issues and then of proposed governmental remedies that may well come at the expense of some other interest group.

NEEDS ANALYSIS

Organizations generally first become involved in government relations because of an internal need associated with a specific issue or group of issues. Later, if the needs and issues become chronic and their impacts severe, the organization begins to explore the value of a long-range capability to deal with all relevant issues as they unfold, evolving through a progression of strategies.

There is an important distinction between needs and issues. *Needs* are internal to the organization or interest group. *Issues* are matters of public debate preceding governmental decision-making. Issues flow from and interact with interest group needs.

For instance, a company may perceive an internal need because of the cost or burden created by an existing law or regulation. The internal need is translated into an external issue once the company takes steps to repeal or amend the governmental requirement.

The converse situation may also occur: The issue may produce an internal need, perhaps as a consequence of new, burdensome legislation arising out of another group's desire for change.

Internal needs can also become translated into positive opportunities to reduce costs, open up markets, or seek other advantages, by taking the initiative to seek new legislation or amendments to existing law.

Almost every issue involves change and confrontation. One group's changed economic or social circumstances may lead it to seek remedies in changed law. Since other groups may well prefer the status quo, they resist change; the result is confrontation. It generally falls to government to resolve the conflict, sometimes through the legislative process, sometimes through the judicial.

Defensive Needs

The most familiar governmental problems to businesses are the ones that add to costs and to the difficulties of managing the organization. Some flow from existing laws or regulations, others from proposals for future action by government.

Such issues are often characterized by a complaint:

- Why do we have to put up with this unfair regulation?
- Why are they planning to impose this costly new tax?
- Why must we fill out all these cumbersome government forms?
- Why is the government planning to put us at a disadvantage with our competition or the unions?
- Why do we have to comply with these expensive safety, environmental, and consumer requirements?

Nonbusiness organizations have their own complaints, of course:

- Why are companies allowed to engage in this or that unfair or unhealthy labor, environmental, or consumer practice?
- Why does the government permit or even authorize this social, economic, or cultural wrong?

In each case, the answer is usually that the law was made either when circumstances were different or as the result of a conflict between two (or more) interests in which one side lost.

The more significant question is, "What can be done about it?" The answer usually involves changing the law, and that means lobbying lawmakers to do so. It is important to keep clearly in mind that any legislator can introduce a bill. Getting it enacted is extraordinarily difficult, the reason the vast majority of legislative proposals are stillborn. To kill a bill, it need only be stopped at any one of the many hurdles it must overcome between introduction and final passage. (See Chapter 6.)

Marketing Opportunities

Nonetheless, interest groups of all kinds seek new legislation (or regulations) to achieve change that they believe would have positive effects on their own internal needs. For example, a company or an industry that finds itself barred by law from entering a market may initiate proposals to revamp the law in order to expand its marketing opportunities.

The banking industry, for instance, was long barred from operating across state lines and from diversifying into other financial activities. Relentless campaigns, some in Washington and some in the states, eventually brought about a long series of changes to accomplish the diversification goals of major banking companies. This occurred only over the opposition of other financial interests with little desire to see potent new competitors enter their particular fields of business. Bankers prevailed over securities brokers in a major federal legislative battle in 1988 but lost to independent insurance brokers in the same contest.

At the end of Prohibition, to take another example, New York State was faced with the question of which kinds of retailers would be allowed to sell alcoholic beverages. Taking Solomon's sword against the contested infant, the legislature permitted alcoholic beverage stores to sell liquor and wine but forbade them to sell beer. Food retailers were allowed to sell beer but not wine and liquor. Ever since, food retailers have been struggling for the right to sell wine as well as beer. Liquor stores have tenaciously opposed not only this change but even a compromise that would let both kinds of retailers sell all alcoholic beverages.

A more recent example is federal deregulation of telecommunications, which eliminated regulatory boundaries among long-distance, local telephone, cable television, and other industries. While the concept was widely supported, intricate and agonizing negotiations over key provisions produced important gains for some, major losses for others. Near the end of the process, AT&T withdrew its support for the legislation, which was nonetheless enacted over its objections.

As the examples illustrate, a bill or regulatory proposal to accomplish a change in the law very likely means goring someone else's ox. People and interests become accustomed to living and operating under sets of circumstances that may be altered by legislative or regulatory changes. Legislation that would benefit one set of businesses may be harmful to another. A consumer group that favors new labeling or advertising requirements runs up against the companies whose marketing practices would be regulated. Anti-smoking advocates take aim not only at cigarette manufacturers but also at the government programs that encourage farmers to grow tobacco. An issue that is defensive to one group may be offensive to another—often literally.

Newer industries sometimes have an easier time with government regulation than more established ones. The computer software industry, otherwise largely unregulated, successfully sought federal protection against software piracy, both in the United States and internationally. On the other hand, biotechnology companies are heavily regulated because they fall under the jurisdiction of laws on the books before the technology arose.

Assessing Needs

The questions that produce a needs assessment are these:

- What proposals are governmental policy-makers considering that would increase business costs or restrict our operations, marketing, or profitability?
- What changes in existing governmental requirements could lower our costs of doing business or decrease restrictions on our operations?
- Are there changes down the road in the public environment that could significantly affect us for better or worse?
- What legislative or regulatory changes would open up markets for products or services from which we are presently barred?
- What changes would facilitate our achieving other, or non-business objectives?

It is one thing to state needs and quite another to satisfy them. For each need, there exists at least one real or potential issue. To be actionable, organizations must define their issues clearly and carefully.

Defining the Issues

Once needs have been stated, the next step is to list all the issues that satisfy (or challenge) those needs.

An issue may be defined very broadly. For instance, "all legislation that would restrict the company from marketing its products." This is an appropriate and usable definition if the issues have potentially severe impacts on the company's basic business. Tobacco companies, faced with innumerable proposals to limit smoking, define their issues in such broad strokes. So do casino gambling operators.

Or, the issue may be specific: legislation to increase the minimum wage . . . bills regulating solid waste disposal . . . proposals restricting the union's ability to organize . . . regulations imposing mandatory television v-chips or program ratings.

The issue may also be stated in great detail: Section 17 of S. 1234, to increase the sales tax to 9 percent on widgets retailing for more than $3000.

Whether stated broadly or narrowly, it is important that the issue be expressed clearly and coherently so that the organization can frame a workable position. The purpose, after all, is to have a definition on which a policy can be based and that is actionable. (If the bill is amended to raise the sales tax to only 8.5 percent on widgets selling for over $2,500, is it no longer of concern?) But at the other extreme, defining the issue as "all sales tax proposals" may be meaningless or unworkable.

INTERNAL IMPACT ASSESSMENTS

Issues vary in their impacts. It is important to establish the inherent significance of the issue, that is to put a value on the organization's stake in it. Without such a value, it is difficult to gauge the effect, both short term and long term, of the issue on organizational plans. The relative values of issues can also help evaluate priorities for the allocation of resources among different needs and issues.

Like the financial executive referred to earlier many corporate and organization leaders instantly grasp the anticipated impact of an issue—or at least think they do. This is hardly a sophisticated internal analysis, however, and certainly not adequate as a rationale for external consumption. Indeed, the more important the issue, the more important it is to research its impact with great care.

Sources of Impact Data

For Companies Businesses are most commonly affected by economic issues for which a quantitative value can usually be established: What is this tax costing us? How much would our costs of compliance be reduced if this regulation were amended? What is the size of the market that would be opened up to us if this law were repealed? What will it cost us if this law is enacted?

Within companies, the best judges of an issue's probable impact are those most likely to be affected by it. Tax lawyers and accountants can give the hardest assessment of a tax bill's probable consequences. Purchasing agents will usually best understand the effects of a legislated increase in raw material costs. Personnel and labor relations professionals are the best source for analysis of a proposal to increase benefits or the minimum wage. Marketers are likely to be the experts on legislation affecting consumer packaging or labeling. The general counsel's office is still another source of invaluable input and assistance on most issues. Sometimes, internal issue experts like these, with their own specialized sources, may be the first to spot a new issue while also serving as effective resources on issues identified by others.

The important point is that all relevant sources within the company that have useful expertise need to be consulted in assessing an issue's impact. (After all, they will usually be the people who have to live with the problem on a day-to-day basis, long after government relations professionals have gone on to other issues.) Other people who should be consulted are those whose involvement is valuable for internal political reasons.

Where feasible, issues should be measured in comparable terms. It may be difficult to work with a list of issues if one is measured in terms of potential market, another in sales, a third in costs, and a fourth in tax impact. Wherever possible, these varying measures should be reduced to a common denominator, perhaps profits.

For Membership Organizations Within trade associations and other membership groups, the process of assessing an issue's impact is not very different than the corporate process. Issues are almost always referred to the specialized committees or task forces that are a major component of almost all organizational structures. In some cases, members may be polled, formally or informally, by the staff to gain an understanding of an issue's anticipated impact. The query may go directly to known experts within the membership or may be channeled via official representatives, depending on the association's structure and procedures.

To the extent applicable, these member inputs should be quantified for the reasons set forth above. In practice, though, quantitative data is more likely to be available from large corporate members with their greater resources than it is from smaller companies or from individual members, or the information may be considered proprietary. For such reasons, if the issue is sufficiently important, other analytic techniques may have to be considered. An accounting firm could be asked to collect data from all members, or a representative sample of them, on a confidential basis. Or an economic consultant could be commissioned to undertake an economic study of the industry.

These techniques may or may not be appropriate for individual membership organizations that wish to determine the quantitative impacts of an issue on their members. Assistance from economic consultants should be sought to evaluate these other kinds of quantitative impacts. After-tax consequences are not an appropriate measure for such groups, but an effort should be made to develop some quantifiable common denominator.

Issues Difficult to Quantify

The problem is more difficult for noneconomic issues, but no less important. Without some means of issue valuation, it is hard to compare needs, judge resources, or rank priorities.

An environmental group, for example, may be concerned with stopping a nuclear power plant, preserving an endangered species, and cleaning up a source of toxic waste. Without some valuation of these issues, it will find it difficult to establish its priorities, allocate its existing resources, or know where to apply new ones.

Clearly, of course, subjective judgments always play a role, but the less issues lend themselves to quantification, the greater the subjective element and the greater the risk the organization may make incorrect assessments.

Many issues, however, are difficult to quantify, especially those that are essentially social or political. Groups dealing with abortion rights, whether pro or con, are involved with moral questions that for them transcend statistics. A civil rights organization trying to get a favorable nomination confirmed or an unfavorable one blocked is dealing with a political issue on which emotions can run high. Sometimes, the emotional intensity of issues can be higher than their intrinsic importance, thereby possibly jeopardizing a rational allocation of resources.

For precisely this reason, some effort to evaluate inherent significance on a quantitative scale is even more important on social and political issues than on economic ones. (This is not to say that economic issues lack emotional content, as anyone who has ever been involved in such contentious issues as right-to-work can testify.)

Issues can be evaluated on a linear scale that provides a basis by which to test resources and priorities. One way to get started is to undertake a Delphic survey. Although the process may be a bit complicated, it can be a worthwhile first step, followed thereafter by a simpler version once the issues evaluation approach is in place:

1. Select a panel of people to survey. This could be a group of managers or executives, in the case of a company. In the case of an association, it could be a board of directors, a government relations committee, a specially chosen representative task force, or even the entire membership. Executive judgment will determine if the panel needs to be statistically representative of the whole, or if it should be composed of technical experts or decision makers.

2. Ask the panel to assess the organization's basic needs, using the needs analysis described earlier.

3. Based on those needs, poll the panel again to develop a comprehensive list of issues. To make the process workable, a tentative list of actual issues should be suggested, allowing each panel member to add other issues.

4. Edit the resulting issues list to be sure each is descriptive and workable. The editing should be as objective and fair as possible; the process is defeated if obvious distortions or biases are injected.

5. Poll the group a final time, asking now that each panelist assign a value to every issue (on a scale of one to ten if the list is short, or one to one hundred if it is long). Little harm is done if a panelist gives the same score to more than one issue; if enough people are polled, the values will sort themselves out in the aggregate.

6. Compute the score for each issue and then rank the list by these total values.

7. Develop priority rankings for each issue based on these values, modified as necessary by assessments of the political factors affecting each.

Let's take the XYZ Corporation and see how it handled this process. In Step 1, XYZ created a panel consisting of officers, department heads, and key managers. In Step 2, a statement of company needs was developed and then, in Step 3, a tentative list of issues. The issues were edited in Step 4 and in Step 5, then once again presented to the panel, this time for the value rating computed in Step 6.

By the end of the fourth step, the company's panel had narrowed its issues to the following list:

- Sales tax increase: The company's products may be less attractive to its customers if sales tax increases raise their cost.
- Widget use licensing: The widgets XYZ makes may not sell well if consumers must be licensed in order to use them.
- Employee education tax: The company makes educational grants to its employees and does not want them to have to pay income taxes on those grants.
- Bars to raw material imports: Import restrictions on raw materials the company buys from overseas would raise costs.
- Gizmo safety regulations: New safety regulations would impede the marketing of gizmos, a product made by another firm that competes directly with widgets. Safety restrictions imposed on gizmos but not widgets would give XYZ competitive advantages.

The XYZ Company panel gave the following values to its issues, with 10 being most important and 1 least:

Sales tax increase:	6
Widget use licensing:	9
Employee education tax:	2
Bars to raw material imports:	8
Gizmo safety regulations:	4

Comment Because licensing requires a substantial prepurchase effort by the consumer, the panel viewed it as a major deterrent to the marketing of XYZ's widgets, substantially more so than an increase in the sales tax, even though that would increase the price consumers must pay. Almost as important are the proposed raw material import restrictions because of the increase in costs and ultimately price to consumers. While placing safety restrictions on the competitive gizmos would give XYZ an edge in the market, there are difficulties in doing so; besides, the sword has two edges, and XYZ could be the company affected next time around. While it wishes to benefit its employees and their education, the impact of the proposed tax is spread among many companies and, in any event, is clearly of less importance to XYZ's interests than the other issues.

The panel survey procedure brings out the relative intrinsic importance to the company of the issues. From time to time as new issues arise, the panel can be asked simply to rate these questions on the linear scale.

Political Considerations and Other Factors

The opinions of these experts will be a weighty factor in determining the position the company should adopt on the issues—but they should not be decisive. Experience and expertise in engineering, marketing, or the law do not necessarily endow an executive with political judgment. Political factors, such as evaluations of the issue's legislative significance, may not bear on internal issue assessments, but they are a critical element in determining the company's tactical position.

The widget licensing proposal, for example, may be less significant as a local bill pending before the Omaha City Council than as a federal issue. On the other hand, the Omaha bill may become *more* important if it is clearly going to pass while the federal legislation is going nowhere. Political factors like these must be taken into account, and the panel may not have the expertise to do so. This, therefore, is a task for government relations professionals.

In addition to political considerations, other impact factors should be evaluated. These might include consistency with previous issue positions, public and consumer image, and legal matters—or implications for employee morale, stakeholder and community relations, or some other aspect of the company's business.

Public opinion surveys can aid in developing issue positions and strategies. Many groups establish their positions based almost totally on their own internal needs, with insufficient attention to what will "sell" politically. Sometimes this is necessary, but often alternatives are available that are not adequately considered. Opinion polls can help direct strategies in directions that legislators may find more palatable politically, or indicate to the company or organization areas in which better public communications are needed. *Statistical modeling* of survey data can help pinpoint strategies that may sway significant population subgroups.

Focus groups (small panels of people chosen to approximate the characteristics of the population at large) can provide opportunities for in-depth discussion of these same topics at less cost than polls, although also with somewhat less accuracy. An advantage of focus groups is that they are a cost-effective way to get the thinking of constituents in the home districts of key legislators, and thereby provide guides to issue communications targeted to altering public opinion in those districts.

The final ratings of priorities should be based on evaluations of both the intrinsic importance of the issues and the judgments made on these political and other factors.

ESTABLISHING ISSUE POSITIONS

The issue has been researched, its potential impact evaluated, its prospects assessed—all within the parameters of the organization's needs. Now, how should all this information be pulled together to facilitate determining a position on the issue? What are the alternative choices?

Options Papers

An issue options paper can focus the available information and distill out the alternatives in a way that will facilitate decision making. Note the model options paper shown on p. 51. It is relatively brief, even sketchy. Supporting documents can be appended, but the shorter the document the more likely it is to be read and utilized.

The options paper pulls together in concise form the basic data relating to the issue—bill numbers, sponsors and opponents, key provisions, arguments pro and con, and the like. It also requires that thought be given to several important considerations.

Probable Impact What is the likely impact on the company or organization, together with an assessment of *potential allies*, that is, other interests likely to be similarly affected? If the impact would be shared among others in the company's industry, this is probably an issue for a trade association. If the impact would be shared among companies outside the industry or with nonbusiness organizations, major tactical considerations will include utilizing a coalition. If the impact would be both high and unique to the organization, then a major lobbying campaign will have to be geared up.

Although the impact description should be concise within the options paper, it should be backed up with the research described in Chapter 3. This information might be included as an appendix to the options paper. It will also provide crucial raw material in preparing the *position paper* described below.

Likely Supporters (and Their Rationale) What other legislators (especially leaders and committee chairmen) can be expected to support the sponsors? What is their justification for the bill and the major arguments they are likely to use? What other interest groups might back them, and why? Which major elected officials, departments, and agencies will lend support? Similar questions for the *opposing* side also require answers.

Alternatives Are there other bills that are preferable—or perhaps some form of executive or regulatory action? Is there a better way that could be implemented voluntarily?

Decision Options On the basis of all the foregoing questions, it may be that a decision is made to flatly oppose or support the bill. Possibly, though, that decision might be different if the bill is amended in some key respects. Perhaps flat support (or opposition) is to be the "going-in" position, but depending on various tactical considerations, a fallback posture (or series of fallbacks) should also be adopted, so that if the other side seems likely to prevail, harm will be minimized. Fallback positions are also important, so that the organization's lobbyists will know how to negotiate or compromise if key provisions are amended.

Priority or Value Rating The rating assigned the issue (as discussed earlier in this chapter under "Impact Assessment") indicates the importance of the issue for the budgetary allocation of personnel and other resources.

Responsibility for Implementation Responsibility should be specified and, in most cases, will be that of the government relations staff. However, if this is a state or local issue in a decentralized company, it might be a local manager who has been assigned certain government relations responsibilities. In dispersed organization models (see Chapter 5), it will be a designated issue coordinator. In trade associations or other membership groups, implementation will be assigned to the appropriate staff member or department.

MODEL ISSUE OPTIONS PAPER

Date:

Issue name:

> Senate Bill No.:   House Bill No.:
>
> > Main sponsor(s):   Main sponsor(s):
> >
> > Date introd.   Date introd.

Key provisions:

Probable impact on our organization:

> Is impact unique to us or shared with others? Who?
>
> Other factors bearing on our decision:

Likely proponents (legislators & interest groups):

Rationale and arguments pro:

Likely opponents (legislators & interest groups):

Arguments against:

Alternatives (legislative or other):

Our position options:

> Support
>
> Support if following changes made (or not made):
>
> Oppose
>
> Oppose if following changes made (or not made):

Other considerations:

Decision: Priority:

> Fallback positions (if needed):

Implementation by:

Comments:

DECISION-MAKING SYSTEMS

Final decisions on issue positions typically are made in corporations by the chief executive officer, unless he or she chooses to delegate this responsibility. Delegation might be made to another corporate officer or, in the case of decentralized companies, to the head of the operating division or unit affected by the issue. This power can also be delegated to the Government Relations Committee (see Chapter 5), but approval by the CEO of the company's position at least on major issues is good management practice. Of course, this is essential where two or more units within a multidivisional company have different views on an important issue.

Trade associations and other membership organizations generally have established processes for the adoption of issue positions. The process usually involves staff research and political inputs to a committee or task force that recommends a policy or position for ultimate decision by the executive committee or board of directors. Occasionally, policy decisions on major issues may be put to a vote of the entire membership. (See Chapter 11.)

Informal decision making can occur on minor issues or those that are essentially variations on established issues. Where it is reasonably apparent to government relations professionals what the position of the company or organization is likely to be, an informal check with the appropriate corporate or association official can be sufficient to establish a position on the matter.

Informal decision making may also be essential when time is a vital factor. This often occurs near the end of a legislative session when issues crowd each other and bills are rushed through for final passage or defeat. The company or association should have procedures in place so that lobbyists will know which individual to call to get a fast decision on a position. This kind of situation also illustrates the value of pre-established fallback positions, enabling the lobbyist to make decisions on the spot when legislative circumstances require.

Position Papers

Once a decision has been made concerning the organization's position on the issue, the options paper—backed up with the basic research, particularly the detailed, quantified impact assessment—becomes a statement of the organization's position.

There is a need at this point for a document that clearly and concisely lays out this position for external use. This position paper can be used with a variety of audiences:

- Legislators, legislative committees, and staffs
- Executive and regulatory agency officials
- The press
- Trade associations and potential allies

- Grassroots program participants and other company stakeholders
- Organization members

A position paper should be concise, brief, and written in clear and persuasive language suitable for a lay audience. It must be factual and accurate in content, and reasonable and moderate in tone. Firmness and conviction are always appropriate—shrillness, hysteria, and threats never are. Length should be no more than two pages, going to three or (at most) four only if absolutely necessary. (Readers' attention spans tend to vary inversely with length.)

The position paper also can be the basis for testimony on the issue at public hearings, speeches, press releases, employee and shareholder publications, and similar communications avenues. (See Chapter 15.)

Preparation of the position paper need not be difficult since it will draw heavily on the research already done for the options paper. It should contain the following elements:

- Description of the issue.
- The organization's position coupled, where appropriate, with a refutation of the other side's arguments. If it is possible to do so, it is well to frame the argument as a question of basic fairness or other moral principles.
- Impact of the issue on the organization's operations stated, as appropriate, in terms of gain or loss in jobs, tax consequences, community effects, impacts on suppliers (especially small or minority businesses), and so forth. Such points tend to have more impact than arguments relating to jeopardized sales or profits, although these will be worth making if they are dramatic enough and can be well documented.
- Documentation is important. Third-party validation of the company's or organization's claims always carries more weight than self-assertions. If the validation originates with a respected and disinterested institution (e.g., university or government agency), so much the better.
- Impact on consumers or the public in general. It is important to show citizens who probably would not perceive a common interest that they do indeed share one with the company or organization. Again, this should be documented or validated by some third party if at all possible.

White papers are more research-oriented versions of position papers. Intended for academics, legislative analysts, and other researchers and audiences interested in a fuller exposition of the issue, they are useful vehicles to communicate research results or other documentation of the rationale underlying the group's position.

THE EVOLUTION OF LOBBYING STRATEGIES

Organizations with similar needs and issues may deal with those issues in very different ways, depending on the strategic posture the company or association has adopted. Strategies affect the ways in which issues are analyzed, the evaluation of their impacts, the positions adopted, and the tactics with which those positions are implemented. It is one thing to respond to someone else's agenda and quite another to develop one's own.

Every organization that deals with government and the public environment has a strategy for doing so. But not every strategy is the result of a conscious and deliberate process.

Business enterprises without significant public policy needs or challenges ignore lobbying and government relations, as indeed they should. Why invest in an expensive capability when there is no need? But once government policies or regulation become a factor in operations or the cost of doing business, companies initially approach their involvement in government relations with a reactive strategy: either seeking to defeat or ameliorate adverse legislation or regulation—or using governmental power to alter some unfavorable social, economic, marketing, or political condition.

As a company confronts more and more issues, it will begin to evolve from a single-issue orientation toward an eventual realization that it can influence the development of issues and the public environment in which the organization operates. The movement from early reactive phases through legislative lobbying into problem solving and proactive strategies is a function of two influences: (1) the scope and intensity of its issues; and (2) cultural disposition and limitations within the organization.

Trade associations and nonbusiness membership organizations may follow a similar evolutionary pattern but are likely to move into the legislative lobbying phase faster than most individual firms. However, they may also be less prone than companies to move beyond that strategy.

There are seven government relations strategies that tend to build on each other more or less sequentially.

Reactive–Crisis This is an unprogrammed, purely reactive activity. Issue monitoring is not systematic. Information on governmental proposals and developments is gleaned almost completely from publications and trade associations. Direct lobbying action is undertaken (either by a staff executive substantively expert in the issue or by retained independent lobbyists) only in crisis situations affecting vital interests and in response to the initiatives of someone else. Involvement in trade associations is passive; the company may be represented on boards and committees, but little effort is made to influence industry positions or actions significantly.

Reactive–Regulatory Monitoring This is a "no-surprises" strategy based on systematic monitoring of key regulatory agencies, including utilization of consultants or tracking services and use of company or organization personnel to cultivate information sources within the agencies. Legislative monitoring is less intense unless there are bills of burning concern. There is much greater involvement in trade association position development and action planning, but the company's own lobbying is still reactive only to crises.

Reactive–Regulatory Lobbying Issues monitoring is now more intense and includes systematic cultivation of personal contacts within key agencies and among other relevant sources, for example, other interest groups and some key legislators and staff. Serious efforts are now made to obtain early warning of potential regulatory action and to influence its direction by frequent, personal, and more-or-less systematic lobbying of regulatory officials and staff. Monitoring of legislative issues is also likely to become more systematic as a by-product of regulatory tracking.

Reactive–Legislative Lobbying By this stage, monitoring of both legislative and regulatory issues is intensive. Major efforts are now being made to lobby on all relevant issues, though still defensively and with the degree of activity proportional to the potential impact of the issue. A political contributions program has been developed to aid friends and expand legislative access. The beginnings of grassroots and coalition activity are found, particularly on top priority issues.

Proactive–Political Grassroots programs to involve stakeholders or members in personal lobbying and political efforts are now extensive, often tied in with community relations activity. Political action now goes beyond simply sponsoring a small PAC to engage in more sophisticated ways to affect election outcomes. The organization lobbies extensively on pertinent issues although pertinence may still be defined in defensive terms. The organization now frequently assumes leadership roles in associations and coalitions and, on occasion, is even willing to act independently if the circumstances warrant.

Problem Solving This is a mixed strategy, comprised of both reactive and proactive elements. There is extensive tracking and analysis of both current and emerging issues. Direct lobbying efforts are now supplemented by active communications programs to help shape or alter public opinion and knowledge, and by cooperative, interactive efforts with other interest groups and government officials to help solve problems at the roots of real or potential issues. There is also a sensitivity to possible needs for voluntary internal change if external circumstances warrant. This is the "enlightened self-interest" strategy.

Proactive–Marketing Issues are now being identified or developed that could lead to expansion of markets or other positive benefits on the organization's own initiative. Lobbying is no longer strictly defensive, and the organization actively seeks adoption of issues on its own agenda, whether legislative or regulatory. The organization utilizes all available government relations tools and techniques proportional to the importance and value of the issue, building on the problem-solving strategy to enhance prospects for success.

Let's look at a model case to see how these strategies evolve.

A Model of Strategic Evolution

Armand Geddon had always limited his involvement with government largely to paying taxes. He prided himself on his total lack of political involvement. ("I never vote; it only encourages them.") His entire adult life had been devoted to building his home security business.

So it was with considerable shock that Geddon learned that his company, Armageddon Industries ("You'll fight to the end to get our products!") was being sued by the Product Regulatory Oversight Department. The complaint charged that the company had violated the law by failing to register its products with PROD.

"We've been in business for fifteen years," an angry Geddon told his lawyer, Juanita Lopez. "I've never heard of such a law. Why are they attacking us?"

"Don't take it personally, Mr. Geddon," Lopez replied. "They're just enforcing the law the legislature passed two years ago to regulate security products. Didn't your trade association or your government relations people tell you about it?"

"I don't belong to trade associations—waste of money," the indignant Geddon responded. "And I don't have any government relations people. Why should I? I don't have any relations with the government."

"You do now," Lopez said. "Let me talk to the people at PROD and see what can be done."

Lopez persuaded PROD officials to levy a minimum fine and took care of registering Armageddon's products to get the company in compliance. A few weeks later, she visited Geddon in his office to get his signature on the final papers.

"You really need to keep on top of what PROD is doing, Mr. Geddon, to make sure you know what's happening that could affect you in the future. Perhaps you ought to hire a specialist to monitor these things."

"I don't want to add to staff," Geddon said. "Too much overhead already. You do it for me."

So for several years thereafter, Lopez kept track of PROD's activities and sent him memos whenever there was something she thought he should know. She persuaded Geddon to join the Protective Engineering Systems Organization (PESO) so he would get news on legislation, but she suspected that he rarely read the material.

Then one day, Lopez called Geddon. "Did you see this week's trade association bulletin?" she asked.

"Getting ready for next week's sales meeting. Don't have time for anything else," he said.

"I think you may have to take the time, Mr. Geddon. PROD is proposing government standards for your products. If they're adopted, you may have to redesign your products from the ground up," Lopez told him.

"Let PESO handle it," Geddon said. "Isn't that what they're suppose to do?"

PESO did handle it, and the regulations were substantially modified before they were adopted. Unfortunately, Armageddon had some features on its products that its competitors did not. Since no one from the company attended PESO's meetings on the subject, the association did little to take care of Armageddon's unique needs. The result was new PROD standards that raised Armageddon's costs by 7 percent.

After Geddon's blood pressure came back down, he thought hard about the experiences he had been having with PROD and PESO and decided to ask Lopez to meet him for lunch. "Well, I can't say you didn't warn me," he said to her. "We obviously have to do things differently. Do you have any suggestions?"

Lopez told him it was time to hire a government relations specialist who could devote full time to Armageddon's growing problems. "That's exactly what I've been thinking," Geddon said. "I'd like you to take the job." Lopez agreed, left the law firm, and became Armageddon's first Director of Government Relations.

She drew up a list of federal and state agencies whose activities could affect Armageddon and developed a program to monitor them. She also subscribed to several publications that cover Congress and the state legislature and retained lobbying firms to watch out for anything that could affect the company. She even succeeded in persuading Geddon to become active in PESO. And Lopez herself decided to get involved in local politics.

By the end of her third year, Lopez had built an effective government relations program. She had developed a substantial network of contacts among officials in several key agencies, and she was frequently asked for information by them. Armageddon's lobbying firm had played an active role in PESO's fight against a provision in a tax bill that would have denied tax benefits for the industry's R&D expenses. And Armand Geddon, by now actually chairman of a PESO committee, had given a couple of speeches to local chambers of commerce on his committee's work. Working through several legislators in whose campaigns she had been involved, Lopez had gained a public commitment at a legislative hearing from PROD's new head that the agency would consult Armageddon and other PESO members before developing new standards and regulations affecting the industry.

By her sixth year, Lopez had two assistants who handled most of the regulatory lobbying and issues research. Armageddon was using computerized tracking services to monitor legislative and agency activities, and Lopez herself did a considerable amount of legislative lobbying. She also developed plans for a political action committee but complained to her husband that she was having difficulty getting Geddon to take time from his duties on PESO's board of directors and his chairmanship of the state chamber of commerce finance committee to discuss the PAC.

Two years later, Armageddon was confronted with a major issue. Legislation was introduced to require that home-security device companies be required to obtain a homeowner's written permission before a sales presentation could be made. Not all of Armageddon's competitors kept to the ethical standards Armand Geddon had always insisted on, and some unpleasant publicity had produced this proposal. Lopez persuaded companies in several other, unaffected industries that legislation like this could easily be amended in the future to cover them and accordingly put together a coalition that succeeded in defeating the bill after several months of hard lobbying. "It would have been easier," she told Geddon, "if all our PAC contributors had good personal relationships with their legislators." Just beginning his term as chairman of PESO's board of directors, Geddon promised to get the association involved in designing a plan for a grassroots program for its members.

Lopez, by now Armageddon's vice president for public affairs, decided that something had to be done both about the industry's image and also about some of the underlying ethical problems. She had no problem persuading Geddon to make an ethics program a major goal for PESO. She also retained a consulting firm to develop a solid public affairs program for Armageddon. As a result, a community relations home and neighborhood safety program was upgraded, a scholarship program for talented minority students was instituted, and the company took the lead in persuading the city to redevelop the blighted, high-crime waterfront area near its plant into a major hotel and office building complex.

A year later, she had lunch with Armageddon's marketing vice president. "You know, if this company is going to continue growing, we'll need a new line of business," he told her. "Why don't you do something about that state law that bars home-security device companies from getting into the office security business?" Lopez went back to the office with a major new lobbying project.

On her twelfth anniversary with the company, Armand Geddon and his wife took Juanita and Hector Lopez to dinner. "I'd like your advice on a matter," he said. "I've been thinking about stepping down as chief executive of Armageddon. The company is doing well, and the new office security business has already increased revenues by 20 percent. Benson is ready to move into my job. But the real question is this: With the waterfront project doing so well, several of the city's top business and labor leaders have asked me to think about running for mayor. What do you think?"

Lopez smiled. "We've come a long way from the time when you didn't even want to vote. Can I manage your campaign?"

Comments on the Model and the Sequential Strategies

Not all companies and organizations will move through each strategic phase to the next as Armageddon Industries did. Some will vault one level or another in their progress. Some will also freeze their development at a particular stage. The perceived importance of their issues may not provide sufficient justification for the incremental resources and effort each additional strategic level requires. The corporate culture may be disinclined toward a high public profile or toward political involvement. There is also the comfort factor: Many executives are personally uneasy with a broad-spectrum strategy that requires extensive interaction with the public sector and with unfamiliar interest groups. Others feel, with equal force, that publicly visible organizations cannot shun opportunities to influence the external environment in which they operate lest they abdicate the field to competitors and adversaries.

Moreover, depending on issues and circumstances, some organizations may blend parts of different strategies without necessarily adopting all the components at any one time or may fluctuate in their embrace of a particular strategy according to changes in the internal or external environment.

No outsider can judge the correct strategy for a company or any other organization. The "wrong" strategy is the one settled on through inertia or emotion. The "right" one is the strategy adopted rationally, deliberately, and by plan on a basis that is consistent with the organization's internal needs, culture, and vision of its future.

The importance of sound strategies is that they influence the way the organization perceives the internal impact of relevant issues, the positions it takes on those issues, and the action programs it adopts to implement its positions.

Chapter 5

Organization and Resources

Set thine house in order.

—II Kings 20:1

There is nothing more difficult to take in hand, more perilous to conduct, or more uncertain in its success, than to take the lead in the introduction of a new order of things.

—Machiavelli

Lobbyists often characterize government relations as akin to fire fighting, describing their activities as running around dousing brush fires wherever they may flare up. But even the possibility of an occasional small blaze requires some advance preparation, if only so that an extinguisher be kept handy. Moreover, insurance needs to be taken out against possible losses, and affirmative fire prevention programs should be developed to minimize the likelihood and severity of problems. All these measures notwithstanding, the probability that a certain number of major conflagrations still will erupt is the reason fire departments are organized.

Government relations needs to be organized as a system for very similar reasons. Issues need to be managed. That requires planning, programming, budgeting, and implementation. It also requires evaluation and mobilization of resources within a system that either already exists in satisfactory form or needs to be reorganized or even developed from scratch.

This chapter deals with those problems, focusing on the resources and forms of organization needed for an effective "fire-fighting" program.

ORGANIZATIONAL CULTURES AND MANAGEMENT SUPPORT

The essential elements in any organization's government relations program are top management support, top management support, and top management support.

Strong support from senior management is no assurance that a government relations program will succeed, but it does give it a healthy start and facilitates a favorable allocation of other necessary resources.

Without support from the top, however, no government relations program can have much hope of success. Resources available to the program will be scant. Understanding and cooperation from other segments of the organization will be given grudgingly at best. Lobbyists, assuming any are even tolerated in the organization, are likely to be viewed as practitioners of black magic whose methods are mysterious (and probably unspeakable) and who certainly are not to be considered part of the management team.

Organizational Philosophies

The organization's philosophy of government relations is an element of the permanent cultural value system that every organization develops—one that is expressed, but also often reinterpreted, by current senior management. It is therefore subject to substantial modification from the top.

The following statements are stereotypes of organizational philosophies of government relations often expressed by business leaders and (much less often) by the heads of nonbusiness organizations as well:

- "I don't have the time or patience for a government relations program in this company," says the chief executive of Company A. "We're under extreme pressure to cut costs, and there is no place here for unnecessary staff overhead. Besides, that's what we pay our trade associations to do."

- "Government relations makes an important, in fact vital, contribution to our profitability," responds his counterpart in Company B. "It has enabled us to reduce the cost burdens of government regulation. It has lowered our taxes. And it has helped us open up new markets that previously were closed to us. The benefits the government relations function has brought this company have paid for its costs many times over and have contributed substantially to our bottom line."

- "It's all right to have a government relations person in this company," says Company C's top executive, "providing he confines himself to monitoring issues, informing management, and representing us with trade associations. But nobody in this organization is going to lobby any government officials or consort with politicians."

What accounts for these very different philosophies, all widely found within the business community? Sometimes, differences among corporate cultures and experiences. Other times, the values and experiences of individuals. Still other explanations flow out of the varied ways government relations is integrated into corporate processes of goal setting and implementation. In most cases, the truth will lie in some combination of these factors. Each of these merits a more detailed examination.

Corporate Cultures and Business Environments

Each organization has its own culture, its own institutional personality. The longer the life and stability of the organization, the stronger and more distinct its culture and values are likely to be. The attitudes of the person at the top will shape the organization's cultural views and values, but the culture will also influence the boss.

The ability of an organization to affect its external environment is greatly influenced by its willingness to do so, its belief that it can do so effectively, and its acceptance of the merit of the effort. This philosophic disposition, articulated or not, will underlie everything the organization seeks to do. If the organization and its top executives question the appropriateness of trying to alter governmental policy, no comprehensive program can be organized. Government relations will be task oriented, and results will be, at best, only marginally effective.

Different industries are likely to hold different points of view, depending on the frequency and impact of the regulatory experience.

Highly regulated government contractors, for instance, typically must conduct business under government controls that other businesses, operating exclusively in the private sector, would often find unacceptable. Government contractors are subject, by both law and regulation, to more rigid standards of performance and accountability than are private-sector marketers. Their executives frequently are highly restricted in their ability to make even routine decisions without approvals from the government agencies they service. Laws governing prevailing wage rates and other labor practices often have special applicability to companies seeking public business or financing. The effectiveness of government relations is fundamental to the ability of such companies to operate and to obtain and service contracts. Sometimes, though, government contractors may receive special treatment not available to other firms—as when the Defense Department decided to reduce the number of major contractors and facilitated antitrust exemptions for a series of corporate mergers that probably would not otherwise have been allowed.

For public utilities, government regulation has been the way of the world. Perhaps even more than government contractors, utilities have had to account to state and federal regulatory bodies and others in government for virtually every facet of their business. Utilities have also been forced by government on occasion to undo the results of decisions that regulatory bodies had previously approved—a fact of life of which the operators of nuclear power plants are painfully aware. While the recent trend toward deregulation and the promotion of competition has eased some of these burdens, utilities still labor under requirements not commonly imposed on other kinds of businesses.

Retailers and other labor-intensive companies of all kinds must operate within personnel cost structures mandated in great detail by legislation and regulations, even if they are not also subject to the intricate provisions of union contracts.

Pharmaceutical companies, biotechnology firms, and (to a lesser extent) food manufacturers must obtain government approvals for new products and processes, both generally extensive and expensive.

Financial service companies generally must obtain governmental approvals for many new products, business opportunities, and marketing approaches.

Many of these enterprises have some of the most sophisticated government relations programs to be found anywhere and engage in constant efforts to affect the government controls that are such a substantial part of their business environment. Indeed, for some, government *is* the business environment in totality. In contrast, other firms conclude from their own experiences that they can do little to alter and reshape that environment.

Sometimes a CEO will argue that a government relations program to reduce regulatory expenses is unnecessary because such costs are an equal cost factor in all competitors' pricing. However, the converse is also true—everyone benefits when regulatory costs are reduced and productivity improves.

Personal and Corporate Values

Corporate and personal value systems are often a major factor in attitudes toward the company's ability to influence government. A top executive once told the author that he thought business was no more justified in interfering with government than government was in interfering with business: "How can we tell the politicians to keep their noses out of our business if we're down in Washington lobbying theirs?"

Personal experiences can have lasting impacts on executives' attitudes. An executive was invited to testify by a congressional committee on a financial issue in which he was considered expert. Flattered, he prepared thoroughly and presented himself at the hearing. However, during questioning by committee members, he was subjected to a merciless barrage of criticism on a completely unrelated matter by a legislator who once had an unfortunate experience with the company. Traumatized by the incident, the executive left Washington vowing never to become involved in government relations again.

Values toward public affairs can also be shaped by perceptions of others' experiences. A chief executive had spent the early part of his career in Latin America. He observed there that publicly conspicuous companies, especially units of U.S. multinationals, seemed inevitably to become political targets. His conclusion was that the only safe strategy was to maintain the lowest possible corporate profile. He brought this philosophy back with him when he returned to the United States. For the remainder of his career, he vigorously resisted any efforts to lobby on issues affecting his company except through trade associations.

Yet, the woods are equally full of executives who went to Washington or a state capital to lobby an issue on behalf of their companies, found the process successful and rewarding, and became strong advocates of government relations.

The environment in which companies operate also helps shape their willingness and ability to become involved in the business environment. Some public utilities, for example, contribute substantial executive time to socially beneficial community programs, reaping the good will in more favorable marketing and regulatory climates. Participation in public affairs becomes part of the corporate culture for those companies, typically transcending any adverse views held among individual executives.

Indeed, it is the nature of corporate cultures that they tend to foster the careers of executives who share the company's philosophy and to force out individuals whose personal values are too much at odds with those of the organization. One of the best known consumer products corporations in America "breeds" executives known for their nearly total antipathy to government regulation of consumer marketing. The story is told of two rising managers who were part of a trade association committee trying to develop an industry-wide position on an important legislative issue. The two reluctantly went along with the rest of the committee in agreeing to trade off a small degree of government control in order to avoid more stringent regulation. It took personal intervention by industry leaders to save the jobs of the young executives when their superiors learned what happened, but two promising careers were probably stunted.

At the other extreme are companies whose cultural values include the belief that they have an obligation to be "socially responsible" and that profitability is a secondary objective. More common are those enterprises that find that it is easier to be socially responsible when they are profitable than when they are not.

Nonetheless, neither men nor companies are islands. Businesses operate in an environment comprised of many other institutions and value systems, not all of which are favorably inclined to a laissez-faire philosophy. Government relations can provide an antenna into that environment, picking up the signals of competitive and adversarial institutions seeking public policy changes. That information is not only lobbying intelligence but, if received early enough, can be valuable input for strategic and business planning.

Gaining Management Support

Both association and company executives tend to be strongly preoccupied with current issues, and effective government relations professionals therefore devote the bulk of their efforts to those problems that affect the organization's one- to three-year objectives. This does not mean that issues larger than the company's immediate interests should be neglected. Tending to macroissues is one of the reasons trade associations and umbrella business groups exist.

Moreover, analyzing new and emerging issues is an important function that can alert senior management to long-term changes in the business environment. If the company wishes to play a proactive role in dealing with such issues or to become involved in larger social and economic concerns, that is the "fire prevention" function to which government relations and public affairs should make major contributions.

But the CEO and the corporate culture have to be ready to accept such activities. Many a program has stumbled and even been shut down because the public affairs department was perceived by operating personnel to be more concerned with changing the world than protecting the bottom line.

The role of a chief executive is to direct and shape government relations as a bridge to, and from, the world of public policy—supporting the function within the organization and participating appropriately in its external activities when CEOs can make their own unique contributions.

Whether corporate value systems tilt toward pragmatism or in more ideological directions, the most successful government relations efforts will be those that are deeply rooted in the mainstream of corporate objectives and strategies. Most companies believe that their primary purpose is to generate a profit for the benefit of owners, to strengthen the business, and thereby to assure the economic well-being of their employees and the communities in which they operate. The government relations function must be intimately involved in serving that purpose if it is to be accepted, effective, and successful.

Wise government relations executives will therefore devote considerable energy to assuring that their efforts concentrate on those issues with the greatest impact—both short term and long term—on corporate profitability and other basic business objectives, quantifying the results to the maximum extent possible. If new to the organization, they will take great pains to learn its culture, absorb its folkways, and adapt their personal styles as appropriate to the circumstances. Strong programs of communications to senior and operating managements are essential to help build and maintain essential support and to gradually reshape company values adverse to the government relations process.

Lobbying, in other words, begins at home. Here are some possible steps:

- Shore up support by helping executives and managers achieve their business objectives, the ideal approach in today's hard-nosed corporate environments. Integrate government relations plans and programs with corporate and operating unit business needs and objectives. This applies not only to the top executives but also to their likely successors, those a tier or two down.

- Help managers understand how the political, legislative, and lobbying processes work—how they affect the organization's goals—and how the organization can influence them. Giving them the flavor and nuances of the system is more important than a civics lesson. So are actual case studies, showing how the company has benefited from particular lobbying activities.

- Keep top corporate and divisional executives personally informed of important developments. If something significant happens on an issue important to the chief financial officer or the head of a division, call or e-mail the individual personally with the news before they see it in your newsletter or in the press. Use this personal approach to cultivate not only the CEO but also the people a level or two down from whom the next CEO is likely to be drawn.

- Develop a company newsletter reporting on the importance and status of issues affecting the business. This is also a good place to highlight the achievements of participants in the grassroots program. Publishing this material on internal e-mail or the company's intranet allows it to be updated as frequently circumstances warrant.
- Solicit lobbying participation. Even if executives or managers are not yet participating in a grassroots lobbying program, nothing will give them a better feel for the lobbying process than a few trips to discuss issues impacting their business objectives with legislators.
- Organize political education seminars. Management meetings at which important federal or state legislators speak are an excellent way to build greater awareness of the importance of government relations and enthusiasm for it. Invitations to a private lunch or dinner with the speaker before or after the program are an effective way to strengthen personal support and relationships, if they can be arranged under circumstances that do not violate pertinent federal or state laws. (See Chapters 8 and 9.)
- Budget travel time to visit major company facilities, to brief local managers on important issues, individually or as a group. The personal relationships built by such visits are value added to the educational and informational benefits. Nothing can be more helpful to government relations managers than peers in other parts of the company who champion the department's work.
- Where possible, tie these meetings in with plant or facility visits by legislators. This strengthens relationships all the way around—with you and the local managers, with you and the lawmaker, and between the managers and their legislators.
- Undertake benchmarking studies (see below) to strengthen performance.

GOVERNMENT RELATIONS STAFF

No government relations or broader public affairs effort ever has enough personnel to cover all the issues assigned its staff. Once a decision to hire a staff has been made, sophistication and awareness increase, and the number of issues in which the organization takes an interest constantly grows. The perceived importance of many issues also increases within the organization. The overall effect is a staff that almost always has more on its plate than it can ever digest.

The questions management must therefore answer are these:

1. What are the objectives we want the government relations function to achieve?
2. How much staff, with what kind of skills, is needed to do the job?
3. What other internal resources are available to accomplish objectives?
4. What external resources will be needed—or can be utilized more cost-effectively than internal ones?
5. How should resources be organized?

A government relations staff can actually be quite small and still accomplish its objectives—if it is well organized and if other organizational resources are effectively utilized. Of course, there is no optimum size. Staff size depends on the size of the company; the number, intensity, and geographic scope of the issues; overall affordability; and the manner in which the organization is structured to handle the basic functions of government relations.

Here are the key functions of a government relations staff, noting for each the nature of the staff role.

* **Issues research and analysis and development of positions**
    Staff role: Direct implementation optional; coordination mandatory.
* **Direct lobbying**
    Staff role: Direct implementation optional; coordination mandatory.
* **Trade association liaison**
    Staff role: Direct implementation optional; coordination mandatory.
* **Grassroots lobbying**
    Staff role: Direct implementation and coordination mandatory.
* **Coalitions and alliances**
    Staff role: Direct implementation optional; coordination mandatory.
* **Political activity**
    Staff role: Direct implementation and coordination mandatory.
* **Internal and external communications**
    Staff role: Direct implementation optional; coordination mandatory.

Examples abound of almost every conceivable organizational form, as we shall see in a moment. Nonetheless, the staff must provide at least a coordinating role for each core function; for several, direct staff implementation is essential, for reasons to be discussed. (Geographic scope may make a difference here. Companies that engage in international government relations often structure that function differently than they do domestic activities. In three out of five companies, the staff does not currently play even an advisory role in international government relations.)[1]

Staff Role Comments

Research The staff must coordinate the process of defining needs, identifying and analyzing issues, and establishing the organization's positions. It must assure that the necessary issues research is performed, whether within the government relations staff, by others elsewhere in the organization, or by purchase from the outside. (See Chapters 3 and 4.)

Direct Lobbying The staff must decide, too, how direct lobbying is to be handled—whether the ball will be carried by the company's personnel, handed off to retained lobbyists or trade associations, or shared.

Even if the company takes responsibility for all or part of the direct lobbying, the staff may or may not do the actual personal contact work. As discussed more fully in Chapter 7, direct lobbying is a function that requires great skill and experience. It may be more cost-effective in some cases to utilize outside lobbyists than to develop those skills in house. That is surely true when issues arise in remote locations or require exceptional technical or political expertise. On the other hand, inside lobbyists will tend to have a much better understanding of the organization. Supervision and coordination of outside lobbyists is a critical staff responsibility.

Trade Association Relationships A function often assigned to government relations personnel is liaison with trade associations to ensure that the company's legislative positions and those of its associations mesh. As discussed in Chapter 11, assigning government relations staffers to be the company's formal representatives is a questionable course of action. However, the *coordination* of liaison relationships is a critical staff function.

Grassroots Lobbying The government relations staff plays the key role in building and coordinating the grassroots network. Management of the network, communications to it, and effective utilization of it on appropriate issues are essential staff functions. (See Chapter 13.)

Relations with Other Groups Coalitions should be developed with other groups (both business and nonbusiness) that share an interest in the issues. The optimum liaison with each group will be an ad hoc choice. If a company has a consumer affairs director, for instance, that individual is probably the right person to maintain relationships on legislative issues with consumer organizations. In some cases, outside lobbyists may be the most appropriate liaisons where there already are good relationships with specific groups or the lobbyist represents the organization in a distant location.

While one or several people may have responsibility for maintaining these relationships on a day-to-day basis, the *coordination* of coalitions must be responsibility of the senior government relations staff executive. A country may have many ambassadors; it has only one foreign minister. (See Chapter 12.)

Political Action Political activities must be closely and professionally managed, either totally within the government relations staff or, at the very least, by experts who share that staff's reporting relationship. Political fund-raising and disbursement are sophisticated and highly regulated activities. Transgressions can jeopardize the entire government relations program and result in legal problems and unfavorable publicity for the entire organization. Note that this should not preclude the active involvement of members or employees in both fund-raising and disbursement—for example, the members of a political action committee (PAC)—but the program must be managed carefully and with political sensitivity. (See Chapter 14.)

Communications Public relations or employee relations personnel, or outside firms, may prepare issues information for dissemination to internal or external audiences—but it is critical that the communicators take close guidance on issues and political matters from the government relations staff. Not only facts, but also nuances, are critically important in these communications. (See Chapter 15.)

Staff Organization

There are at least three models for organizing the government relations function.

Centralized This is the traditional form, used by two-thirds of U.S. companies and by most membership organizations.[2] In a centralized structure, the government relations staff reports to a common executive and serves the entire company or organization. Staff members may have functional responsibilities or be organized by geographic scope or by issue categories, or some combination.

Centralized departments may be headed by an officer or other executive whose sole responsibility is government relations—or comprise a unit within a larger public affairs structure. (Corporate public affairs functions often include, in addition to government relations, activities such as community relations, philanthropic programs, public and investor relations, and the like.)

Centralized corporate staffs are most frequently located at the company's headquarters, but in a few firms they operate out of the Washington office. In other instances, the head of the Washington office is the company's top government relations executive, but a portion of his subordinates are at the headquarters location or perhaps elsewhere.

Decentralized In many companies, government relations is the responsibility of individual operating units. Since these units typically have broad profit-and-loss responsibility, they are assigned whatever staff functions are necessary to achieve that responsibility. (Of course, they also have the latitude to decide *not* to exercise those functions, including government relations.) Sometimes, too, government relations personnel are assigned within individual corporate staff departments, usually those that are broadly affected by government policies (e.g., labor relations, taxation, etc.). A small central government relations or public affairs staff may (or may not) exist at the corporate level in such companies, primarily for purposes of coordination but also to handle company-wide issues. Somewhat more than a quarter of companies use a decentralized organizational form, most of them larger corporations.[3]

Dispersed A few companies use a third model in which each operating unit or staff department is responsible for coping with any issues that may arise to affect it. In each such unit, government relations is handled on a part-time basis by *issue coordinators*—individuals with substantive expertise who manage that issue for the company. Under the dispersed model (sometimes also called "the quarterback system"), issue coordinators have strategic responsibility for their issues. They may be responsible for undertaking or obtaining the necessary issues analysis; be deeply involved in formulating policy, positions and strategy; play the principal implementing role through direct lobbying, trade association liaison, coalition-building, and the like. Central coordination of the issue coordinators, if it exists at all in this organizational form, is provided by an inter-departmental committee or perhaps a single individual at the corporate level who may devote all or perhaps only part of his or her time to this responsibility. (The dispersed model can also function as a supplementary adjunct to a central government relations department or to a Washington office.)

Large companies may have *hybrid* structures, with one division's lobbying functions centralized, a second decentralized, a third using the dispersed model, a fourth leaving everything to its trade association, and a fifth doing nothing whatever.

Which organizational model is "correct"? There is no such thing as an ideal structure for government relations. Even within the same organization, what is ideal at one point in time may become quite imperfect at another.

The correct model is the one that will achieve the organization's objectives within the context of its culture.

For most membership organizations, the centralized form is typical; few have staffs large enough to be decentralized, let alone dispersed. The very largest, however, have sometimes taken different paths. The U.S. Chamber of Commerce, a multiissue business organization, has long followed a form that is partly dispersed and partly centralized. Issue experts, diffused among several departments, are responsible for research, alliances, and general strategy for their issues. They share responsibility for direct lobbying and membership communications on their issues with a central Legislative Department that also manages grassroots programs. Political action is the responsibility of another department.

Within individual companies, the organization of the government relations function is likely to adhere to the firm's current overall organizational philosophy. For many large multidivisional companies today, this often means decentralization. Since the government relations function may not be a fulltime responsibility in a decentralized structure, it is sometimes combined with other related activities such as legal, public relations, or community relations. In the dispersed form, government relations is always only one of multiple individual responsibilities.

The advantages of both the decentralized and dispersed forms are that the government relations process is never far removed from the substantive expertise on the issues. Advocates of both forms also believe costs are less; but depending on the sophistication of internal accounting, it may be only that costs are less visible than they would be under a centralized system.

Two prime hazards need to be guarded against with both noncentralized forms. The first is potential lack of coordination. At its worst, this can take the form of two operating units within a company taking opposite stands on the same issue. Even short of this extreme, however, there is a need for consistency of positions and mutual support in their implementation.

The second problem is that lawmakers and other public officials are unlikely to appreciate the niceties of corporate organization and may question why they should be asked to take their time to see several people from the same company on different issues when a single individual could cover them all.

This is not to say that centralized structures are necessarily the best. Centralized government relations departments can become too concerned with governmental and political process at the expense of issue substance. They also have been known to lose touch occasionally with some of the operating realities of the business, particularly in multidivision companies.

In most companies, it is the responsibility of government relations or public affairs personnel to identify issues for top corporate and operating managements, often including forecasts of developments and emerging issues. Less frequently, they participate in planning processes or comment on the plans of others. These are important roles that can be fulfilled in different ways, depending less on the form of organization than on perceptions of the value management places on the judgment and expertise of government relations executives.

Corporations and associations seeking organizational models will find numerous permutations and examples. There is no universally optimum government relations structure. What works, works.

Coordinating Systems

Regardless of whether government relations is organized along centralized, decentralized, or dispersed lines, coordinating mechanisms are essential. Such systems should take guidance from, and communicate with, all relevant operating unit and corporate staff executives. A permanent government relations (or public affairs) committee provides such a mechanism.

This committee should meet regularly to approve company policies, positions, and implementation plans; review the status of issues; and generally stay posted on the significance of developments and the outlook for each issue. On major matters, committee recommendations should be submitted to the chief executive for final approval. (In some organizations, the CEO may choose to be a member of the committee.)

In organizations where government relations is centralized, an important purpose of the committee is to help the department stay close to its constituencies. The head of the Government Relations Department should chair the committee. Members should include his or her principal subordinates plus the heads of operating divisions or units, and those corporate staff executives deeply involved in public affairs (for example, the general counsel plus managers in charge of public relations, environmental affairs, regulatory compliance, human resources, tax matters, and the like).

In decentralized or dispersed organizations, the committee's functions would be the same but with a few differences in composition. Membership would include all the above individuals (to the extent their roles exist) plus the issue coordinators. If there is a senior government relations executive, that individual should chair the committee; if not, another appropriate corporate executive should do so, making sure that the system functions as it should on the issues.

Reporting Relationships

An important consideration is the organizational placement of the government relations staff.

If the chief executive wants the function to be important—and to be *seen* as important—it should not be run by a manager three or four reporting levels down. If the function is truly important to the organization, it should be directed by an executive reporting directly to the CEO or at most one level down. The further removed government relations is from the top, the lower the perception of its importance within the organization; in this context perception *is* reality. In over half of companies in 1996, the senior public affairs officer reports to top management, to lower-ranking executives in the rest.[4]

The reporting relationship should be dictated by the importance of the function and the organizational needs and public issues with which it is concerned, *not* by the size of its staff or budget.

Compensation and Titles

Compensation (salaries plus bonuses) for corporate executives in public affairs and government relations varies by geography, size of company, size of department, gender, and other factors, according to 1995 and 1996 studies. These surveys, updated every two years, are commissioned by the Foundation for Public Affairs, an arm of the Public Affairs Council.[5]

Compensation for the top public affairs position in 1996 ranged from $41,000 to $700,000. The low range and the median are about a third higher than they were in 1988, but the high range has nearly tripled during that time, implying that companies for which public affairs is of great importance are willing to pay top dollars for top people.

Shown here are the national medians of total cash compensation (salary and bonus, if any). All data are for 1996, except for the Washington office positions, which were separately surveyed a year earlier.

Top public affairs executive	$197,803
Top federal government relations executive (headquarters-based)	148,080
Head of Washington office	179,235
Deputy head of Washington office	150,000
Top state government relations executive	121,500

Since these figures are medians (the number which 50 percent of the data fall below and 50 percent rise above), actual compensation diverges substantially from these numbers. The FPA surveys contain considerable additional data, both for these positions and for others in corporate public affairs.

The senior public affairs or government relations position carries the title of vice president or higher in about three-quarters of the companies in the FPA survey. This is a significant upgrade in status compared to a decade ago.

Program and Budget

If a government relations department is to be run cost-effectively, it should operate by both program and budget.

There is a logical progression in the development of these management tools: Organizational needs lead to issues. Planning the management of those issues, coupled with issue priority ratings, results in a program. The program, together with the dollar estimates of the costs needed to implement it, produces a budget.

Both program and budget should be multiyear if they are to be useful planning guides. Three years is the practical outside limit. Multiyear programs and budgets are usually prepared on a rolling basis: The old year drops off as a new third year is added; the new first and second years are amended as needs and resources dictate.

The priority or value rating system discussed in Chapter 4 provides a guide for the allocation of resources, both internal and external, including personnel.

Few substantial issues are settled within a year or two, least of all contentious ones. In formulating the program, the best estimate possible should be made of the length of time required to resolve the issue. In the case of long-term issues—those that are very controversial or defensive, the timing of which really rests in the hands of legislators or other interest groups—the estimate can be only approximate. It may be sufficient to note in the program that the issue is likely still to be alive at the end of the third year.

The program should contain the outline of a battle plan for each major issue, sketching out the resources to be applied. The time period during which particular resources will be needed should be indicated.

Major line items in government relations budgets may include the following:

- Salaries and bonuses
- Employee benefits and perquisites
- Travel and entertainment
- Consultants and independent lobbyists
- Publications, subscriptions, specialized computer software, and on-line and tracking services
- Dues and professional training
- Rent and other costs of satellite offices (in Washington and state capitals)
- Coalition expenses
- Political action committee administrative costs
- Grassroots program costs

A rough rule of thumb for government relations budgets is that their total is about twice personnel costs (salaries, bonuses, and benefits). Corporate budgets in 1996 ranged as high as $15 million and more, with larger companies generally having larger budgets; the median was in the $1 to $2 million range.[6]

Utilizing Other Corporate Resources Staff and issue coordinator responsibilities and deadlines should be identified in the program to ensure accountability for performance. Other resources required to accomplish performance by deadlines should also be noted. (See the model below.) These include *internal* resources—those within the government affairs department—as well

---

MODEL GOVERNMENT RELATIONS PROGRAM
XYZ Corporation

ISSUE: *Widget Use Licensing*

OBJECTIVE: (1) Oppose all legislative/regulatory proposals to require licenses for widget use. (2) Support efforts to repeal existing license requirements.

VALUE RATING: 9

PRIORITY: *High* in Ark., Pa., Utah, Seattle, & Boston — serious threats. *Medium* in Ariz. & Tenn. — repeal interest growing. *Low* elsewhere including Congress — little activity.

COMPLETION DATE: Open — long-term problem.

ACTIONS PLANNED:

> *Research* — Impact paper by Jones of Law Dept. & Smith of Marketing Dept. Legislative analyses commissioned in three High states & two High cities. Background papers underway for Ariz. & Tenn.

> *Direct Lobbying* — G.R. resp. in PA (Hodges) & Seattle (Dixon). Local lobbyists hired in Boston, AR, & UT. Local legal counsel monitoring in AZ & TN. Trade assn. field staff helping as feasible.

> *Grassroots Lobbying* — Employees in Philadelphia, Seattle & Nashville plants being alerted to contact legislators; information booklets already distributed. Other action plans in preparation.

> *Coalitions* — Widget user groups to be formed, using warranty records as base. Unions closely involved. Negotiations underway with ACLU & consumer groups.

> *Political* — Good access where needed.

> *Communications* — P.R. Dept. (Harrison) developing targeted messages for stockholders, employees, public officials, & press in High & Medium locations. Outside P.R. firm providing backup, speech material, & media interviews.

RESOURCES: *G.R. Dept.*: Mason, mgr.; D'Elia, back-up. Field reps: as noted above. Outside lobbyists as noted. *Other internal*: P.R. (Harrison - 1/2 time + outside firm as needed); Law (Jones - 1/4 time); Marketing (Smith 1/8 time); Data Proc. (3 person-days); Human Res. & Investor Rel. personnel (as needed).

COSTS: See budget for data by year & quarters

BENEFITS: See Marketing Impact paper for estimates of potential revenue preserved or regained.

as those resources elsewhere in the organization on which the department can call as required.

This latter point can be a critical element in cost-effective government relations management, as the following examples indicate:

- The existing data processing system can be utilized for highly sophisticated communications to a variety of constituents and audiences.
- Grassroots lobbying lets the organization utilize its members—or the company's managers, employees, and stockholders—as a trained, enthusiastic volunteer cadre of lobbyists who can be mobilized issue by issue.
- Coalitions and alliances can sometimes permit a sharing of costs and resources among the participating organizations to accomplish common objectives.
- Trade association memberships can be managed to maximize the value of the dues and executive time invested.

The ability to transform such resources can maximize the capability of the government relations staff to achieve program objectives with minimum budgetary impact. These nondepartmental resources should also be detailed in the annual and three-year programs. The budget includes those current or planned internal expenses needed to make the most effective use of external resources and otherwise to achieve objectives.

A very substantial number (three-fourths) of companies today take this concept a step further by outsourcing a variety of government relations and other public affairs activities.[7]

This kind of program and budget requires strong support from top management. Without such support, inadequate funding and organizational politics will cripple the achievement of government relations goals.

Performance Evaluation

Judging both the effectiveness of the government relations function and the performance of its managers is more difficult than evaluating business functions that usually are appraised quantitatively. Government relations personnel can—and should—be evaluated, but fair measures of performance must reflect the nature of the function.

If a hundred adverse bills died in a particular legislative session, it is unrealistic to give the government relations manager full credit for all the scalps. For one thing, most of the bills might have died anyhow for lack of general support. For another, credit that may be deserved perhaps should be shared with other organizations that worked equally hard. It may be more significant that an important favorable bill was passed, if only because enacting legislation is usually much harder than defeating it; but if it took three years to get this bill passed, does the manager get an incomplete in each of the first two years and A+ in the third? Lobbyists at best are persuaders; decision-making power lies exclusively with public officials.

The advantage of a formal annual government relations program is that it can be used to hold personnel accountable for performance: What was to be done? By whom? By when? With what resources? Were the goals accomplished? How well? On time? Within budget? More than 70 percent of companies use preset objectives to measure performance.[8]

For this approach to work, the program must be quite specific. Each task, function, or role should be assigned to a named individual. Each should agree in advance with the statement of his or her accountabilities. A computer can then print out a list of responsibilities and accountabilities.

At year's end, the manager will have a basis for evaluating individual performance: Was the grassroots training seminar actually organized by July 24? How good a job did Smith do on the project? The PAC fund-raising drive under Jones was to raise $50,000 by September 1; what factors explain why only $40,000 was raised and only half the fund-raising budget was spent?

This approach assumes that an executive whose program is regularly meeting its objectives on schedule and on budget is probably also achieving positive results over time in the areas where measures are softer and less direct. The same concept can be used by the CEO to appraise the effectiveness of the department as a whole.

A growing number of companies take evaluation of government relations effectiveness to more sophisticated levels. For example, quantifying the performance of the department as a whole in various ways is a distinct trend in corporate government relations, used by about half of major companies. Many define the department (or perhaps just the Washington office) as profit centers, quantifying issues as best they can to aid in prioritization, resource justification, and year-end evaluation. In some instances, the quantification process allows the calculation of return on investment—that is, costs as a percentage of the dollar value of the benefits gained from the advocacy process.[9]

A variation on this theme positions the government relations function as an internal consulting firm retained by the company's operating units to lobby on their issues. The operating groups finance their share of the department's costs based either on the numbers of hours spent on their behalf or as a percentage of the department's budget. In some companies, operating divisions satisfied with the lobbying result actually pay the department a bonus. This approach permits "customer satisfaction" surveys to measure the quality and value of services provided. (Indeed, a few firms also survey legislators, asking them to appraise the effectiveness of the company and its lobbyists.)

Implicit in this concept is that the business units are the "clients" of the government relations department. In some companies, the internal government relations staff must actually compete with outside vendors. If operating managers in these companies feel they can get better service externally, they have the latitude to outsource their government relations needs.

Who are the prime clients of public affairs? The chief executive in 70 percent of companies, business units in more than half, and other staff departments in a third.[10]

Benchmarking

A growing trend in corporate government relations is systematic compari-son with the highest-performing companies. Benchmarks are not a fixed stan-dard but, rather, a moving target. As the best-performing companies improve, those emulating them also are strengthened.

In reality, no single government relations staff excels at everything. At any time, one company's staff may have the best tracking system for current is-sues, another a superior program to identify emerging issues, a third a top-flight grassroots program, a fourth an optimum program to involve managers in precinct politics, and so on.

Benchmarking can also be used to compare the roles and relationships of the top government relations executive with superiors and peers, with operat-ing units and other staff departments in corporate planning processes, and so on. It can examine the best practices in such areas as outsourcing, the supervi-sion of consultants in international public affairs, candidate interviewing tech-niques for PACs, or the management of crisis planning. Benchmarking lends itself to comparative evaluations of performance in any of the major fields of government relations or their smallest aspects.

The basic benchmarking process follows these steps:

1. Identify and prioritize the areas to be studied. Generally, these will be those fields of activity in which government relations executives or their superiors feel are in greatest need of improvement.
2. Identify the companies that are considered to be the best performers in each field.
3. Determine the best measures (preferably quantitative ones) that will facilitate optimum comparisons.
4. Analyze the data, pinpointing strengths to be maximized and weaknesses to be corrected.
5. Plan improvements based on the data and budget for them.
6. Communicate with subordinates, peers, and senior management at every stage, so that everyone involved supports the process and the action plan that results from it.

The value of benchmarking is that, over time, it provides a continuing way to bootstrap the government relations function to ever-higher levels of perfor-mance. It also assures top management that it has the best government rela-tions operation possible, relative to its own evaluation of needs and affordability. Benchmarking is therefore still another way to win the confidence of the company's operating managers and chief executive.

TECHNOLOGY IN GOVERNMENT RELATIONS

While the number of companies and other organizations making use of new technologies is rapidly growing, the vast majority still do not utilize all the new tools available to them. For the vast majority of companies, high tech in government relations means little more than fax, voice mail, and e-mail. At the same time, the scope and breadth of technological tools are mushrooming at an astounding rate. Indeed, nothing in this book is likely to be outdated as quickly as this section—technology books are often obsolete before they can be published.

Only a few years ago, business cards listed name, title, address, and telephone number. Then fax numbers were added. Today, they often show a pager or cellular phone number, an Internet e-mail address, and sometimes the company's homepage address on the World Wide Web.

Every office has a fax machine today. Most computers come equipped with an internal modem that, combined with appropriate software and a telephone line, can be used to send and receive faxes. An increasing number of organizations are now using *broadcast fax*. This requires a more complex modem or communications server, generally servicing the organization's computer network but also accessible from individual workstations on the network. Broadcast fax rapidly transmits a document to hundreds or thousands of recipients whose fax numbers have been preprogrammed into the system, at about half the cost of first-class mail (even less if sent at night when telephone rates are cheaper).

No technological development has more significance for government relations, however, than the ubiquitous *Internet* and the various management tools it provides and facilitates. Still, only 10 percent of corporate public affairs departments were making use of the Internet in 1996.[11] For government relations practitioners, the Internet can be used to research any conceivable subject; monitor public affairs developments worldwide; track the progress of issues almost instantaneously; manage crises; communicate with public officials, candidates, and the press; and stay in virtually constant touch with participants in grassroots programs. Given the Internet's exponential growth, it is only a matter of a few years before any computer-literate individual in the world (including developing countries) will be able to contact any other individual or organization anywhere—on any subject.

The Internet has experienced its most exponential growth since the advent of the *World Wide Web*. The Web is simply a way of organizing information (text, graphics, or audio) on the Internet. Data on the Web are stored on *homepages*, each of which has a specific address. The Web is based on the concept of hypertext (or more precisely hypermedia because it also handles graphics and audio), a technology that allows links between information stored on computers anywhere in the world. Most homepages incorporate *hypertext links* to other homepages with related information. Pushing a hypertext button on the screen immediately takes the user to another site. *Search engines* facilitate locating information on particular subjects or from particular sources, again *anywhere* on the Internet.

The Internet lets users view color images of the paintings in the Louvre, hear the president's state of the union address, and download information on a lawmaker's voting record and issue positions. Virtually every legislator has an e-mail address, and many have their own homepages.

A rapidly growing number of interest groups and public policy organizations are creating their own homepages that include government relations and political information. Information can be available to anybody with access to the Web—or access can be limited to specific individuals, such as members or employees with a password. Access can also be sold to for a fee.

Anyone with a few of days of widely available training can design and program an organization's homepage. Or the organization can pay a modest fee to have it created. Once created, the homepage must be stored or *hosted* on a server (a network computer). The organization may use a commercial Internet service provider or it may choose to host its own homepage. Fees for both homepage creation and hosting vary greatly and depend on factors of size and complexity. Software to track the number of times a homepage has been accessed (called "hits") is readily available and can be acquired at little or no cost. Companies providing hosting services also typically provide more detailed information on the hits—including which data were accessed and the identification of the user's system (but not the user itself). An organization may also invite people who visit its homepage to sign a "guest book." Thus, a vast amount of information can be collected regarding who is interested in the organization and what information is evoking interest. The key to obtaining frequent "hits" is to update the information, both text and graphics, frequently.

The standard for modems is currently 28.8 bps (bits per second). In the near future, this is likely to rise to 56.6 bps or even faster. Anything slower than 28.8 bps will be costly in terms of time required to access the information needed. Technologies such as *ISDN*, a digital service, allow access at greater speeds and substantially reduce the time required to view and download information.

A growing number of companies and organizations are building their own miniversions of the Internet. *Intranets* enable e-mail, departmental homepages, and a variety of other features *within* the organization. Corporate and departmental intranets were used in a quarter or more of companies in 1996.[12] *Extranets* allow such communications with specified outsiders, such as vendors or customers.

Organizations may also use the Internet to establish forums (or mailing lists) to share information about specific topics, such as government relations programs. Participants subscribe to a *list;* they may contribute information, post questions, and receive information on the topic via e-mail. All information to "the list" is sent to a central address from which it is distributed to subscribers.

A personal computer with a modem permits government relations practitioners to utilize *on-line tracking and issues management programs*. (See appendix.) Several firms offer the ability to monitor in real time the status both of legislation and often of regulations in the various states and at the federal level. Other services offer specialized software programs that permit users not only to download this information but also to edit, manipulate, and analyze it according to their own special interests.

Software to manage grassroots programs and political action committees is also available. Grassroots management programs can be simple or as complex as relational databases that let membership organizations or companies identify the congressional or state legislative districts of their members or employees. They thus permit grassroots communications to highly targeted lists of participants; for instance, all or selected constituents in the districts of House Commerce Committee members. These programs can also be used to manage coalitions. Some of these programs can also maintain data on previous legislative contacts by specific participants, together with legislators' responses, so that appropriate personalized mail-merge letters or broadcast fax bulletins can be automatically prepared and sent.

Programs to manage PACs can tie into payroll deduction plans, monitoring contribution levels and facilitating solicitation campaigns, including automatic generation of thank-you letters. They can manage information on contributions to candidates and party committees—and also permit on-line filing of reports to the Federal Election Commission (FEC) and, in some cases, to the FEC's state counterparts.

Packages combining several of these government relations software programs are available, allowing them to be integrated for analysis and communications. The Public Affairs Council is a good source of up-to-date information on such programs. Costs are in four or five digits, depending on the complexity and sophistication of the program, but they are highly cost-effective in terms of both speed and personnel time saved.

Some associations and large companies maintain their own *private on-line services*, permitting users to access a variety of legislative or regulatory information. For example, NAMnet, a service for the members of the National Association of Manufacturers, tracks federal legislation and issues legislative alerts for its grassroots network. It also provides users with issue analyses from independent think tanks, the NAM's analyses of congressional voting records, and texts of legislative publications. Information on the status of certain state issues from the NAM's state affiliates is also available on NAMnet. Corporate systems usually use internal e-mail or their intranet for these systems.

Pagers and cellular telephones are commonplace today. People walk the streets of every city and lurch down every highway, oblivious to the world around them as they carry on telephone conversations. Business luncheons are constantly interrupted when someone has to answer an urgent page. The impact of these devices on the pace and civility of life is a topic for another discussion, but the fact is that no one need ever be out of touch with home or office anymore.

A related technology now on the market is the *personal digital assistant* (PDA), a wireless, hand-held computer. A PDA can receive news about particular subjects personalized to the user's requirements, (e.g., developments on particular issues). It allows the user to receive e-mail, utilize a stylus to send hand-written messages, browse the web, and use basic word processing, spreadsheet, and contact management programs.

Coupled with advances in cellular technology and personal communications services (*PCS,* a wireless communications technology), a PDA will allow a lobbyist roaming the corridors of Congress to receive "personalized" information, such as the status of legislation in the California legislature, the European Commission, and ultimately any parliament on earth—and take immediate action accordingly. The PDA can be used to make appointments, call meetings (both automatically recorded on a built-in calendar), buy airline tickets, or make credit card purchases.

It is likely that at some point PDA technology will incorporate portable telephones and allow the use of the instrument as a portable answering machine if the user is unable to accept a call.

The days when lobbyists lined up at pay telephones to report on important news from some legislative hearing—or to learn the status of another issue—are gone forever.

NOTES

1. James E. Post and Jennifer J. Griffin, *The State of Corporate Public Affairs: 1996 Survey Results* (Washington, D.C.: Foundation for Public Affairs, 1997). Fig. 10.8. Contains a survey of more than 260 companies by Boston University School of Management.

2. Ibid., Fig. 4.1.

3. Ibid.

4. Ibid., Fig. 2.1.

5. Hay Management Consultants, *1996–1997 Compensation Survey of Public Affairs Positions* (Washington, D.C.: Foundation for Public Affairs, 1996); idem, *1995–96 Washington Office Compensation Survey* (Washington, D.C.: Foundation for Public Affairs, 1995). Both reports also show data on long-term compensation (e.g., stock options) and perquisites.

6. Post and Griffin, *Corporate Public Affairs,* Fig. 5.1.

7. Ibid., Fig. 11.3.

8. Ibid., Fig. 13.1.

9. Ibid.

10. Ibid., Fig. 11.1.

11. Ibid., Fig. 12.1.

12. Ibid.

Chapter 6

Politics and the Legislative Process

Man is by nature a political animal.

—Aristotle

Laws are like sausages. It is better not to see them being made.

—Bismarck

Government relations professionals deal with elected officials, particularly legislators. That means they deal with politicians. Politics is part and parcel of the legislative process, as we shall see in this chapter's discussion of the ways legislatures go about their business, the staffs they hire to assist them, and the considerations that affect their votes.

LEGISLATIVE INFLUENCES

Among the fifty-one national and state legislatures, there are very broad similarities in the legislative process but also innumerable differences in detail. The "typical" legislative process is widely taught in elementary and high school classes. In reality, however, there are significant differences in legislative procedure. The crucial details differ greatly—not only from legislature to legislature but to some extent even from chamber to chamber in the same state.

For example, every legislature (except Nebraska, which has a unicameral legislature) requires that a bill pass both houses in identical form to be enacted, but the procedures to resolve differences vary. Congress and some state legislatures provide for formal conferences between the two houses; others do not, relying, in effect, on informal negotiation. Recorded roll-call votes are common in some legislative bodies, rare in others. Many—but not all—use electronic tally boards for such votes.

Good lobbyists sometimes know the fine points of legislative procedure better than many lawmakers. An understanding of these often intricate rules is an essential requirement for the lobbying process.

In some state and local legislatures, bills may be "pre-filed" (introduced before the legislative session begins) but during the session may be introduced after a deadline only under restricted conditions; in other legislatures, including Congress, bills may be introduced at any time during the session. The rules of Congress do not permit pre-filing.

In addition to the vast body of formal procedures, every legislature has customs and folkways that are at least as important as the formal rules. For instance, legislative hearings may be quite common in one legislature and virtually nonexistent in another. Committee meetings may be open to the public or closed. Strategic decisions on controversial issues, which are generally made out of public view, may be reached in closed-door party caucuses, in a Rules or Policy Committee, or by the majority party leadership.

Intellectual command of these technical details, formal and informal— essential for lobbyists—has often meant the difference between victory and defeat on an issue. The good news is that the minutiae of the legislative process seldom change significantly. Once they are mastered, keeping up is fairly easy. The political environment, on the other hand, is highly fluid—as placid as the sea, or as violent.

The Role of Legislative Staff

If Napoleon's army traveled on its stomach, legislators travel on their staffs. In both Washington and many state capitals, service in the legislature is virtually full time, and for many it has become a career. Congressmen and state legislators are highly, sometimes completely, dependent on competent staff personnel.

Lobbyists are also dependent on legislative staff people. Friendly staff can help lobbyists get in the door, hostile staff determinedly keep them out. Personal, cordial relations with the staff are as essential as they are with legislators themselves. Lobbyists make a point of knowing and cultivating the staff experts on their issues, whether personal aides to the legislator or committee staff members.

Cultivating means not just personal relationships, but professional ones— providing the staff member with useful data about both the interest group and its issues, and getting important information back in return. Working with helpful legislators almost always really means working with their legislative aides to assure that every necessary or useful detail to advance the interest group's position is carefully handled.

Professional legislative staffs are of two types: (1) personal staffs to individual members; (2) committee and general legislative staffs.

Personal Staff

Aides help their legislators with all their duties, many of which relate only marginally to legislation. Such staff functions typically include

Scheduling This includes booking appointments and filling the calendar with constituent visits, lobbyist appointments, speaking engagements, and the like, both in the district and in the capital—as well as keeping track of legislative committee meetings, floor sessions and other scheduled official duties.

Casework This is assistance to constituents with problems they may be having with government agencies. These range across the entire spectrum of governmental activity, from helping with a delayed pension or Social Security check or facilitating the award of a government contract to getting a pothole fixed or obtaining an official publication. The quality of such services is a significant influence in voters' decisions on election day and a major reason why incumbents are usually re-elected.

Legislation This consists of providing issues research and tracking legislation. The size of personal legislative staffs may range from one individual to dozens, depending on the legislative body and the lawmaker's interests and responsibilities. The legislator's seniority is often a factor in the size of these staffs. Staff aides usually specialize in particular subject areas, again depending on the legislator's needs and interests. Lobbyists make a particular point of knowing well the staff assistant who covers their issues. A telephone inquiry to the legislator's office is sufficient to learn which staff assistant handles which issues.

Committee and General Legislative Staffs

Each legislative house has staff people who handle administrative and legislative details for groups of legislators or for all of them. Sometimes these staffs serve only the members of their political party; in other situations they perform without regard to partisanship. In addition, most legislative committees have their own expert staffs. Committee staffs are often controlled by the committee chairman unless the staff is partisan, in which case the ranking minority legislator on the committee will control his or her own party's staff. In some legislative bodies, committee staffs report to a senior staff official who serves the entire house (or all of the party's members); even in such an arrangement, most staffers typically are assigned to specific committees.

These staff members specialize in particular areas. Most are issue or subject specialists. Some specialize in bill drafting, either preparing bills for individual legislators or approving the legal form of bills drafted by others on personal or committee staffs. Still others manage the legislative calendar of the committee or full house, or provide policy, political or parliamentary advice to the leadership.

It is no putdown of legislators to say that their legislative staffs do most of their thinking for them. These individuals not only put lawmakers' ideas in bill form, but also advise them about substance. They research the issues, receive—and commonly solicit—information and inputs from lobbyists, weigh the effects on key constituencies, negotiate with interest groups and with their counterparts on other legislators' staffs, write the speeches and the press releases, and do whatever is necessary to make their boss look good. Whenever there is an unusually able legislative leader, lurking just over the shoulder is a highly skilled and knowledgeable staff expert.

It is interesting how many legislative staff people later become lobbyists because the personal characteristics are so different. Obviously, intelligence, honesty, and total loyalty to the boss are essential. But good staff aides also have to be self-effacing, not a trait normally associated with lobbyists. They must be able to act as surrogates for the legislator in meetings or before audiences, but they also need to know when to fade anonymously into the background. They act as policy and political advisors to their lawmakers and, truth be told, often are the brains behind them. "Staffers do not sit on the throne, but they know the secret passageways, the trapdoors, the hidden tunnel system. They can brag that they have friends in low places, that they know where the bodies are buried because they know where they buried them."[1]

Sometimes, these staff assistants (both personal and committee) are actually the intellectual founts of the issues their legislators champion. They may search out public problems and devise legislative remedies, acting in some cases as in-house lobbyists for particular causes or points of view, working closely with allied interest groups. Activities of this type are perfectly legitimate, so long as these aides act with the full knowledge and consent of the legislator they assist and represent.

The lobbyist seeking the originator of a particular issue often therefore need look no further than the legislative sponsor's staff. Harder—because it takes considerable time and effort—is the essential development of good personal working relationships with these individuals.

Legislative Voting Influences

Since at least the time of Edmund Burke more than two centuries ago, political scientists and philosophers have argued about the theory of legislative representation. Burke held that legislators are "trustees," elected by their constituents to rely on their consciences and best judgment in deciding what is in the public interest. The contrasting view is that elected representatives are "delegates," chosen to advocate the interests of their constituents and to vote as a majority of them wish, reflecting and representing constituents' opinions rather than legislators' personal convictions.

To some extent, actual practice lies somewhere between these poles. Lawmakers have their own political philosophies and ideologies, which significantly influence their positions on issues and their voting behavior. A skilled politician is a leader who has a knack for convincing the voters that their views are identical with his or hers, who can shape and mold public opinion, as well as be influenced by it. A lawmaker with a reputation for great conscience can get away with voting on an issue or two in opposition to the desires of the people back home. But legislators who make a habit of voting as they think best and not as their constituents wish tend to have brief careers.

However, this last statement does not take into account electoral politics and the competitiveness or safety of the legislator's seat. An economic analysis of legislative voting affirmed what lobbyists and politicians have long understood intuitively: "The more electorally secure the legislator, the less account she takes of constituency interests in her voting decisions."[2] In other words, she is freer to be a "trustee" if her district is relatively safe. But that still leaves open the question of what interests she *does* take into account.

One of the most critical judgments lobbyists must make is understanding the influences likely to be the determinants of each legislator's voting decisions on particular issues. The variations will be substantial, depending on the legislator's political vulnerability, the character of the legislative body, the time and political climate, the issue, the role of various interest groups, and, of course, each lawmaker's own ideology and personality.

While personal philosophy matters greatly as an influence on legislative voting, so does public opinion in lawmakers' constituencies, especially if they feel reelection is at risk. The legislator whose reelection campaigns are always a battle is much more susceptible to constituency contacts and press and public opinion than one who rarely has to worry about coming back for another term.

The 1996 minimum wage issue in Congress is a good illustration. When the voters in enough congressional districts became convinced that an increase was fair, necessary, and overdue, that factor overcame the ideological antipathy of the House Republican leadership and of many members. This was especially true of those legislators who felt their reelection prospects were endangered in the upcoming congressional elections. Every legislator's staff keeps careful tallies of constituent communications on current issues (including the increasing number arriving as e-mail). Both the volume and the intensity of the messages from back home are major determinants of legislative voting behavior.

Related, though usually of lesser impact, are media coverage and editorial pressures, both locally and to some extent nationally. An editorial in a local newspaper that the legislator knows is a strong influence on both opinion leaders and the general public back home will have some impact, but for the most part editorials are a weak force.

Among constituents, the opinions of major campaign contributors and campaign volunteers tend to carry greater weight than those of uninvolved citizens.

Because legislators like to be consistent in their voting, another key influence is the positions they have taken in the past on related issues. But since it is impossible for them to be expert on every issue that comes before them, they are influenced by legislative staff issue experts or those with friendly outside organizations, and by committee recommendations.

The views of respected colleagues with similar philosophies who are known for their expertise on an issue are one of the strongest influences on legislative voting. It is common on any complex issue to see legislators rush onto the floor for a vote about which they know little, take a moment to learn how a particular colleague is voting, vote the same way, and rush back out again. Lobbyists know if they can persuade a couple of these legislative opinion leaders to their side, a number of other votes will come with them, almost automatically.

Lawmakers frequently bring other votes with them for another reason, a practice called "log-rolling." Legislators who agree to vote for a narrow issue that primarily helps another member or for a public works project in someone else's district can call in these legislative debts when they have their own pet parochial issues.

Another substantial influence often is the legislator's political party. The views taken by party caucuses, leaders, activists, and platforms are significant shaping forces on legislative voting. If the lawmaker is of the same political party as the president or governor, party loyalty will be an important influence.

A classic case is that of Democratic Representative Marjorie Margolies-Mezvinski. She was elected in 1992 in what historically has been a philosophically moderate Republican district in the Philadelphia suburbs. When President Clinton's tax and economic legislative package came up for a vote in the House the next year, she was lobbied intensely by Democratic leaders and White House lobbyists to support her party and its president. Reluctantly and at the last moment, she did so, and the bill passed the House by a single vote. Her vote became the overriding issue in her 1994 reelection campaign, and she was defeated by her Republican opponent. The obvious moral is that party loyalty sometimes asks too much.

That lesson was largely ignored for a time among the large class of freshman Republicans elected to the House in 1994. Arguably, one of the most intensely ideological groups ever elected to Congress, the freshmen took highly conservative positions on issue after issue, often crossing swords with powerful pressures in their districts to do so. Several publicly and defiantly maintained that they had been elected to change America, and they were going to do so even if it resulted in their defeat. No "delegates" they!

All that changed after the budget crisis and two shutdowns of government agencies, a political and public relations debacle for Republicans at the hands of the Democratic president. The GOP's rout had a significantly moderating effect on the views of the freshmen; they had lost on substance, and they had lost politically. By the summer of 1996, with the November elections looming, trusteeship had departed the House of Representatives. Legislation was passed increasing the minimum wage, on health care, and on the environment—bills that surely would have been killed twelve months earlier. Most of the freshmen went on to win reelection in the fall.

Political consultants are increasingly a factor in the positions legislators adopt. Once used only during campaigns, political strategists and pollsters now frequently are on year-round retainer to many legislators. They advise them on public attitudes, strategy and tactics, fund-raising techniques, ways to minimize the candidacy of possible opponents, and the potential political impact of major issues. Legislators frequently seek their advice before deciding how they will vote, especially on controversial subjects.

The positions taken by particular interests may be a major force, a minor one, or have no effect whatever, depending on the legislator's relations with and attitudes toward the group. Liberals whose views are in sympathy with such interests as labor unions, environmental organizations, and trial lawyers—and who have benefited from their political support—generally are receptive to the positions taken by those groups. Conservatives who have good relations with various business groups give their advocates a cordial and sympathetic hearing and tend to support their positions absent some other overriding influence.

However, even very conservative legislators can be prone to support the position of a labor union if the union local in their districts has a large, politically potent membership, more so if they feel vulnerable, less so if they feel safe. Liberals may be disinclined to support the positions of national business groups but may go out of their way to be helpful to a particular industry or a company that is a significant employer in the district.

Interest groups affect legislative positions in other ways, too. Lawmakers sitting on committees of particular concern to an interest group are more likely to draw campaign contributions from that group's members, and this likelihood is further increased if the legislator's voting record is supportive of the interest group's positions.[3] Members of the House Ways and Means and Commerce Committees (and their Senate counterparts) receive more contributions from business political action committees than do members of, say, the Foreign Affairs Committee. Those business contributors are likely to be even more forthcoming if the legislator's votes are mostly supportive of business positions.

Here again, though, vulnerable incumbents have to balance their need for campaign contributions against an assessment of the impact of their votes at home. If Congresswoman Jones's vote helps a large and supportive agribusiness company but hurts the farmers in her rural district, she will have some fast talking to do when campaign time rolls around. Her need for campaign funds only partly offsets her need for her constituents' votes. If the conflict is too great, she will look for some other industry or interest group with which to establish an alliance. Reelection, not campaign contributions, is her bottom line.

Do members of Congress vote the views of their contributors more than they do their own convictions? Even political contributors think so. A January 1997 *Washington Post* sample survey of people who donate to federal campaigns indicated that they believe senators and representatives vote at least half the time as contributors wish. Only 11 percent think this does not happen often. On the other hand, only 9 percent said they personally contribute to influence legislators' positions or actions.[4]

A number of interest groups use issue advertising in certain publications in an attempt to affect legislative opinion on particular issues. Most legislators say that this is the weakest influence of all on the positions they take. In specific cases, though, it has been known to work quite well. A lobbyist who was working hard to gain the support of a particular member of Congress discovered that she always listened to the same radio station while driving to her office in the morning. The lobbyist had an issue ad developed and played it on that station for several weeks during the morning rush hour. The maneuver worked, and the legislator came over to the lobbyist's side.

Issue ads can have an indirect influence on legislative decisions. Most lawmakers themselves may not respond, but occasionally the public will. If a legislator gets a substantial amount of constituent mail on the issue, the ad has served its purpose.

POLITICAL INFLUENCES

Lobbyists can no more shun politics than they can shun legislation. They need not participate personally in politics, though some do, but they must constantly take political considerations into account as they seek to affect the public policy process. Politics infuses and colors that process, and in fact energizes it.

Private-sector executives, particularly those in business, often have little understanding of politics, but sometimes they show great disdain. "Politicians have no conception of the bottom line," is an oft-heard comment. Nothing could be further from the truth. Political figures have a bottom line that is every bit as critical to them as the statement of profit or loss is to business people.

Election or re-election is the political version of the bottom line. Winning is every bit as critical to a political career as financial results are to a career in business. As dollars are the units of economics, so votes are the currency of political power.

The ebb and flow of political power pervades the legislative process. Every piece of legislation is considered, not only on its substantive merits but also in terms of its impact on power relationships. How will it affect the individual legislator's re-election prospects? If not a likely re-election problem, could it be a problem within the lawmaker's party as a possible danger to renomination? How will the various interest groups important to the legislator's success regard the issue?

Even legislators from safe seats must consider the effect an issue might have on prospects for retaining, or gaining, control of the legislative house in the next election. Next to a legislator's personal re-election prospects, political control of the chamber is always the overriding consideration. Control means the leadership. It means chairmanships of committees and subcommittees and command of their staffs. It means personal perquisites of many kinds.

Most important from the standpoint of this book, it means power over the levers of legislative process and public policy.

This drive for control and power also extends to the presidency, governorship, and other elected executive offices—and to regulatory and judicial offices as well where these are filled by election instead of appointment. Success in these elections for the legislator's party means enhanced personal influence and the opportunity to assist political friends and allies by helping to place them in key appointive positions. *Clout* is the term frequently used to describe this kind of influence and power.

Bipartisanship and Legislative Coalitions

Party loyalties notwithstanding, politics also involves personal and working relationships that often extend informally across the aisles that separate Republicans and Democrats in most legislative bodies. These cross-party relationships can also profoundly affect legislation. Legislators of different parties sometimes share a common point of view or an interest in a particular subject or engage in the favor-trading that is such an ingrained part of the political (and lobbying) process. Personal friendships and mentor relationships may also cut across party lines. The Republican leader of the U.S. Senate, Trent Lott of Mississippi, is a prime example. Senator Lott began his career as an aide to a conservative Democratic member of the House from his home state, and to this day he maintains close personal relationships with members of Congress in both parties and both houses.

Coalitions of Republicans and Democrats often form on various issues or subjects. Members of both parties will typically be found on both sides of issues, ranging as widely as capital punishment, environmental control, economic development, immigration reform, and fiscal policy.

In Congress, bipartisan coalitions frequently dominated the legislative process in the years following World War II. The master coalition was made up of Republicans and conservative southern Democrats who together determined the fate of many a piece of legislation for several decades. In later years, as these southern Democrats retired, they were, more often than not, replaced by Republicans who were typically even more conservative than the Democrats they succeeded.

After Republicans won control of Congress in 1994, a band of about two dozen conservative Democrats (not all of them southerners) organized themselves into the "Blue Dog" caucus to seek some leverage on close issues.[5] (Self-protection was another motive. A half-dozen southern Democrats in both houses switched parties after Republicans won majorities.) At the beginning of the Congress elected in 1996, in which the GOP majority in the House was reduced, the Blue Dogs and a group of moderate Republicans agreed to cooperate on legislation. The New Democrat Coalition, another caucus of somewhat less conservative House members, was created in 1997 with similar goals: to nudge Democratic policy toward the right.

Ideology and Partisanship

Notwithstanding such efforts, bipartisanship in Congress (and many state legislatures) is fading as the Republican and Democratic parties become polarized ideologically. In the 1940s, 1950s, and early 1960s, both parties at the national level ranged the spectrum from liberal to conservative; but that situation changed forever in 1964. The Republican presidential contest that year was a bitter ideological battle between conservative Senator Barry Goldwater of Arizona and liberal Governor Nelson Rockefeller of New York. Goldwater defeated Rockefeller decisively, and conservatives have dominated Republican politics ever since.

Goldwater was beaten badly in the November election, but he carried several southern states and energized the resurgence of the Republican Party in the South. A prime example is Mississippi, which up to that year had elected no Republican to any significant office in almost a century. A generation later, both the state's U.S. Senators were Republicans (one of them the Senate majority leader), as was the governor and two of five U.S. Representatives (plus a third after the '96 elections); both the chairman and the co-chairman of the Republican National Committee were from Mississippi.

This pattern has repeated itself all over the south. After the 1996 elections, seventeen of the region's twenty-four U.S. Senators were Republicans, representing ten states; and Republicans predominate in House delegations throughout the South. In 1997, the governors of nine of the region's twelve states were Republicans, and Republicans controlled at least one house of the legislature in a half-dozen states.

These southerners have moved the GOP steadily rightward. Republicans in the west and midwest have always been competitive, and many of these states are also represented in Congress by staunch conservatives. Today, there are no liberals left among Republican members of Congress, and the band of moderates is steadily shrinking.

At the same time, the Democratic Party's center of gravity in Congress has moved steadily leftward as conservative Democrats switched parties or were replaced by Republicans. Most newly elected Democrats have tended to be liberals, just as most new GOP members of Congress have been conservatives. The pundits and political scientists who long hoped for a clear ideological distinction between the two major parties have finally gotten the polarization they wanted.

Which brings to mind the old maxim, "Be careful what you wish for lest you get it." As the parties have polarized, partisanship has grown more intense and bitter. Comity and civility have declined, and debates over contentious issues are increasingly shrill and angry—none more so than that over the House Ethics Committee's report on Speaker Newt Gingrich that opened the 105th Congress in 1997. The debate surrounding the committee's recommendation that he merely be reprimanded (and thereby allowed to continue as speaker) rather than censured was intensely partisan and savage, perhaps even more so than the debate over the ouster of an earlier speaker, Jim Wright (which Gingrich himself had engineered a few years before).

The intensification of partisanship complicates life immeasurably for lobbyists. When Republicans took control of the House in 1995, they centralized control in the leadership to an extent not seen in this century. The number of committees was reduced, and limits were placed on the number of terms a member could chair a committee. Committee chairmen, power barons under the Democrats, were stripped of much of their ability to control the content and flow of legislation. On certain issues, special task forces were established to do end-runs around established committees and subcommittees if those chairing them were considered insufficiently reliable.

All this meant that some lobbyists had less maneuvering room than previously, while life was simplified for others. Advocates who were accustomed to spending most of their negotiating time with committees now found that the fate of their issues rested largely in the hands of the speaker, the majority leader, and the majority whip. Conservative interest groups, ranging from the Christian Coalition to antitax movements, rapidly developed intimate relationships with the new House leaders. Major business associations met weekly with the leadership to coordinate direct and grassroots lobbying but sometimes found it necessary to accommodate their positions to conform to the party line. Labor and liberal interest groups for the most part found themselves and their agendas out in the cold.

An exception occurred in 1996 when issue ads and other pressures engineered by the AFL–CIO to increase the minimum wage grew to the point that the leadership could no longer control the rank and file. Moderate Republicans joined with Democrats to pass the bill. The unions then turned on many of these moderates, even some who voted to raise the minimum wage, and made them targets of a $35-million campaign in the fall elections. Labor succeeded in defeating some House Republicans but failed in its goal of regaining control of Congress for the Democrats. (Senate Republicans actually gained two seats.) Labor's campaign left GOP survivors embittered; some vowed never to allow a union lobbyist in their offices.

The minimum wage vote represented a weakening of leadership control, returning to the pattern that had typified pre-1994 Democratic congresses. Leadership control was further weakened after the House reprimanded the speaker. House committee chairmen began to flex their muscles again. The chairman of the Ways and Means Committee quickly moved to assert his prerogatives by arranging a personal meeting with President Clinton absent any other GOP leaders, the first time that had occurred since the Republicans took control of the House.

Legislative Politics When Party Control Changes

Lobbyists tend to make political contributions to gain access to important legislators, rather than for reasons of ideology. (See Chapter 14 for more on this topic.) When a legislative body has been controlled by one party as long as the U.S. House of Representatives was controlled by the Democrats (forty years), the effect of a sudden change can be wrenching, even shattering, for many lobbyists. They had had long, established relationships with the chairmen of the committees and subcommittees handling their issues; now those legislators were occupying minority seats on the committee, with little voice in decisions. Almost worse, the majority of Democratic committee staff aides they had worked closely with were now out on the street, looking for other employment. The climate was only slightly better in the Senate. Some corporate and trade association lobbyists had gotten their jobs because of their Democratic connections, and many of those on the staffs of liberal interest groups were Democratic activists. What were those party ties worth now?

Aggravating the situation, most of the new leaders were not just Republicans but ideologically conservative and highly partisan Republicans who were demanding that interest groups, especially the business community, demonstrate loyalty and helpfulness to them. In this case, loyalty and help meant political contributions—contributions to pay off the debts of newly elected GOP freshmen, contributions to help build their treasuries for the 1996 campaign, and contributions to Republican Party committees. The word went out that lobbyists who gave to Democrats need not expect Republican support on their issues.

Some Washington reps responded pragmatically. "What's new?" asked one. "I gave to the chairman of the House Ways and Means Committee before the election. I give to the chairman of the House Ways and Means Committee now."

Others responded eagerly. Groups of association executives and Washington reps began meeting weekly with the new leadership to help move the GOP agenda, even if it sometimes meant compromising the legislative goals of their own interest groups.

Politically active Democrats among Washington's lobbying corps burrowed in and kept their heads down, hoping things would change back in the 1996 elections. They didn't, of course, but at least they still had the White House and the administration to rely on—for whatever good it did them with re-elected GOP leaders again demanding the heads of Democratic lobbyists representing companies and associations. It remained to be seen whether liberal Democratic lobbyists, including those in the business community, would find ways to accommodate to the GOP majority and whether the legislative agendas of nonconservative interests would fare any better than they had in the previous two years.

Pragmatic politicians tend to forgive and forget; "What have you done for me lately?" tends to be their watchword. But partisan ideologues have long memories. And congressional Democrats have become as partisan and ideological as the Republicans. Lurking in the back of every lobbyist's mind is the fear of what will happen when the Democrats regain Congress, as they surely will some day. Will it be the same situation all over again, just in reverse?

Party Loyalties and Party Control

Party loyalties are usually strongest on issues relating directly to electoral prospects or legislative control, but even here there may be occasional breaches.

The former speaker of the California Assembly, Willie Brown, long a power in the Democratic Party, was originally elected to his post by a coalition of Republican and Democratic legislators opposed to the incumbent speaker; the Republicans were temporarily able to share power until the new speaker succeeded in consolidating control among his fellow Democrats. As an exquisitely ironic climax to his legislative career, at the beginning of his final term Brown maneuvered Republicans out of a newly won bare majority by persuading a couple of Republicans to vote for him. When he departed the legislature to become Mayor of San Francisco, he even managed briefly to deliver the speakership to one of these apostate Republicans.

Bipartisan coalitions in leadership contests have also been found from time to time in Connecticut, Kentucky, New Jersey, North Carolina, Tennessee, and other states. Although the phenomenon remains unusual, it seems to be increasing. It has never occurred in Congress in modern times—which is not to say it never will.

Divided Government

At the national level and in many of the states, government has been divided more often than not, with one party controlling the executive branch while the other has a majority in at least one house of the legislative branch. The federal government has been divided in this way for thirty-two of the last fifty years. Some voters actually desire this state of affairs. Polls conducted after the 1996 campaign found that 16 percent of the electorate may have voted for Republican congressional candidates because they believed President Clinton would be reelected, certainly enough to assure that control of Congress stayed in Republican hands. A poll for NBC News and *The Wall Street Journal* in January 1997 found that the public, by almost a two-to-one majority, thinks divided government works just fine for the country.

In some states, divided government has become institutionalized. New York is the ultimate example. There, Republicans have controlled the state senate for a generation while Democrats perpetuate their majority in the lower house. The situation continues in election after election regardless of which party wins the governorship, the product of agreements between the parties to manipulate legislative redistricting in such a way that each party is able to maintain control of its house.

The world of lobbying is more complex when government is divided in this fashion. In 1997, neither party had full control of the governorship and both houses of the legislature in thirty-one of forty-nine states (omitting Nebraska where the one-house legislature is nonpartisan). If both legislative houses are controlled by, say, the Democrats but the governor is Republican, interest groups must worry constantly about a veto of the bill they worked to get through the legislature. The strategic problems of getting anything enacted are even more difficult if the legislature itself is divided, as it was in eleven states in 1997.

Divided government plus partisan ideological polarization makes bipartisan coalitions harder to assemble. Consider the difficulties of passing a reduction in business taxes in a state where one house is dominated by conservatives
who believe high taxes on companies deter economic development while the
liberal majority in the second house wants to maintain or even raise high business taxes to finance a tax cut for low- and middle-income individuals.

TECHNOLOGY IN POLITICS

Technology is even more pervasive in politics today than in government
relations, and political applications will continue to increase. Several states
are experimenting with universal voting by mail, and many people argue that
voter turnout can only improve if ballots can be cast from home. If anyone can
vote by mail, why not let them vote from their PC?

Congressional and legislative redistricting is important to interest groups that
want to elect as many of their own people as possible. Technology has simplified
this process enormously. Street-by-street computer maps are available from the
Census Bureau. Software is available that allows interest groups, political parties, and legislators to integrate political and demographic data with computer
graphics. Users can thus adjust hypothetical district lines on computerized
maps to see instantly what the effects of changes would be on voting behavior
and population characteristics. These systems have been used not only to con-
struct redistricting plans but also to challenge existing plans in court.

The Internet and other technologies described in Chapters 5 and 15 will
also become media of increased utilization in candidates' campaigns and in
the legislative process.

NOTES

1. Joel Achenbach, "The Staffers of Life," *The Washington Post*, January 6, 1997,
p. C-1.

2. Dennis Coates and Michael Munger, "Legislative Voting and the Economic
Theory of Politics," *Southern Economic Journal*, January 1995.

3. Kevin B. Grier and Michael C. Munger, "Committee Assignments, Constituent Preferences, and Campaign Contributions," *Economic Inquiry*, January 1991.

4. *The Washington Post*, February 11, 1997, p. A-9.

5. The term *blue dogs* is a double pun. For generations after the Republican-
sponsored Reconstruction period that followed the Civil War, many southern voters
would not consider any Republican candidates for elective office, no matter what
their qualifications. It was said that these southerners would vote for a yellow dog if
it was the Democratic nominee—hence the term, *yellow-dog Democrats*. The other
half of the pun comes from British politics. The color of the Conservative Party is
blue, that of the Labour Party (which had its origins in the socialist movement) is red.

Chapter 7

Direct Lobbying

There go the people. I must follow them for I am their leader.
—Alexandre Ledru-Rollin

Direct lobbying typically involves personal, face-to-face communications. It has two essential functions:

1. The collection of unpublished intelligence about issues and other governmental and political developments of significance to an interest group (analysis of published information is the task of issues research, described in Chapter 3).

2. The communication of the interest group's positions on issues to lawmakers or other government officials with the intention of shaping or reshaping public policy.

Lobbyists therefore need simultaneously to be both intelligence agents and sales people. This requires a fairly unusual combination of personal traits and capabilities:

- Personal integrity
- Strong communications and persuasive skills
- Empathy
- The ability to listen
- Intimate grasp of both formal legislative procedures and informal folkways
- Political sophistication
- Intellectual strength and substantive competence
- Strategic skill

THE LOBBYIST'S CREDENTIALS

As government and politics become increasingly sophisticated, the personal credentials essential for effective and successful lobbying have also expanded.

Modern lobbyists must be superb communicators yet know how to listen. They must not only be armed with an intricate knowledge of governmental and political processes but also be able to deal with increasingly complex issues and new technologies. They must have a strong strategic sense, be flexible and adroit, yet possess high personal integrity.

These qualities merit closer examination.

Communications Skills

Government relations is, in a sense, a specialized form of marketing. In that same sense, direct lobbying is often face-to-face selling.

The same qualities required to be successful in sales are needed in a successful lobbyist: cordiality and charm, persistence, understanding of the product (i.e., the position the "issue sales person" is advocating), and the persuasiveness needed to make the "purchaser" (the public policy-maker) want to buy the "product."

Empathy, the ability to see situations from the viewpoint and self-interest of others, is also an invaluable trait. The lobbyist needs to understand not only the positions of the opposition to counter and defeat them but also their attitudes and even feelings. And empathizing with the self-interest of legislators is important to winning their friendship and support.

Although lobbyists typically communicate one on one with policymakers, they also frequently speak before audiences and write for publication. The lobbyist must therefore be effective when speaking to larger audiences, whether giving legislative testimony or spaking to various groups. The ability to express highly complex issues, arguments, and developments in clear writing is important both as a vehicle of persuasion and as a means of keeping clients, members, or headquarters executives fully informed about what is happening and what it means.

The lobbyist must know how to listen, for two reasons. First, lobbyists need to be sensitive to the reaction their message is creating, a reaction that may not be verbally expressed. (The ability to listen carefully to what clients or superiors are communicating is critical, not only to success but sometimes to survival.) Second, and even more important, a major part of lobbyists' effectiveness lies in the ability to gather information about developments and outlook. This requires a personality that makes others *want* to share information with them.

Personal Integrity and Political Ethics

Because the ability to communicate and persuade is such an essential trait, lobbyists of the nineteenth and early twentieth centuries sometimes offered little besides personal charm and a political background. To this day, the popular image of lobbyists, like that of politicians, remains a shabby one. Occasional deviations from ethical standards do occur. Moreover, the populist streak in the American national character seems always ready to assume the worst in its leaders (which did not keep the voters from reelecting President Clinton, despite the allegations of personal and ethical lapses laid at his door). Still another factor is the news stories generated by journalists obsessively preoccupied with any hint of transgression. Today, the press is ready, indeed eager, to report cases in which ethically challenged public officials and lobbyists have traded on relationships and reputations, campaign contributions and cash for personal gain.

Lawmakers, in consequence, perhaps anxious to prove their own virtue, have written ever-tightening ethical standards into law. Special prosecutors abound, and hardly a day passes without some news story reporting on the progress of yet another investigation involving public officials, campaign contributors, and lobbyists.

Yet, the fact remains that the vast majority of both politicians and lobbyists are people of integrity, in this writer's thirty-five years of personal experience. Indeed, often those whose personal ethics are suspect are also those who are the most loudly sanctimonious about the need for higher ethical and political standards. But even lobbyists and politicians whose personal standards might bend more easily than most know that in today's hypersensitive ethical climate they must conduct their professional lives with the virtues of Caesar's wife. The merest hint of scandal jeopardizes their entire careers. Operating as they must in an environment in which a publicly shady reputation is the kiss of death, yet in which compromise is an integral skill of success, continuing to meet those ever-rising ethical standards is a constant challenge.

Professional Competence

The legislative process is highly complex and growing more so—technically, politically, and substantively. The effective lobbyist must be competent in all these areas.

A clear grasp of the technical details described in the last chapter, both the formal and the informal ones, is an essential trait. Mastery of the process has very frequently made the difference between victory and defeat on an issue. For that reason, lobbyists typically (though not invariably) have spent a substantial part of their careers in politics or on legislative staffs. Sometimes, they are former legislators themselves or have held other elected or major appointive positions in government. They are intimately familiar with political nuances and relationships because they frequently have been part of the process themselves, as they often still are.

Lobbyists, too, often have clout and know how to use it. Although lobbyists as a group tend to stay out of intramural legislative power struggles in order to maintain their good will with all sides, it is not at all unknown for lobbyists to play a role in some battles for leadership or the choice for a committee chairmanship or other key post. As a generalization, labor lobbyists seem more inclined to act as power brokers of this kind than do business lobbyists.

As issues grow ever more complex, the ability to grasp their substance is as important to lobbyists' success as legislative and political savvy. When federal or state bills on tax policy, labor relations, environmental control, education, health, resource management, economic development, international trade, and a host of other issues commonly run now to hundreds, sometimes thousands, of pages, the lobbyist must become expert on the finest details. Indeed, it is frequently in the fine print that wins and losses are determined and measured. For instance, an entire specialty of tax lobbying today centers around obtaining tax changes that sometimes benefit only a single company or individual even though the language may appear to be written in general terms.

Most legislation integrates in some fashion with existing public policy, often amending current law or superseding a regulation or executive action. The lobbyist must be able to analyze these legal connections. Moreover, legislation invariably involves change—change in social or economic practice or behavior, change in governmental programs and priorities. Change that affects people's lives and livelihoods must be carefully and competently analyzed—an imperative for both lobbyists and lawmakers.

Increasingly, the intellectual ability to handle issues of great complexity is an essential quality in a lobbyist. It is quite likely that lobbyists of the future, particularly in Washington and the capitals of the larger states, will be specialists in particular substantive fields rather than the legislative generalists that they traditionally have been. Lobbyists sometimes develop a "buddy system" in which one partner contributes technical expertise, the other the political contacts. (The staffs of most associations and growing number of Washington corporate offices are organized by issue specialties.)

Notwithstanding the growing importance of substance, the legislative process, as we saw in the preceding chapter, remains intensely political and competitive—competition between the parties, between individual lawmakers who covet higher office, between contending interest groups, between lawmakers and the press, between committees vying for jurisdiction, between the two houses, and between the legislative and executive branches. Lobbyists unable to grasp the niceties and nuances of this competitive environment will never get past their first issue.

The best lobbying often requires considerable creativity in legislative problem solving. If a particular position cannot be implemented, ingenuity and expertise may produce a very different approach to accomplish the goal, or at least to reach an acceptable compromise.

Legislative leaders need the skills to resolve differences in order to develop a compromise that can gain a majority of votes. As often as not, the hands of equally skilled lobbyists working behind the scenes are as instrumental as those of the lawmakers in fashioning a successful compromise that still meets their clients' needs.

(A wonderful story is told about a debate in the New Jersey Senate that was considering a proposal to end a long deadlock with the other house on an issue. After several years of dispute, several lobbyists and legislators came up with a compromise, one the Assembly reluctantly agreed to accept. A cantankerous senator rose to object. "I'm not against compromise," he said, "but why should we compromise with them? Let them compromise with us.")

Although compromise lies at the heart of all successful negotiations, knowing when not to compromise is no less important. An association executive had long been involved in a difficult and testy issue. After several years of negotiations, lawmakers offered him a take-it-or-leave-it deal that would benefit a major portion of his membership but leave the rest out in the cold. After a sleepless night, he rejected the deal because it would have split his association badly. He became a hero to the members he had protected; most of the others never forgave him.

Lawyer or Not?

The increasing intricacy of many issues raises the question of whether a lobbyist need necessarily be an attorney, a member of a profession focused on detail. In many cases, lawyers make effective lobbyists for many of the same reasons that attorneys predominate as legislators: They generally combine an orientation to substantive detail with knowledge of existing law and public policy, and they often are skilled advocates—but not invariably. Lawyers make good lobbyists only if they combine substantive ability with legislative and political skill and with that specialized form of advocacy needed to "sell" effectively in one-on-one communications.

Conversely, nonattorneys may be excellent lobbyists if they possess these traits. Clearly, though, the lobbyist who is not personally trained in the law needs ready access to an attorney for aid with analytical research and drafting legislative language.

Making the Presentation

Lawyers or not, lobbyists must know how to present their case to a legislator. That means understanding all sides of the issue to be able to rebut the arguments of the opposition if the need to do so arises. It means knowing how the issue affects the legislator being lobbied, so that the lobbyist can play to strengths, without putting lawmakers in difficult situations in their districts or at odds with positions on previous issues. It means making a carefully prepared presentation, backed up by a position paper to be left with the legislator or staff. Finally, it means knowing how to follow up appropriately; if he or she can close a deal on the spot, fine and good; but if not, the lobbyist must understand how and when to pursue the matter to gain a favorable decision.

However, the most finely honed persuasive skills are rarely enough in themselves to prevail on an issue. There must also be a belief among lawmakers that the lobbyist's positions represent the views of involved stakeholders—

preferably those of vocal ones in large numbers—and that the public interest will be served in some way. It is hard to win on a visible issue if there is no legislative perception of larger public gain. Interest groups often do win on very narrow issues, but seldom if there is an inadequate defense to widespread public criticism.

Strategic Skill

Legislation always involves struggle. Issues that benefit one interest group will usually do so at the expense of another. Even where no organized opposition exists, the forces of inertia must always be overcome. "If it ain't broke, don't fix it," remains a common legislative maxim.

The ability to strategize is therefore an essential skill among both government relations practitioners and legislators. Depending on the issue, the lobbyist may function as both advocate and strategist—or the strategic general may be the client or a senior corporate or organizational government relations executive. Whoever calls the tune must, like a skilled lawmaker, be able to plan and execute legislative campaigns—marshaling backers, neutralizing opponents, enlisting allies, mobilizing publicity and public support, and knowing how to use time and other resources for maximum effect. A well-honed strategic sense is therefore a vital quality in the lobbyist or government relations executive in charge of a legislative campaign.

SELECTING AND ORGANIZING LOBBYISTS

Companies and membership groups in need of lobbying services must deal with some basic questions:

- Should lobbyists be in house or retained?
- Should in-house lobbyists on federal matters be based at corporate or organization headquarters or in Washington?
- Should state lobbyists be retained or in house—at headquarters or the state capital?
- How do we choose the right person?

Scope of Exposure on the Issues

The answers to these questions depend on the breadth of the issues confronting the organization or company. Issues tend to fall into one of four categories, each of which requires a different kind of lobbying service:

1. The unique issue
2. Clusters of recurring issues
3. Epidemics of related issues
4. Ongoing general exposure

The Unique Issue

This is the bill or regulation that occurs in a single legislature or agency, perhaps arising out of a special local situation of some kind. Once dealt with, the issue is unlikely to recur, in this jurisdiction or elsewhere.

In such situations, the best solution is to retain a knowledgeable lobbyist experienced in that issue or that governmental body. How much backup that individual will need is a function of the political or technical complexity of the issue, but most unique issues can be dealt with readily by a single competent lobbyist.

The Cluster of Recurring Issues

These are legislative or regulatory problems that continue to crop up within a single governmental jurisdiction—local, state, or national. The cluster may require special technical expertise or an insider's knowledge of how decisions are made in complex or exotic governmental environments—for example, Congress, the Pentagon, the California State Treasurer's office, or the legislature of Suffolk County, New York. The issues themselves may be on related topics or disparate ones.

If the issues are expected to be short term, a retained lobbying firm is probably the most convenient and cost-effective solution. However, if the issue cluster gives indications of settling in for the long haul, then it may be worthwhile to add an experienced local lobbyist to staff.

Retained lobbyists, consultants, and technical experts tend to be expensive; some charge by the clock and others by the issue or project, but most prefer a retainer (often sizable) covering a legislative session or calendar year.

The question of whether to rely solely on them or to open a government relations office staffed with full-time employees is, in part, an economic cost-benefit decision. But there may also be considerations of visibility and image. Even if a closely calculated economic analysis does not seem to justify a full-time office in Washington or the state capital, the company or organization may still consider it worthwhile "to show the flag," that is, to become known as a permanent and involved member of the government relations community.

The Epidemic of Related Issues

Sometimes issues that treat the same problem or subject matter arise more or less simultaneously in a number of governments around the country. Examples include casino gambling, highway speed limit changes, drinking-age increases, mandatory personal leave, and AIDS issues.

In such situations, the affected company or interest group is likely to have the substantive expertise on staff (or be able to develop it quickly) but may not know its way around the various state legislatures or agencies. The larger the number of jurisdictions in which the issue is active, the more likely this is to be true. In these cases, retained lobbyists may provide a different kind of service. Instead of handling the issue largely on their own, they may act as guides for the client's in-house experts—teaching them the governmental and political fine points of lawmaking in that state or community and introducing them to the right decision makers and staff.

At this point, there is likely to be a need for an additional resource: an individual to *coordinate* the lobbying activity in the different states to assure compatibility among positions, actions, and agreements. The client's substantive expert may or may not have the political sophistication or broad-gauge understanding to be able to provide such coordination. Typically, this is the role of an in-house public affairs or government relations manager.

In actual practice, the company's government relations manager tends to provide both the substantive expertise and the multistate coordination, operating through retained local counsel in each state or locality. If the number of jurisdictions is so large that one person cannot simultaneously be the traveling in-house expert and the provider of policy coordination, then the functions will be split, with the coordinating role residing with the headquarters-based government relations manager. In some organizations, this executive directs an in-house group of regional lobbyists, each responsible for a state or group of states. Another option is the use of a state government relations consulting firm, as discussed in Chapter 9.

Permanent General Exposure

Because of the nature of their operations or interests, many industries and organizations must deal continuously with a wide variety of issues at the federal, state, and local levels. Large manufacturers, for instance, are constantly confronted with labor, tax, and environmental issues wherever they have facilities—and with consumer and marketing issues wherever their products are sold.

The greater the number of issues or jurisdictions facing the organization and the more complex and varied the issues, the more likely it is that the company will move away from sole reliance on retained lobbyists and in the direction of having its own on staff. The variety of issues may be broad, but each is unlikely to be unique. Staff personnel can develop familiarity with a number of issues and travel to the fires wherever they break out—through a regional manager system or by utilizing on-site independent lobbyists as guides to the local scene.

Lobbyists and Relationships

One additional factor should be considered in deciding whether to retain an outside lobbyist or hire one onto the staff. Each prospect has his or her own set of personal skills, talents, contacts, and expertise. Retaining the outsider means *renting* those credentials. Bringing such an individual on staff, however, enables the company to develop *equity* in its government relations program.

Independent lobbyists may represent Client A on Issue X today and Client B on Issue Y tomorrow. They may often talk to a legislator about the needs of both in a single visit, thereby making maximum use of their time as well as the legislator's. But it is the lobbyist, and not the client, who tends to have the relationship and visibility with the lawmaker.

On the other hand, when a government relations executive of a particular company or organization goes to visit the legislator or official, the situation is reversed. The company or group has now begun to develop its own visibility, in the person of its full-time representative, and to build its own network of relationships.

Such relationships take time to cultivate. With the independent lobbyist, the client can get instant access—but it is the lobbyist's access, not the client's. The organization gets the best of both worlds when the individual it adds to staff brings along knowledge and connections. But even if the staff lobbyist is new to the local scene and the relationships therefore take a while to develop, once built (and maintained) they become an asset of the organization.

Personal access to legislators, staff, and other public officials is essential to success in direct lobbying. Personal access flows from relationships developed over long periods of time between individuals who have come to trust and rely on each other. The legislator or official has learned that the lobbyist is discreet, loyal to friends, a source of reliable information on issues and their background, interested in the official's career, and frequently politically supportive. The lobbyist, in turn, has learned that this lawmaker or staffer, that public official, is a reliable source of accurate and authoritative information on a particular subject, often inclined to be helpful to interest groups with a shared point of view, and keeps promises.

Like any other political relationship, theirs is pervaded by discretion, a degree of trust and particularly mutual back-scratching—the informal exchange of favors and mutual aid. Perhaps the lobbyist has aided the legislator with fund-raising or some other political chore, or helped a career agency official win a promotion. The legislator may have recommended the lobbyist for a job or to a client. This favor exchange operates on a rough barter principle. An accounting is rarely kept, but neither side can go to the well too often or drink too deeply before it starts to dry up. The requests made must be appropriate both to the stature of the favorgiver and to the nature and sensitivity of the relationship.

A critical ingredient is the lobbyist's knowledge that the good will of the relationship is more important than any one issue. The story is often told of the lobbyist who was asked by his client if he had convinced Senator X to support their bill. "I saw him," the lobbyist replied, "but I recommended that he vote no."

"Why on earth did you do that?" asked the incredulous client.

"Because this issue would hurt him back home. He'll help us behind the scenes if he can, but we need him back here after the election more than we need his vote on this bill."

This is the stuff of politics. It is the stuff of lobbying as well.

THE COLLECTION OF INTELLIGENCE

Gathering unpublished information on political and issue developments and their significance is, in many ways, the most important single function direct lobbyists perform. Intelligence collection depends much more on the lobbyist's personal relationships than does even the ability to open doors and sell the organization's message. Most lobbyists spend far more time collecting, and disseminating, information than they do advocating positions and points of view.

Good lobbyists develop networks of contacts with whom they frequently touch base—people who can alert them to new legislative ideas still in gestation, the rationales and motivations of sponsors and opponents, the issue's political prospects, and the like.

The singular value of back-channel information of this kind is its timeliness. Early-warning information is particularly useful because it can so often facilitate remedial action while issues are still in their most formative or vulnerable stages. As a result of private information, bills are much more susceptible to being killed, stimulated, or reshaped before formal introduction than they are once they have seen the light of day.

The liability of private information is that it may sometimes be speculative and subject to considerable change. Its reliability is only as good as its source, and developments that can outdate it may occur moments after the lobbyist leaves the source's office. The lobbyist's ability to evaluate the validity and usefulness of private information is a talent that is hard to teach and that comes through judgment and experience.

Private information is at least as important on executive and regulatory issues as it is in the legislative process.

In the case of regulations (the agency equivalent of legislation) and other formal agency actions, proposals are typically published for a period of public comment before being finalized and officially promulgated. A published regulatory proposal, though, usually represents an all-but-final agency position; and it is often more difficult for interest groups to alter it than to amend a bill introduced in the legislature. Once top officials go public with a proposal, they are committed to it. But if the official and the agency can be reached before they take a position on the public record, they will be much more open to data, points of view, and other inputs. Obtaining private information on proposed regulations before they are issued for public comment is therefore particularly valuable to interest groups.

Much the same phenomenon is found among executive branch personnel during the policy development process. Whether the embryonic policy issue relates to possible legislation, agency actions, or a future speech or other public pronouncement, officials are loathe to share their thinking lest it be revealed prematurely or in a way that opponents can use to embarrass them. Indeed, the more sensitive the subject, the greater the reluctance to discuss it. Yet this is precisely the stage at which policy is most susceptible to—and will benefit from—the information and insights that lobbyists can provide.

Individual legislators are not greatly different in this respect. Their views are likely to be most malleable before they take public positions on a particular issue.

There is much more of a difference, however, between the view of a single legislator and the final decision of the legislative body, on the one hand, than there is between the attitude of a top official and the final decision of the agency or department, on the other. A far greater share of legislative decision making occurs during publicly conspicuous processes (such as hearings or committee and floor debates) than during agency decision making. The portion that is *not* visible, though, is just as critical to the outcome of the issue as it is in the departments and agencies.

The problem illustrates why personal relationships are so important in lobbying. When a relationship of confidence and trust exists, the legislator or other public official knows that he or she can tap the lobbyist's best information and advice on an off-the-record basis, comfortable in the knowledge that confidences regarding still-fluid ideas will not be revealed or their source embarrassed. The lobbyist's reputation and access are totally on the line here; a confidence breached is a lobbyist ruined.

But there are degrees of confidentiality. The information may be for the lobbyist's ears only, not to be revealed even to the group he represents. Or it may be shared with the group off the record. Of course, the more people and groups with whom the idea is shared on this basis, the greater the risk that it will be leaked to opponents or the press.

An official may also serve his own political purposes by *wanting* a leak, exposing the policy concept to debate while retaining the ability to deny its parentage if it proves unpopular; "launching a trial balloon" is the term for this kind of leakage.

In every case, the lobbyist has to understand the basis on which the private information is shared. Mistakes can be disastrous in terms of their impact on continuing relationships. When lobbyists lose their access to private information, their sources are reduced to press handouts.

Types of Data

Private sources should not be wasted in the collection of standard data. Information on the status or contents of a bill, for instance, is readily obtainable from published sources. Hearing schedules or floor calendar questions are either published or generally available to anyone who calls appropriate legislative staff. The same is true in the agencies on regulatory matters.

Back-channel sources should be reserved for sensitive questions not readily answered elsewhere: What are the inner politics of this issue? Is the best person to talk with Senator Smith a particular colleague, or is there someone among his family, friends, or business contacts to whom he is especially responsive? Why is Representative Jones dragging her feet in committee on this issue if her enthusiasm is really as great as her press releases say? Is there some kind of political connection between this bill and a seemingly unrelated issue? Interest group X is opposed to this bill, but not as opposed as it is to another bill; are the makings of a deal in the wind? Will the governor support our bill if we lobby for his budget? Will we antagonize important legislators opposing him if we do?

The list of such questions is endless, but to an extent they tend to fall into three rough categories:

WHY questions—relating to political aspects of an issue

WHETHER and WHEN questions— pertaining to legislative outlook

HOW questions—involving lobbying and legislative decision making

These categories are very approximate, however. In practice, there will be much overlapping, and some questions will fall into none of these groupings.

It is essential to note that the most important information may never appear in print or may be questioned and denied if it does. Such data are typically unpublished and private, available only through back channels of varying degrees of sensitivity and reliability.

LOBBYING APPLICATIONS

Direct lobbying seeks to influence public decision-making in a variety of ways:

- By influencing specific legislation
- By affecting pending regulatory matters
- By helping shape executive branch policies and programs, including budgets
- By impacting decisions on key personnel appointments
- By offering opinions on pending judicial cases
- By influencing outcomes on government grants and contracts

Direct lobbying is only one of the techniques utilized to accomplish these purposes, although it is the one most frequently used—on minor issues, probably the only one. The more important the issue is, the more likely that grassroots lobbying, coalitions, communications tools, and the other techniques of government relations will also be utilized.

Legislative Lobbying

Whether the issue involves proposals for new law, amendments to existing statutes, or the appropriations process, all legislative work, and therefore all advocacy, begins in committees or subcommittees, then moves to the floor of that legislative body. At every stage, lobbyists engage in a constant process of personal communication, seeking "face time" with those lawmakers and staff personnel who will have the most to say about the bill.

Communications may begin with legislators known to be interested in an issue, perhaps to persuade them to introduce a particular bill or to dissuade them from doing so or to state agreement with the position they may already have taken. It can be assumed in the discussion that follows that the lobbyist and the lawmaker are in agreement about the need to pass new legislation. (The process is not greatly different if they want to oppose a particular bill.)

The lobbyist may offer various forms of support: To assist the legislator's staff in the drafting of the bill; to encourage other legislators to cosponsor the bill; to aid in lining up votes in subcommittee and full committee, and eventually on the floor; to testify on behalf of the bill at legislative hearings; to help drum up support among constituents, various other interest groups, and the press; to work with the leaders of the house and sympathetic lawmakers in the other house; to encourage officials in the executive branch and pertinent agencies to back the bill; and so forth.

The lobbyist then proceeds to do each of these things. Other key legislators (pro and con) will be identified, and personal meetings will be sought with each or, more frequently, the individual on their staffs who has responsibility for the issue. In each of these meetings, the lobbyist will state the case for the bill, provide a position paper or some other form of backup data, and present whatever reasons can be mustered (both substantive and political) to obtain support from the legislator. If the advocate obtains a commitment, he or she may urge the legislator to join the lobbying effort by encouraging likeminded colleagues to add their support.

A growing number of lobbyists use a touch of technology, such as a colorful graphic presentation on a laptop computer, to outline their arguments and bolster their case with statistical charts and graphs and other supporting material. The printed version of this presentation can provide the necessary and inevitable handout.

This same process of personal communication carries through every later stage of the legislative process. Advocates focus first on persuading a majority of subcommittee members to support the bill, then on working to get it approved by full committee members, and finally on enlisting a majority of the entire legislative body to vote for it. Lobbyists frequently assist legislators in preparing speeches for floor debate when their issue comes up and may try to generate favorable press coverage of the lawmaker's statement.

Assuming the bill is passed, the entire lobbying process then begins all over again in the other house.

At every stage of lawmaking, amendments to the bill are inevitably proposed; some will strengthen the bill, others weaken it. In either case, the personal communications begin anew, to persuade legislators to adopt the lobbyist's position on pertinent amendments.

On many issues, lobbyists work alone or in partnership with advocates for allied interests. On major issues, they usually have considerable support. The company's top government relations executive or the head of the association is likely to become deeply involved in the development of strategy and issues research, as well as the mobilization of grassroots, coalitions, public relations, and other support activities. Other staff lobbyists may divide up the direct lobbying responsibilities, and sometimes an outside lobbying or law firm is signed up to help in various ways. Generally speaking, the more significant the issue, the greater the resources that will be brought to bear.

If the issue is important enough, the company's chief executive will be brought in for heavy lifting with legislative leaders and other top lawmakers. Trade and other business associations often encourage CEO involvement on key issues. The Business Roundtable, whose members are the chief executives of America's largest companies, facilitates lobbying by these corporate leaders on major issues affecting the business community.

From start to finish, direct lobbying involves face-to-face discussions between advocates and legislators or their staffs. These meetings often occur in the lawmaker's office, but almost any venue is appropriate. Lobbyists seek out their targets at legislative committee meetings, as they enter or leave the floor, and wherever else they find them—at social gatherings, fund-raising receptions, trade association meetings at which a lawmaker is speaking, and so forth.

Entertainment of legislators, previously a favorite technique of lobbyists, is much more difficult now for Congress and many state legislatures. Laws defining ethics and banning gifts limit or even prohibit what formerly were a prevalent lobbying vehicle. Nonetheless, lobbyists have always been creative in finding or manufacturing opportunities to meet with lawmakers.

Legislative Hearings

Public hearings at which both the public and relevant interest groups can testify on pending legislation are utilized by every legislative body, some frequently, others occasionally. Hearings are usually conducted at the committee or subcommittee level.

Lobbyists often take advantage of these opportunities. The lobbyist may choose to be the witness or to obtain someone else who can state the case more persuasively. Witnesses may be experts on the issue from within the company or industry or academics from a university or think tank. Sometimes the best witness is an influential constituent of the committee chairman or of a wavering committee member.

Unless the issue is one with unique or special impact on the company, individual corporations do not usually participate at hearings, preferring to let staff executives of the industry's association testify. That, after all, is a principal reason trade, business, and professional associations exist. On the other hand, sometimes the best witness is an executive of a member company who can state with authority what the impact of the legislation will be. Occasionally, an affected interest group will make a strategic decision not to testify if it believes its cause will be hurt more than helped.

The hearing process usually involves an opening statement by the witness followed by a period of questions from committee members. Effective lobbyists orchestrate this process with considerable care—assisting the witness with the statement, planting questions with supportive committee members, perhaps making sure that interested journalists attend to report on the hearing, and the like. Planting questions intended to bring out the weaknesses in the opposition's case is commonplace.

Despite the use of terms like "witness" and "testimony," very few legislative hearings are actually conducted under oath. Investigative hearings, such as those probing into some alleged scandal, often require that witnesses be sworn in, however.

Appropriations

Many lobbyists involve themselves in the process of appropriating funds for various regulatory and executive branch agencies. They may seek full or increased funding for a particular program that benefits the interest of their company, industry, or other interest group, or to reduce or eliminate funding for a program they oppose. Sometimes, they try to get language inserted into the appropriations bill to influence how the program is carried out, or to alter the way a law is enforced.

Even if the interest group has no special stake in an appropriations bill, its advocates may lobby for it to build good will with an agency whose funding is threatened. This is especially true if the interest group and the agency are part of an "iron triangle" (discussed later). Rarer, but not unknown, is lobbying to reduce the appropriation for a hostile agency.

Direct lobbying on appropriations utilizes the same techniques applied to other forms of legislation.

Other Arenas of Direct Lobbying

In addition to legislative advocacy, direct lobbying is utilized to affect policy in the executive branch, independent agencies, and (occasionally) the judiciary. It is also often used to procure government contracts and grants.

Executive Departments and Agencies

The elected chief executives of federal, state, and local governments, the individuals who head the principal departments and agencies, and their top staff personnel are all deeply involved in the public policy process in ways that both rival and interact with the legislative branch. Policies that require legislative approval are frequently initiated in the executive branch. There is substantial interaction between the branches of government during the give and take of the legislative process. Executive officials frequently play essentially a lobbying role to get a final product consistent with their policies. Indeed, the most vigorous and assertive lobbyists prowling the corridors of any legislative body are quite often representatives of the president or the governor. The favor-trading game is played for bigger stakes when the executive branch is involved. The White House or the governor's office can offer or deny special treatment for a lawmaker's pet issue, a key appointment for a political supporter, or a public works project that would be highly popular back home. Private-sector lobbyists can seldom match such inducements.

Following enactment, executive officials are responsible for enforcing or otherwise carrying out the new law, though often with considerable latitude as to how to do so.

Lobbyists for private-sector interest groups seeking to influence executive branch policies engage in the same kind of personal communications advocacy they use in legislative lobbying. They meet with appropriate officials to influence their positions, to gain their support and perhaps active participation, or to try to neutralize their opposition—whether to influence them on a legislative matter, on an executive policy decision, or on a regulatory issue.

Once a bill has been enacted, interest groups work to affect development of the responsible agency's rules, regulations, and procedures concerning implementation or enforcement. Later, if particular regulatory compliance problems arise, they are likely to be in frequent contact with the agency to assure at least evenhandedness, if not the most favorable possible enforcement policies, and may seek help from friends in the legislature to bring about such a situation.

Lobbyists also get involved in a variety of other types of executive actions. For instance, they may try to shape the budget, to the extent that it affects government programs in which they are interested.

Regulatory Agency Lobbying

At every level of government, there are agencies that exercise authority over some aspect of the economy or society. Such agencies are most commonly involved in fields directly or indirectly affecting public and consumer health and safety, but they also regulate many aspects of business and the economy. Civil rights and employment conditions are common examples of government involvement in social fields.

These agencies are generally granted broad authority by the legislature to both write and enforce rules, regulations, and standards. Thus, the Securities and Exchange Commission issues regulations controlling stock market transactions or the marketing of mutual funds. The same agency then enforces its own regulations, investigating possible transgressions, prosecuting violators in trial-like proceedings, and imposing penalties. The SEC's operations are not different in principle from those of a local agency regulating restaurant sanitation.

Lobbyists seek to influence the actions of these agencies in many of the same ways they use to affect executive and legislative decision-making. Lobbying can occur at two stages of regulatory action: rule-making and compliance.

In the rule-making stage, the agency develops rules or regulations over a particular problem area. This process is essentially legislative: A problem will be identified and a possible solution conceived, formulated, and publicly proposed. Except in emergency situations, the proposal is offered for public comment, either at hearings or by mail. Following the comment period, the proposal may be modified before final adoption. The agency's final action can often be appealed to the courts.

At each step in this process, the lobbyist can provide information and analysis to influence the proposal. Early information is particularly important because there are fewer stages in regulatory rule-making than in the legislative process and because lobbying is sometimes virtually prohibited in some later stages if it involves private communications with an agency official. Psychologically, politically, and procedurally, the earlier lobbyists can begin influencing the thinking of agency officials, the more successful they are likely to be.

Within the bounds governing each agency's rule-making procedure, the lobbyist can use all the available tools. The research function is essential. Direct lobbying and the use of coalitions are always appropriate, subject to some restrictions. The intervention of influential legislators can be enlisted. Public communications can be helpful and sometimes a necessity. Grassroots lobbying and political action may or may not be effective; some state and local regulatory officials are elected, but others are appointed, sometimes for fixed terms to insulate them from political pressures. (At the federal regulatory level, all such officials are appointed.)

For all that it often involves highly technical matters incomprehensible to any but experts, regulatory policymaking on occasion can be very political indeed. The White House and members of Congress (or their state and local counterparts) may offer their own views, perhaps privately, perhaps publicly, often stimulated to do so by an affected interest group. The public comment period provides opportunities for interest groups to generate grassroots communications, though these comments need to be more substantive and informed than legislative mail usually is.

Now and then, an interest group may persuade a regulatory agency to let it develop a voluntary program to deal with a public problem. In 1996, the Federal Communications Commission allowed the television industry to develop a system of voluntary ratings for children's television programs, although it then engaged in some lobbying of its own to affect the industry's product.

Lobbyists are likely to play a much more informal role in the regulatory compliance stage. Because no department or agency ever has enough funds, employees, or other resources to saturate the field it is regulating, such bodies depend on voluntary compliance, often supplemented by informal (even off-the-record) warnings. Lobbyists who are well acquainted within the agency may be quietly told that such-and-such an action or practice by the lobbyist's client, company, or members could well result in an enforcement proceeding if it is not changed. More often than not, the entire matter is satisfactorily worked out. Many activists consider such informal communications improper and sometimes technically illegal, but the practice is necessary to insure that regulatory objectives are met with minimum economic, social, and political strain.

Iron Triangles

Another kind of political influence pervades many regulatory situations. Regulated sectors develop strong common interests with career officials in the regulatory agency, as both groups do with certain legislators (and staff) who have a strong constituency or committee interest in the regulated field. These relationships are called "iron triangles," and they carry mutual self-protection and favor-trading to an almost institutional level.

Iron triangles abound at all levels of government. Here are a few examples:

- Veterans' organizations like the Veterans of Foreign Wars and the American Legion, the U.S. Department of Veterans Affairs, and congressional committees with jurisdiction over veterans matters
- Teachers and their unions; federal, state, and local educational agencies; and friendly legislators
- Truckers and the Teamsters Union, legislative allies, and regulatory agency officials
- The environmental movement, including individual organizations, the Environmental Protection Agency (and many comparable state agencies) and its legislative and agency friends; Vice President Gore has been a leading player in this iron triangle
- Consumer groups, state and federal consumer protection agencies, and supportive legislators
- Farm associations representing particular commodities, their friends in Congress, and the Agriculture Department bureaucrats regulating those commodities. Agriculture as a whole operates as an iron triangle, but those involved with particular commodities (peanuts, tobacco, or milk, for instance) constitute smaller triangles within the larger one

Favor-trading is strong, not only within iron triangles but among them, to leverage and broaden support. A new Senator from California once devoted his maiden speech to raisins, their nutritional benefits, their importance to his state's economy, and so on. When he was done, a senator from Alabama stood up to praise the speech and to tell the world that he agreed with every word. Afterward, the Californian thanked him, adding, "But I'm puzzled. I wouldn't think a senator from Alabama would be interested in raisins." The southerner replied, "I'm not. But I *am* interested in peanuts."

Iron triangles are perhaps the ultimate form of coalition politics and involve every form of government relations activity. The regulated group is usually highly organized, vocal and communicative from the grass roots, and politically active on behalf of friendly legislators and other elected officials. The legislators assure that the regulatory agency gets the funding and resources it needs and often give career boosts to cooperative bureaucrats. The legislators involved use their legislative oversight and appropriations authority to hold the agency in line, if need be, to make sure that constituents' interests are protected. Agency officials provide useful research and other assistance to the legislators.

Lobbyists play a significant role in iron triangles, acting both as representatives of the regulated group and frequently as liaisons among all the partners in the relationship to make the system work.

Variants of iron triangles are the "issue niche" and the "policy community." Issue niches "often involve highly technical choices that only a handful of interests care about or understand."[1] Although they operate in policy areas that may be equally arcane, policy communities are broader, with memberships that represent interest groups, federal agencies, congressional committees, and think tanks. Both exist for the purpose of formulating proposed policies on which all can agree before the proposal becomes widely visible or publicized. Because policy communities are more diverse than issue niches, they may be less successful in working out agreements; but if they do, they have a greater chance of legislative success. "The extensive Medicare-based policy community includes hospitals, some physicians, the AARP, a House Ways and Means subcommittee, and many other actors"[2]

Lobbying on Personnel Appointments

Interest groups frequently try to influence key departmental, agency, and judicial appointments to assure that friendly people are named—or at least that hostile ones are not. Presidents, governors, and mayors frequently ask for interest group inputs before making certain appointments that affect them. As often as not, the prospective appointee is someone prominent in an iron triangle of which that group is part.

Such campaigns are usually conducted behind the scenes to minimize embarrassment to the personalities involved if someone else is picked, but highly controversial appointments or nominations from time to time have become major public issues. Any or all of the tools in the lobbyist's kit may be utilized as appropriate to the circumstances to influence the choice.

For instance, several nominations to the Supreme Court were the subjects of major lobbying campaigns to deny them Senate confirmation. The battles over the Court nominations of Robert Bork by President Reagan and Clarence Thomas by Presiden Bush illustrate the intense use of various tools of government relations by both supporters and opponents. Similar tactics were used in forcing President Clinton to withdraw the nomination of Lani Guinier to head the Justice Department's Civil Rights Division. Tactics in these situations typically include these:

- Intensive research into the nominee's personal and professional background, writings, and past decisions
- Direct lobbying of vast scope, targeted not only at members of the Judiciary Committee but at all senators
- Extensive coalitions among interest groups, organized largely along ideological lines
- Extensive, orchestrated public hearings.
- Grassroots lobbying on the part of many of these groups to muster massive communications from their members to senators
- Political finance, at least to the extent of pointed reminders to senators of the strong interest, both pro and con, of past contributors and support groups
- Communications utilizing advocacy advertising, promotion of major press editorials, and the placement in news stories of research results

Major campaigns like these are relatively uncommon, but in some respects they are easier to organize than battles over legislation. Personality issues are easily painted black or white and, therefore, more readily communicated. There are few gray areas or questions of complex amendments to confuse the public. Compromises and tradeoffs often may be arranged for nominations to lesser offices; but the more controversial the individuals involved, the harder it is for the normal legislative and lobbying processes of compromise to come into play. In many ways, highly controversial battles over nominations resemble the politics of elections more than they do the normal legislative processes.

Indeed, a 1986 campaign to remove several California Supreme Court justices was an election in reverse, with the voters of that state using their power to disapprove the judges' continuance in office.

Procurement Lobbying

A specialized field of lobbying influences legislative, executive, and sometimes regulatory decision making to obtain government contracts or funding for companies or organizations. The spectrum of this kind of lobbying is enormous:

- Defense contractors not only solicit Pentagon business to build a new weapons system but also lobby Congress and the White House to get the system authorized and funded in the first place.
- Universities seeking federal or state funds for particular projects utilize independent or on-staff specialists who are expert in the complex processes of obtaining government grants-in-aid.
- Associations of state or local officials lobby Congress to authorize new education programs and then lobby the Department of Education for some of the new subsidies.
- Local agricultural organizations lobby state legislatures and agencies for funds to promote sales of their particular commodities—and national farm-related groups seek federal money so that their members can go abroad to explore and promote export opportunities.

Lobbying the Judiciary

Important court decisions can also be the focus of lobbying. Direct lobbying in such situations is quite formal, taking the form of "friend-of-the-court" briefs and oral arguments before the judges by interested groups who may coalesce for the purpose. Political pressures and grassroots lobbying are inapplicable, and may in fact be self-defeating, in such situations. However, public communications tools are commonly utilized on highly visible issues to influence the judges. News stories and press editorials, for example, played a significant role in a number of Supreme Court cases, including those on school desegregation, abortion rights, capital punishment, assisted suicide by the terminally ill, congressional budget controls, and the legitimacy of special prosecutors.

The courts rarely respond overtly to these tactics, but they have their effects. Judges all the way up to the Supreme Court are known to read both newspapers and election returns and occasionally to shape their decisions in response to public opinion. An unusual case occurred in New York City in 1996 when a federal judge ordered a drug dealer released from custody, expressing ideological bias against the police in his decision. After nationwide criticism, including a White House suggestion that the judge resign, he actually reversed his own order, a rare occurrence.

A different kind of campaign was begun after the 1996 election by a group of attorneys to mobilize press coverage and legal opinion for the purpose of persuading the Supreme Court to reconsider its 1976 campaign finance decision, *Buckley v. Valeo*.

NOTES

1. Allan J. Cigler and Burdett A. Loomis, "Contemporary Interest Group Politics: More Than 'More of the Same,'" in *Interest Group Politics*, 4th ed., ed. Allan J. Cigler and Burdett A. Loomis (Washington, D.C.: Congressional Quarterly Press, 1995).

2. Ibid.

Chapter 8

Lobbying the Federal Government

Self-interest speaks all sorts of tongues, and plays all sorts of roles, even
that of disinterestedness.

—La Rochefoucauld

For many companies and organizations, monitoring and influencing the policies and programs of the federal government is their principal government relations activity. Individuals involved in federal government relations represent business firms, trade associations, labor unions, and numerous nonbusiness organizations, while many others pursue federal government relations as independent practitioners with law firms, consulting and advocacy organizations, and the like.

The business community relies principally on trade associations, discussed in Chapter 11, and on lobbyists based in the Washington offices of large companies.

WASHINGTON CORPORATE OFFICES

Corporate federal government relations personnel are usually based either at their company headquarters or in Washington. The trend toward maintaining full-time offices in metropolitan Washington began in the 1950s and 1960s and has continued into the 1990s; more than four hundred corporations had their own Washington offices in mid-1995, and the number rises annually.

The pattern is by no means one of unremitting growth, however. Some companies have closed their Washington offices, generally for cost reasons (occasionally restarting them later), but the number of companies that open offices far exceeds the number that close them. Even in the same industry, patterns are sometimes mixed. In the late 1980s two major banking institutions (Chase Manhattan Bank and Chemical Bank, which later merged under the Chase name) closed their Washington offices, while their larger competitor, Citicorp, decided to open one—with a staff of twenty headed by an executive vice president.

A 1996 survey of 260 companies of all sizes found that fewer than a third with revenues under $3 billion had Washington offices. The percentage was over 60 for those with $3 to $10 billion in revenues—and 87 percent for companies with revenues over $10 billion. Manufacturers were more likely to have their own Washington office than nonmanufacturing companies.[1]

The pros and cons of having a Washington office have been debated for many years. The arguments in favor relate to the personal relationships and information sources that are developed with much greater ease by a resident— akin to the reasons nations place ambassadors in each other's capitals. An on-site representative becomes part of the local scene and has far greater opportunities to develop contacts than does a visitor from out of town.

A Washington corporate representative explains why: "The effect of the federal government, its scope on all phases of national life is pervasive. It's a taxer. It's a granter. It regulates the workplace and the marketplace. Any organization—be it a trade union or company or association—is taking a chance if it didn't have a presence on the Washington scene and an ability to have an input and to have its interests represented."[2]

The principal argument against a resident representative are the costs of maintaining a Washington office relative to the company's perception of its needs. Some people also believe a matter may be given added emphasis because an executive traveled from corporate headquarters for an appointment with an official especially to discuss it; to the extent this was ever true, it is a minor consideration today. Many companies without a Washington office are headquartered within easy traveling distance of the capital. (Most of the travelers flying into Washington's National Airport, one of the busiest in the country, fly back out the same day.) However, a number of other corporations located within a few hours travel time have chosen to be represented on site.

The pattern seems to be to open an office in Washington once the number of government relations personnel reaches two or three. Actually, a little more than a quarter of Washington offices are staffed by only one or two people, but almost 40 percent have staffs of six or more employees.[3]

Those who have tried it both ways over the years, including the author, generally conclude that in the long run federal government relations are more successfully conducted from a resident office if the organization has ongoing issues in Washington. For example, effective participation in coalitions and trade association activities—techniques utilized more and more in government relations— is harder for the traveler, even the regular commuter, than for the resident.

Direct lobbying is a prime function for many Washington-based government relations offices, but not necessarily the most important. For companies particularly, a major Washington staff role involves tracking issues and analyzing federal policy developments and proposals affecting their organizations and then communicating that information back home.

Often, the initial justification for a Washington office—indeed, sometimes for the federal government relations function itself—is the need to focus on regulatory issues, primarily to keep posted on government requirements with which the company or industry has to comply. Involvement with the process tends, sooner or later in most organizations, to evolve into a desire to influence regulatory decisions before they are made—and later still, to attempt to shape the legislative decisions on which regulatory programs are based. Ultimately, the organization may seek to broaden its influence through both grassroots lobbying and political activity.

Thus, the evolutionary pattern of federal government relations for some companies may look something like this:

Regulatory Monitoring   >   Regulatory Lobbying   >   Legislative Monitoring   >   Legislative Lobbying   >   Grassroots Lobbying & Political Action

The pattern is hardly universal, though. For some organizations, the focus has always been primarily legislative. Others choose not to go beyond lobbying and enter the political arena. Still others deal only with regulatory matters. And there are some who engage only in monitoring, leaving all lobbying to their trade associations.

On the average, Washington office personnel spend about one-quarter of their time on issues-monitoring and another quarter on advocacy, including developing contacts and relationships among people in Congress, the White House and executive branch agencies, and political party committees. Another quarter is divided among state and local government relations, association liaison, coalition activity, marketing support, and legislative and business planning and reporting. The final quarter involves providing information to corporate policymakers and other managers and networking with the media, think-tanks, and anyone else who is a real or potential source of information and support.

Procurement lobbying occupies a large amount of time for Washington representatives who work for defense contractors or other companies for whom the federal government is a major customer.

If the Washington office has only one or two people, of necessity they are generalists. Those with larger staffs specialize in some way, most often by subjects and issues, developing substantive expertise in particular topics. Others divide the work by whom they lobby: one or two for the Senate, several for the House, a couple for the agencies with which the office deals, and so on. In a third structure, each person represents the interests of one or more of the company's business units or operating companies. Some offices combine these organizational forms in one way or another. Functions like PAC and grassroots network management are handled in some instances by Washington office personnel, in others by those in corporate headquarters. In one large company, PAC management and state government relations are the responsibility of a manager based at the firm's California headquarters, although he reports to the head of the Washington office.

Corporate downsizing has seriously affected a number of Washington offices. They have had to learn how to do as much, or more, with less. In some cases, staff of company business units have assumed certain functions (e.g., issues tracking or regulatory compliance) formerly handled by the Washington office. In others, liaison with the member of Congress who represents a particular facility is now handled by someone based at the plant rather than in Washington.

CHOOSING A WASHINGTON REPRESENTATIVE

Selecting a Washington representative for a company or organization based in another city involves much the same criteria as those used in selecting a lobbyist elsewhere: integrity and intelligence; experience and understanding of the political and public policy processes; and the other qualities described in the preceding chapter. An important additional consideration, however, is political sophistication to a higher degree than anything found in the capitals of all but the largest states.

Washington is, after all, the capital of the world's most powerful country. To influence national policy is to affect a trillion-dollar economy and the lives of more than 260 million people, a heady experience for anyone whose personal mark has been left on an act of Congress.

It may be unfashionable to say so, but Washington is the major league of government relations, just as it is of politics. Few members of Congress retire to run for the state legislature, although some do leave to become governors or mayors of the largest cities. State legislatures are the breeding grounds for future members of Congress, not vice versa. When members of the House of Representatives want to move up, they usually run for the United States Senate, not for local office. (To be fair, a former U.S. Senator is currently in the New Hampshire legislature and a former House member now sits on the Los Angeles City Council, but these truly are rarities.)

An indication of the importance of federal government relations is the incredible wealth of commercially published information (described in Chapter 3 and in Sources and Resources), more than is available about any state or any other country. Because information is the currency of government relations, lobbyists (including association executives) are the primary consumers of all these data. They need to know who sits on the committees that decide the fate of their issues and who are the key staff people; what the status and prognosis of their issues are; what substantive and political analyses of these subjects exist or who could be persuaded to study them; who in the White House, the departments, the agencies, makes policy in their fields of interest and who has the responsibility for executing the laws they influence. The Washington lobbyist also has a great need to acquire and analyze a vast amount of detailed intelligence both about his or her issues and about the legislators and other policymakers who decide their fate. The collection of this information, whether obtained from published sources or through personal and informal contacts, consumes a considerable portion of any lobbyist's time, but perhaps more so in Washington than anywhere else because the number of potential sources is so great.

Nevertheless, it is important to remain aware that "government affairs is more than just tactics (tracking issues, lobbying, organizing grass roots activities); rather, it is a strategic function that uses creatively executed tactics to help the company achieve business goals."[4]

Notwithstanding its political sophistication, Washington can be quite parochial. This is not as contradictory as it sounds. Anyone who has spent time in any of the nation's major cities has experienced their insular sides. New York, the economic capital of the nation, if not of the industrial world, frequently exhibits its provincial qualities to visitors. (A friend who has spent his entire life in New York City likes to describe people who live outside Manhattan as "bridge and tunnel folk.")

The nation's capital may be the focus of the world's constant attention, but political Washington possesses many of the characteristics of a village. It has its own culture, its own ways of doing business, and a certain disdain for people who do not appear to grasp the finer points of politics and government "inside the Beltway."

Those who are part of the village—members of Congress and their staffs, administration officials, lobbyists, journalists, politicians, association executives, think tank academics, and the like—gossip intensely about everything from political and policy developments to people's personal lives. It may never be reported in the media, but "everyone knows" that lobbyist X has moved in with top official Y, that two members of the House are having an affair although one of them is married, that columnist Z is going on a "study retreat" to dry himself out, who it was that persuaded a certain cabinet secretary to reverse her department's policy on a major issue, that the White House will withdraw a particular judicial nomination next Tuesday despite its strenuous public defense of the nominee, the real reason behind Senator Alpha's retirement announcement, what the Secretary of Commerce told *The Washington Post*'s editorial board that never got into the paper, why a certain angry congresswoman will make sure that the President's pet widget reform bill never gets out of her committee—on and on ad infinitum.

Much of this may seem like petty gossip, but all of it has policy and political implications. A juicy tidbit to one person is valuable intelligence to another.

Veteran practitioners in Washington's village understand its culture and know how to make it work for them, striving constantly to build and maintain a strong network of contacts and relationships. They have breakfast with this one and lunch with that one, stop at a couple of political fund-raisers, and then head off to somebody's dinner party—all for the purpose of preserving and widening relationships and acquiring potentially relevant information. It is an unfortunate commentary on the village's culture that *who* you are seems to be less important than *what* you are; everyone laments that they never see a certain former legislator or official anymore, but few take the trouble to look her up now that she is out of office—unless, of course, she has moved into another part of the village by becoming a lobbyist, the head of an important association, or an influential journalist.

Newcomers seldom have the political and social relationships to gain early acceptance in the village and access to its denizens. It takes time and a certain personal style to accomplish that and to grasp the nuances and niceties that make the system work.

Any company preparing to open a Washington office is likely to consider whether it is better to transfer an experienced corporate executive to Washington or to hire someone with political sophistication and an existing contact network. The question is sometimes put this way: Is it better to get someone who knows Washington and teach that individual the company or transfer someone who knows the corporate culture and teach her or him Washington?

Clearly, an understanding of the company's culture and problems is critical to success in government relations, perhaps more so today than ever. Nonetheless, the style and business of even the largest corporations are easier to learn and absorb than are the culture and process of Washington.

Of course, individuals who have grown up in the company and also are experienced in federal government relations, even if they are commuters to Washington, fit in with both cultures and are therefore in an ideal position to hit the ground running.

Assuming that such paragons are not available, what traits and talents should a company look for in a Washington corporate representative (or just "Washington reps," as they are usually termed)?

In addition to possessing the qualities described in Chapter 7, senior Washington reps have come to head up their companies' Washington offices through one of two principal routes. They have had extensive government experience or they have come up through the government relations ranks in their companies. Those with direct public policy experience have often been recruited from the staff of an important congressional committee or a powerful member of Congress. A few are former members of Congress. Frequently, they have come from a policymaking position in an executive department or regulatory agency, perhaps from the White House itself. Some come from trade association staffs where they have developed extensive government relations expertise and connections. Many are attorneys, many are not.

Although it is not common, a few rotate between top government jobs and their companies. The legendary Bryce Harlow, probably the most respected Washington rep of his time, became the head of Procter and Gamble's Washington office after serving on the White House staff under President Eisenhower.

He left P&G to become a top aide to Presidents Nixon and Ford, eventually returning to his former position at the company. With such exceptional experience and contacts, it is said of Harlow that there were few people he did not know, no one he could not reach, and almost nothing he could not accomplish.

Another route to top Washington office positions is illustrated by one company's vice president for government relations, who was a lobbyist in the company's Washington office for many years. She was named to the top position when her predecessor suddenly retired after only a short time in the job. Coming up through a series of operating positions in the company, he reportedly had little taste for government relations or for Washington. She demanded the job and got it.

There are a couple of significant lessons to this example. First, companies need to be careful about transferring executives whose careers have been spent on the business side to run the Washington office. Some have turned out to quite effective, but others lacked the experience and the attitude to be successful.

The second lesson is that more and more women are moving into senior positions in government relations. About a quarter of the heads of Washington corporate offices are women.[5] The same pattern is found among top corporate public affairs officers, about one-fifth of whom are women.[6] An increasing number of women seem likely to assume top public affairs and government relations positions in the years to come. More and more of them at present fill the kinds of government positions from which the heads of Washington offices are frequently drawn; others can expect to be promoted to the most senior position from the subordinate corporate positions in government relations and public affairs a substantial share of them hold now.

The attention paid to Washington reps in this chapter is not intended to ignore another equally important group of federal lobbyists, association executives. Chapter 12 deals with the role of associations and the people who staff them. Suffice it to say here that trade and business associations, as well as the spectrum of nonbusiness organizations, are among the most powerful lobbies in Washington; and the executives who run them among the most influential of all lobbyists.

Washington reps and association executives concern themselves with all the fields of government relations described in Chapter 7. They seek to influence and shape every bill, major and minor, affecting their constituencies, often including the appropriations process. They work to affect policymaking in the White House and federal departments and the policies of the regulatory agencies, as well as the fine details of the executive branch's implementation of laws and programs. Increasingly, they are making significant efforts to shape judicial case law by challenging in court both acts of Congress and their executive implementation. Where it is applicable to their companies or members, many of them devote considerable time to influencing the federal government's purchasing and grant-making processes.

FEDERAL REGULATION OF LOBBYING

A major attempt by Congress to regulate federal lobbying was enacted in 1946. In 1954, the U.S. Supreme Court struck down many of its provisions as violations of the First Amendment.[7] What remained was widely considered toothless and largely unenforced. It was, in fact, entirely possible to conduct major campaigns to influence federal legislation without being more than nominally subject to the law or even coming under its jurisdiction at all.

In 1995, Congress passed a new law, the Lobbying Disclosure Act (LDA). At about the same time, each house of Congress adopted stringent rules concerning gifts to their respective members; the rules are substantially similar, though not identical. (These measures apply only to the federal government; the states have their own, as described in Chapter 9.) The major provisions of the LDA and the gift-ban rules, both of which took effect in January 1996, are these:[8]

Applicability

- The law defines a lobbyist as one who is employed or retained by a client, makes more than a single lobbying contact on the client's behalf, and spends at least 20 percent of her or his time in a six-month period lobbying on behalf of the employer or clients. Lobbying firms (including self-employed lobbyists) are defined as those with one or more employees who represent someone other than themselves. Religious organizations are exempt.

- Lobbying contacts are oral or written communications to specific categories of federal officials on the client's behalf concerning legislation, rules and regulations, programs, grants, loans, and nominations subject to Senate confirmation. Exceptions are made for testimony at congressional hearings, contacts initiated by government officials, responses to Federal Register notices, petitions to agencies, meetings in which there is no attempt to influence covered officials, and public speeches.

- The categories of officials include the president and vice president, senior White House aides, cabinet secretaries and subordinates down to the level of assistant secretaries (lower in some cases), general counsels, administrators and associate administrators of independent agencies and regulatory agency chairmen, military and quasi-military admirals and generals, some other specified positions, and anyone else in an executive branch policymaking position (which in certain cases includes people with titles like "confidential assistant"). The law also covers contacts with members of Congress, personal and committee staff members, Senate and House officers and leadership staff aides, and staff people working for congressional caucuses.

Registration

- Lobbyists must register within forty-five days of being hired or the first contact, whichever is earlier. Registrations, reports, and terminations of registration are filed with the Secretary of the Senate and the Clerk of the House. Lobbyists must disclose if they have been officials of the executive or legislative branch within the preceding two years.

- Registration is required of lobbyists and lobbying firms that expect to be paid over $5,000 in a six-month period. In-house lobbyists for an employer must register if they expect to spend over $20,000 in the same time frame. (These amounts are to be indexed for inflation.) A single report is sufficient for each client.

- The registration forms ask for personal identification (name, address, headquarters, and so forth), as well as a general description of the business of each registrant and each client.

- Registration also requires identification of anyone else who contributes more than $10,000 over six months to support lobbying activities, and who plays a significant role in planning, supervising, or controlling those activities. Foreign entities that meet certain requirements of ownership or participation must also be identified.

- General areas of policy interest and, where possible, specific issues to be lobbied must be listed.

Reporting

- Reports covering registrants' activities must be filed semiannually, within forty-five days after each six-month period. Reports should list the specific issues (including bill numbers) and specific executive branch matters that have been lobbied, in which house congressional lobbying occurred or which agency was lobbied. If a foreign entity had an interest in a particular issue, that must be disclosed. The names of specific individuals lobbied need not be reported.

- The reports should also contain good-faith estimates of amounts paid or received. Companies and nonprofit organizations can use Internal Revenue Service rules for estimating expenses.

- Noncompliance with reporting requirements is subject to prosecution, following a warning.

Other Provisions

- Recipients of at least $100,000 in federal contracts, grants, or loans may not use those funds to lobby for additional money.

- Certain nonprofit organizations may not receive federal grants, loans, contracts, or awards if they lobby. (Tax laws already limit the amount of lobbying nonprofits may engage in to maintain eligibility for tax-deductible contributions. Trade associations and labor unions that lobby each have a different tax status.)

- The law also affirmed congressional support for the IRS ban on tax-deductibility of business lobbying expenses. (IRS regulations also prohibit deductibility of grassroots lobbying and advocacy advertising costs. Associations that engage in any of these activities must tell their members what percentage of dues is deductible and what is not.)

- Subsequent legislation, enacted in 1996, added criminal penalties (up to five years imprisonment) for knowingly and willfully failing to register and report, or for filing false information.

Congressional Gift Ban

- Senators and their staffs may not accept any gift (including entertainment) worth more than $50, and total gifts in a calendar year may not exceed $100. House members and staff may accept no gifts of any value.

- The rules contain a long list of exceptions or special circumstances under which the gift ban does not apply. For example, it does not apply to political contributions, nor to widely attended events at which the legislator is speaking or performing a ceremonial function.

"The most important fact to bear in mind about the LDA is that it is a *disclosure* statute."[9] Everything in both the registration statements and semiannual reports is considered public information and is available to the press and various research and interest groups.

The lobbying law has not been challenged in court at this writing, so no one yet knows if the federal courts will decide that it is consistent with the First Amendment or not. Because the Senate and the House are empowered by the Constitution to adopt rules governing their members, the gift ban is almost certainly immune to court challenge.

Lobbying Expenses

How much do lobbies spend? The Secretary of the Senate and the Clerk of the House, who are the officers of Congress that collect registrations and reports under the 1995 lobbying law, say they lack the resources to tally and analyze the data. Nor are the more obvious political research organizations in Washington doing so. The Associated Press reported that $63.6 million was spent in 1987 just to lobby Senators and Representatives, but that was under the more limited standards of the old law.[10] Under the new law, $250 to $500 million may be a rough guess, but a guess is all it is. Even if an exact total were to be calculated, it would still be imprecise because grassroots lobbying expenses are not reportable under the new federal law.

One statistic that has been calculated is the number of organizations and people registered under the new law. According to the Secretary of the Senate and the Clerk of the House, there were 3,586 registered lobbying firms in January 1997, and 12,133 individuals registered as lobbyists.[11]

The Law's Impact on Lobbying

The chief impact of the changes is not in the paperwork they produce but in reduced opportunities for interaction between government policy-makers and lobbyists, a result primarily of the gift ban rather than the lobbying law. Lobbyists entertained members of Congress or their staff people partly for good will, to be sure, but also to get them away from the distractions of their offices so that a particular problem or issue could be discussed at length. The legislators or staff accepted the invitations not only to get a better lunch than sandwiches at the desk but also to obtain the specialized information and input that frequently only the representatives of affected interest groups can provide. All this is now much more difficult for both sides.

Partly because of the complexity of the new rules, partly because some officials (who have no expense accounts for this kind of thing) did not want to pay for expensive lunches out of their own pockets, and partly because of publicity about entertainment excesses that preceded their adoption, many in government quickly found the simplest course to be to shun lobbyists' invitations altogether.

Still, ways to adapt can always be found. One Washington organization that decided to launch an annual fund-raising dinner not only asked a prominent member of Congress to speak but also used the occasion to present awards to lawmakers with high scores on the group's voting records. The organization, which structured the details and ground rules in close consultation with the Senate and House Ethics Committees, was very pleased with the high turn-outs by both legislators and lobbyists. Some other groups use PAC dollars to host political fund-raisers for lawmakers as a way to amass good will.

Interest groups in general will find their own ways to live, and even thrive, within the new system. It may be harder for lobbyists to operate than it used to be and for officials to get policy input as easily as they once did, but both will find new ways to achieve their goals. Lobbyists are a creative lot.

A harsher impact of the new law and rules is that they further discourage good people from coming into government. Although the 1995 law was the first comprehensive federal lobbying legislation in half a century, other, narrower restrictions had been enacted previously. Over the years, the tax deductibility of different kinds of lobbying expenses has been tightened or eliminated. Certain executive-branch officials may not become lobbyists for a period of time after they leave government service, and others may never do so. The federal government's chief international trade negotiator may not be an individual who previously lobbied in Washington for a foreign government (although the Clinton administration obtained an exemption in 1997 for its choice of a U.S. Trade Representative). Conflict-of-interest and other rules applying to high executive branch appointments require prospects to fill out extensive documents relating to financial disclosure, security clearance, and the like; many appointees find themselves forced to dispose of certain investments, often at high personal tax consequences.

An unfortunate consequence of all this is that many people who might make outstanding public officials simply refuse even to be considered. Another consequence, for good or ill, is that younger people, who have had less time to accumulate assets or develop career experiences that might pose conflicts, are coming into top White House and administration positions.

One criticism of the former system was that it enabled people to take high positions; gain experience, contacts, and prestige; and then leave government to capitalize on them in the private sector. As humorist Art Buchwald said, "What good does it do for a man to serve his country when he can't sell his connections to the highest bidder once his term is over?"

In practice, the "revolving door" still seems to be turning on well-lubricated hinges. Members of Congress must wait a year after leaving office before they can engage in direct lobbying of their former colleagues, but they can use the time to advise clients on strategy and tactics. Top administration officials may also find it harder to become direct lobbyists, but they too manage to eke out livelihoods. Several former White House aides have thriving firms that "counsel" clients on how to affect public policy or that practice "political consulting." Others have done quite well on the lecture circuit, in trade association management, or in journalism. The host of one Sunday morning Washington talk show was previously a White House aide. Another was once press assistant to a prominent Senator, although he takes pains to note the relationship whenever his former boss is a guest on the show.

NOTES

1. James E. Post and Jennifer J. Griffin, *The State of Corporate Public Affairs: 1996 Survey Results* (Washington, D.C.: Foundation for Public Affairs, 1997), Figs. 6.1–6.4.

2. Ricardo R. Alvarado, of Allied-Signal Inc., quoted in Kirk Victor, "Being Here," *National Journal*, August 6, 1988.

3. Hay Management Consultants, *1995–96 Washington Office Compensation Survey* (Washington, D.C.: Foundation for Public Affairs, 1995).

4. Burson-Marsteller, *B-GRC Benchmark Study* (Washington, D.C.: Burson-Marsteller, 1994). Survey of members of the Business–Government Relations Council, an organization of Washington corporate representatives.

5. Hay Management Consultants, *1995–96 Washington Office Compensation Survey.*

6. Hay Management Consultants, *1996–1997 Compensation Survey of Public Affairs Positions* (Washington, D.C.: Foundation for Public Affairs, 1996).

7. *United States v. Harriss.*

8. This is intended only as an informational summary. Readers should consult competent legal counsel concerning the applicability of LDA and the gift ban to their own particular circumstances.

9. Nancy A. Nord and William H. Minor, "The New Lobbying Disclosure Act: What You Need to Know to Comply," *ACCA Docket*, July/August 1996. Published by the American Corporate Counsel Association. This article is a good analysis of both LDA and the gift ban.

10. Compiled by the Associated Press and reported in *The New York Times*, August 23, 1988.

11. Telephone conversations with the author.

Chapter 9

Lobbying State and Local Governments

> The powers not delegated to the United States by the Constitution, nor prohibited by it to the states, are reserved to the states respectively, or to the people.
> —The Tenth Amendment to the Constitution

No provision of the Constitution has been as ignored throughout American history as the Tenth Amendment. The power of the federal government has steadily grown throughout American history, largely at the expense of the states. States' rights, even more than the slavery issue, was the cause of the Civil War. Supreme Court decisions from the time of Chief Justice John Marshall have decided far more cases in favor of national powers than for state authority.

FEDERAL POWER AND DEVOLUTION

The pendulum of federalism has nonetheless swung back and forth throughout the past two centuries. Periods in which power was concentrated in Washington have been followed by others in which a degree of power went back to the states. We are in one of the latter periods now. Election of Republican Congresses in 1994 and 1996 brought to power conservatives with a strong bent toward "devolution" of federal authority to the states. The Supreme Court under Chief Justice William Rehnquist has decided several key cases in favor of the states.

The philosophic role reversal of the two major political parties in the twentieth century on issues of federalism is not always understood or appreciated. The roots of the Republican Party go back to Alexander Hamilton's Federalists, who favored a strong national government. Those of the Democrats can be traced to Thomas Jefferson and the Anti-Federalists. Lincoln, the first Republican president, fought the Civil War to preserve the union, which is to say the primacy of the national government in preventing states from seceding without its consent.

These polar positions reversed under Franklin Roosevelt. The essence of the New Deal was a federal government strengthened to combat the Depression and then to wage World War II. The Democratic Party, particularly its dominant liberal wing, has largely supported a strong national government ever since. Republicans, especially conservatives opposed to Roosevelt and his ideological successors, today take the language of the Tenth Amendment much more literally than does the Democratic Party.

The trend toward devolution of government programs from the federal to state and local levels actually began in the 1970s. State and local governments have become the growth industry of the public sector. The federal civilian payroll has been essentially static since 1970 while state and local payrolls have nearly tripled.[1] The conservative tilt toward the states is genuine, but the plight of federal finances does make a virtue out of necessity. Congressional enactment of welfare reform legislation in 1996 is likely to trigger a further escalation of devolutionary trends.

As devolution proceeds and more and more government functions flow away from Washington, state finances will become increasingly acute. For decades, Congress was in the habit of imposing program or performance requirements on the states without giving them the funds to accomplish those goals. A ban on unfunded mandates adopted by Congress in 1995 put a stop to that. However, devolution, or perhaps even abandonment of federal programs, will put increasing pressure on the states to assume them, in many cases without adequate funding sources.

Inevitably, as the states assume an increasing share of the costs of welfare and other programs turned over to them by Washington, there will be calls once again for a sharing of federal revenues. During the Nixon administration, federal block grants to the states were initiated, money made available with minimal restrictions. Revenue sharing, initiated by a Republican president in the 1960s for ideological reasons, was terminated two decades later by another Republican, Ronald Reagan, for financial ones.

A shortage of funds, coupled with conservatives' determination to balance the federal budget and their aversion to tax increases at any level, means a reduction in the size of governments at all levels, at least until the winds of ideology shift back to the left.

Federalism and Interest Groups

Liberal interest groups have usually supported federal dominance. Groups with an activist agenda—labor unions, civil rights organizations, and environmentalists, for example—have preferred federal action to that of the states. It is easier, after all, to get legislation through Congress than to persuade fifty state legislatures to act.

Conservative groups, however, are not always of a single mind on this question. Interests opposed to the expanded regulation of business generally prefer that these issues remain with the states because it is easier to oppose them there. Southern and mountain state legislatures, for instance, have generally been more supportive of business interests than of labor unions. The insurance industry, historically comfortable with state regulation, long opposed any efforts to centralize regulation of its activity.

On the other hand, social conservatives (unlike economic conservatives) often prefer federal action on their issues. Pro-life organizations would like the Supreme Court to reverse its privacy rights decision in *Roe v Wade* or, alternatively, want Congress to approve a constitutional amendment banning abortions. Groups supporting voluntary, if not mandatory, prayer in schools also want a constitutional amendment. The reasoning of these social conservatives is similar to that of liberal interest groups a generation ago: Why fight for fifty different laws when you can wage the whole battle in Congress and then get a straight up-or-down vote on ratification of a constitutional amendment in the states?

However, even economic conservatives are not always consistent. Bills concentrating federal power over telecommunications and certain financial securities were both passed by the Republican 104th Congress at the expense of state regulation.

Nor are companies that market nationally always crippled by ideological consistency. Until the middle 1960s, business organizations opposing certain legislative proposals in Congress often used the argument that the subject of the legislation was inappropriate for federal action and best left to the states. This was a useful argument because those advocates knew that the states seldom had much interest in legislating on those topics.

As states became increasingly active in areas of consumer, environmental, workplace, and other issues, many business lobbyists reversed course, urging Congress to enact national legislation that would preempt state action in order to protect interstate and national markets from fragmented regulation. Businesses have also sometimes been reluctant to trade federal deregulation for new (and possibly risky) state and local regulation, especially if they believe they are less influential in the states than in Washington.

Liberal interest groups supported federal preemption, though with a twist, often arguing that federal legislation should preempt conflicting state laws that were less stringent than federal requirements, while leaving the states free to enact tighter standards if they wished.

Many state and local governments have taken a third road, asking that Congress not preempt them at all so that they are free to act in any way they wish, or not to act at all.

Sometimes abetted by Congress, sometimes not, this philosophic conflict is likely to continue well into the next century as state and local governments continue to experiment with widely varying legislative and regulatory approaches. This is particularly true for those states and communities that tend to be regulatory innovators and pacesetters (or, as one disgruntled business lobbyist put it, those "on the cutting edge of trouble"). These are states like California, New York, Massachusetts, Oregon, and Wisconsin, and local governments like those of Berkeley, California, and Suffolk County, New York.

The interests of business will be again caught in the middle. Many business people may be philosophically conservative, but they are operationally pragmatic. It is costly to be compelled to do business under multiple sets of rules and standards, and ultimately both the consumer and economic productivity suffer.

State Legislative Characteristics

It is difficult to generalize about the fifty state legislatures and the 7,500 lawmakers who comprise them. Some are "citizen-legislators" who serve a few terms and then go back to private life; others have become careerists. Some are paid $10,000 or less a year, others more than $50,000. Some legislative houses have twenty or thirty members, others 150 or 200. (The lower house in New Hampshire has nearly 400 members.) On the average, legislatures are in session three or four months, but some meet for as little as thirty days, while others have become virtually year-round bodies. Personal and committee staffs are equally varied in size.

It is not only devolution and state activism that have led to the rapid growth of state government relations. Other factors include

- Increased careerism among legislators, a growing number of whom hold safe seats, who today often consider their legislative pursuits as full-time vocations.
- The enlargement in size and power of legislative staffs, many of whom have become power brokers in their own right, often with their own personal ideological agendas for public policy initiatives.
- The fragmentation of power in many states and its shift away from legislative leaders toward individual lawmakers. Once leadership-dominated power centers, many state legislatures have become bazaars of entrepreneurial activists. There are still some notable exceptions like New York and California, but even in those states changes are trending away from strong power centers.

STATE GOVERNMENT RELATIONS PROGRAMS

State government relations varies in importance to companies, depending on the nature of their business and their exposure to regulation. Public utilities and cable television systems that have operated under monopoly franchises granted by state or local governments have been heavily regulated and need to maintain potent government relations programs. Certain competitive industries, such as banking and insurance, have also operated predominantly under state regulation, and an effective state lobbying capability is critical to them.

Even though many such industries are increasingly being deregulated, the process will stretch out over a number of years, and their need to affect state legislative and regulatory policies will continue for the foreseeable future.

Other businesses, including retailers, manufacturers, and service companies, are sensitive to diverse state and local regulation of marketing, merchandising, health, and safety; they also are subject to a variety of state labor and environmental laws.

In 1996, 70 percent of 260 companies surveyed had formalized state government relations programs—slightly less than two-thirds of manufacturing companies, and about three-fourths of nonmanufacturers—more than 80 percent of larger companies but also 70 percent of companies with revenues under $1 billion.[2]

Depending on the nature and scope of the exposure, state government relations can be carried out in one or more ways:

- By in-house government relations professionals working for an individual company or in some cases for a national association, with responsibility for a single state or perhaps several states in a region
- Through state trade associations, themselves growing in size and importance
- Through independent (or contract) lobbyists retained in each of the state capitals (or localities) in which there is significant exposure
- Through the use of plant and facility managers and other executives at the grassroots level whose responsibilities include some degree of state and local government relations

Modes may differ by industry, by individual company, and even within companies and divisions, depending on needs and resources. If issues are company-specific and sporadic, mostly requiring only monitoring or "light lobbying," it may well be that local operating managers can do what is necessary in addition to their normal duties. Issues affecting an entire industry can be handled by a state trade association if it is effective.

Some companies maintain a network of regional state government relations managers within their corporate government relations or public affairs departments. These individuals monitor developments among a group of states (generally utilizing on-line tracking systems), engage in direct lobbying as required, and often take advantage of their company's grassroots network for support with individual legislators. Sometimes such managers have responsibility for a single state if the company has a great deal at stake there or if it is the only state in which the business operates. In other cases, they may supervise retained lobbyists in one or more of the state capitals for which they are accountable. These retained lobbyists may only assist with the issues-monitoring process, or they may also be responsible for direct lobbying on important issues.

The 1996 company survey found that 85 percent of the firms with formal state programs used either a regional or a state-by-state arrangement, with about equal numbers in each category. Operating units were assigned the responsibility in another 19 percent.[3]

Selecting State Lobbyists

In selecting an outside lobbyist, consider first what you want him or her to do—just monitor an issue or be able to defeat or pass a particular bill. Then seek recommendations of possible candidates from national or state trade associations and other business groups or from other companies that utilize lobbyists in that state. Friendly legislative leaders may be able to recommend people. Eliminate lobbyists who may have real or potential conflicts of interest; that is, they work for companies or other interest groups that may oppose your position. This can be checked out with recommenders, through lobbyist registrations, and in interviews with the candidates.

An alternative way to identify and retain a lobbyist is to make use of one of the state government relations consulting firms that have networks of independent contract lobbyists in each state capital. A client with legislative problems in, say, Hartford, Harrisburg, Sacramento, and Tallahassee, hires one of these firms, which in turn retains and supervises local lobbyists for each of these state legislatures. While not cheap, such services can be more cost effective than a permanent state government relations staff. By relying on such consulting firms, many companies find they can manage state government relations quite well with only a single manager on staff to provide liaison with the consultant and coordination within the company.

"Should you decide to go to an outside firm," says a principal in one of them, "make sure of the following: that there is no charge for the proposal, that it costs no more to work through them than it would cost you to do it yourself, that they are a resource and part of your team (not just a headhunter), and that they have in-depth state experience themselves."[4]

Although an extraordinarily complex or technical issue, such as a matter of tax law, may require a lobbyist with special expertise, lobbyists are usually hired for their legislative contacts, credibility, and ability to get results; the client provides the substantive knowledge. Clients must also manage their lobbyists. They should set goals, establish periodic benchmarks, request reports, meet frequently with them (and with involved legislators), and so on.

Some experts suggest avoiding the best-known or most expensive lobbyists, including former top elected officials (such as former governors) and other "rainmakers" who get the business but may then delegate the actual lobbying to subordinates.

State Legislative Contact Organizations

Washington corporate representatives and association lobbyists make it their business to know the members of Congress who can affect their issues. Lobbyists based full time in a state capital can do the same thing. But government relations managers with multistate responsibilities often find it difficult to maintain all the relationships they need. People whose companies or business associations operate in at least four states, therefore, find it useful to join the State Governmental Affairs Council, an organization headquartered in Washington that maintains liaison with a number of public-sector associations and provides opportunities to become acquainted with key lawmakers and officials *before* problems and issues arise.

The latter include the National Conference of State Legislators, the American Legislative Exchange Council, the National Governors Association, the Council of State Governments, and several of the other intergovernmental interest groups described in Chapter 2 and listed in the appendix.

LOCAL GOVERNMENT RELATIONS

For companies, they key to good government relations in the communities in which they are based (or in which they have facilities) is to undertake an effective community relations program. Community relations means, simply, activities that demonstrate the company's commitment to local needs, causes, groups, and institutions: sponsoring a reading or math program for the local school system or donating classroom computers, stimulating adult literacy in cooperation with community libraries, working with a local anticrime organization to improve safety and support for the police, and so on.

Community relations often involves not only outreach to local government officials, community organizations, and newspapers, but also other efforts to educate people about the role and importance of the company in the local economy.

The value of these activities is that they build support and good will for the organization. This can be invaluable when a government relations problem arises. They also facilitate relationships with local elected and administrative officials prior to an actual lobbying need. These relationships are a precious asset when support is required to pass or kill local or state legislation or regulations. They will be equally important in crisis situations, ranging from a disaster at a local company facility to a plant closing.

The problem is different if an issue develops in a locality where the organization has no facilities—perhaps a proposal to regulate in some special way products or services marketed there. Some local governments practice a high degree of activism and pride themselves on innovating forms of regulation that other localities often then emulate.

In such cases, a state or national trade association may become involved in the issue if it affects a substantial segment of the industry. If not, the only real alternative is to retain a local independent lobbyist. These are prevalent in the largest cities and some smaller ones. They can be identified and screened much as state lobbyists are. As a last resort, some state lobbyists may have the local connections to handle the issue.

STATE REGULATION OF LOBBYING

There are fifty different patterns of state requirements governing lobbying registration and filings—more, if local requirements are counted. Some are vague and loose, others stringent and bureaucratic. Like the federal law, state lobbying regulation laws typically have two kinds of requirements: registration and reporting.

Registration

All fifty states require paid lobbyists to register with a state official if they will be contacting legislators on issues. Thirty states also require registration if the lobbyist will be in contact with executive and regulatory agencies. Typical registration information includes name and address, identification of employer or clients, description of the issues, and sometimes even the names of legislators or officials the lobbyist expects to contact. Many states require an employer or client authorization statement; some require a registration fee. Several states require a photograph of the lobbyist to be published in a directory of lobbyists or used on a badge that the lobbyist must wear. Badges are fairly common.

Reporting

Most states require lobbyists and clients or employers to file periodic financial and activity reports. Some reporting forms are simple, others are very complex. Some reports are carefully checked for accuracy, others merely filed. Some reports must be filed monthly, others quarterly or semiannually, a few annually.

The information lobbyists must file also varies widely: statements of compensation and expenses; whom they have contacted and on what issues; sometimes specific entertainment details (who was entertained, where, when, how much was spent, and so forth).

Although there is a question about how stringent state lobbying laws can become without violating the First Amendment, there has never been a court test of their constitutionality. The Supreme Court emasculated one federal lobbying law in 1954; there has been no court challenge to the 1995 Lobbying Disclosure Act. Lower federal courts have declined opportunities to hear challenges to state lobbying laws.

Each state publishes information on its own lobbying requirements and forms. Sources of this information for each state are indicated in the *State Legislative Sourcebook* and the *Compendium of State Lobbying Laws*. A biannually published reference work is the *Blue Book* of the Council of State Governments. (For citations to these publications, see *State Almanacs and Directories* in the appendix.) The entire September 1996 issue of *State Trends & Forecasts*, published by the Council of State Governments, is devoted to an analysis of state lobbying reform proposals.

In 1996, there were 43,703 registered state lobbyists in the country, a 13 percent increase since 1988.[5] Almost all states prohibit conflicts of interest on the part of state officials and ban receipt of payments, gifts, fees, or honoraria. Many today also regulate lobbying activities by former state officials. Lobbyists are barred in twenty-one states from making campaign contributions during legislative sessions; two states ban them from contributing at all. Most states now prohibit contingency fees; that is, making the fee dependent on whether the lobbyist achieves the client's goal.

An illustration of how stringent state lobbying laws have become occurred in Maryland in 1997. When a state legislator married a lobbyist, she was forced to cancel the wedding reception because her husband's share of the costs would have constituted an illegal gift to his new spouse!

REFERENDA AND INITIATIVES

About half the states extend the legislative process to the polling place by permitting voters to decide the fate of individual issues. "Direct democracy," as some call it, takes two forms, the initiative and the popular referendum. Both are important to government relations professionals in these states because they provide the public with the means either to override an act of the legislature or to circumvent it altogether.[6]

Initiatives

In twenty-four states, the District of Columbia, and many localities, citizens may petition for placement on the ballot of proposed new laws or constitutional amendments. In states with the "direct initiative," the proposal goes directly on the ballot (assuming it gets the required number of petition signatures); and if approved by the voters, it is adopted. Some states have a variation, "the indirect initiative," which requires that the proposal first be submitted to the legislature, which is then given a chance to act on it before it goes to the voters.

Referenda

The term, "referendum," is commonly used to describe any ballot question that the voters are asked to approve—constitutional amendments, bond issues, and the like. Most of these are more accurately described as "referred measures" since they do not involve citizen petitions but are referred by some government body or required by the state constitution.

"Popular referenda," in contrast, give the voters a chance to approve or disapprove legislation already passed by the state's lawmakers. Like initiatives, popular referenda require that a minimum number of voters sign petitions to have the issue placed on the ballot. The popular referendum exists in twenty-five states and many localities.

Both initiatives and popular referenda can result in significant legislation. California, which makes perhaps the widest use of these public policy instruments, has adopted a number of controversial measures over the years, particularly through initiatives. Subjects have ranged from tax limitations to environmental requirements to restrictions on the use of state services by immigrants.

The initiative process can have its peculiarities. On several occasions, California voters have been faced with two different and inconsistent campaign reform proposals, and approved both! (The one with the larger number of votes prevails.)

Recalls

Fifteen states permit the voters to remove elected officials from office, and others require periodic votes on certain officials' continuation in office. These are seldom used but powerful devices. Arizona voters filed enough signatures to force a recall election on their governor in 1988, had the legislature not first removed him from office. In 1986, Californians refused to reconfirm the chief justice and two associate justices of the California Supreme Court, ejecting them from office. Both events were front-page news across the country.

The laws governing initiatives, popular referenda, and recalls vary widely. Petition signature requirements for initiatives and popular referenda, for example, range from 2 to 15 percent of the most recent statewide voter turnout. Signature requirements for recalls are generally higher.

NOTES

1. Tim Clark, Editor of *Federal Executive Magazine*, cited in *ASAE Government Relations*, September 1996.

2. James E. Post and Jennifer J. Griffin, *The State of Corporate Public Affairs: 1996 Survey Results*. Washington, D.C.: Foundation for Public Affairs, 1997, Figs. 7.1–7.4.

3. Ibid., Fig. 7.5.

4. Marcie M. McNelis, *Hiring and Managing Contract Lobbyists* (Alexandria, Va.: MultiState Associates, Inc., 1996).

5. Council of State Governments, *State Trends & Forecasts*, September 1996, p. 14.

6. A useful explanation and analysis of referenda and initiatives is Patrick B. McGuigan, *The Politics of Direct Democracy in the 1980s: Case Studies in Popular Decision Making* (Washington, D.C.: The Institute for Government and Politics of the Free Congress Research and Education Foundation, 1985); see also David B. Magleby, *Direct Legislation: Voting on Ballot Propositions in the United States* (Baltimore: Johns Hopkins University Press, 1984).

Chapter 10

International Government Relations

> International relations have become truly global for the first time. Communications are instantaneous; the world economy operates on all continents simultaneously. A whole set of issues has surfaced that can only be dealt with on a worldwide basis, such as nuclear proliferation, the environment, the population explosion, and economic interdependence.
> —Henry A. Kissinger

A significant phenomenon is the development of global commerce that has gone beyond the regulatory capability of any national government, or even all of them cooperatively. One dramatic example is the Internet, a technology that has mushroomed worldwide, seemingly beyond the ability of governments to regulate it for access or content. The inability of governments to censor electronic communications among groups and individuals may have been a factor in the collapse of the Soviet Union. Another example is the use of satellites that allow communications and electronic commerce even with countries lacking much of an internal telephone system—for instance, virtually instantaneous international currency and commodity trading. *The Economist* estimated that electronic cross-border currency transactions totaled about $1.3 trillion *per day* in 1996. Traders in major Asian, European, and North American cities can rattle national governments in a matter of hours, as the Mexican government learned painfully in 1995.

But most businesses are not immune to government policies and regulation. Major companies operate on a worldwide basis today, for reasons of both efficiency and marketing. Smaller companies in countries around the globe have active and growing export programs. Regardless of where it is manufactured, almost any complex consumer or industrial product is likely to contain components or ingredients from several countries. One way or another, all these businesses are affected by international government relations.

What individual governments do can have consequences a continent away or worldwide. A new social welfare program in the European Union affects not only the companies operating there but also the prices of their exports, producing ripple effects on customers and competitors on every continent. A new food standard from the Food and Agricultural Organization is likely to be adopted by national governments and food manufacturers everywhere. Tax treaties signed by the United States and another government may well have bottom-line implications for businesses in third countries as well. A new wage-and-hour regulation in India would affect not only computer programmers there but also the software purchases of U.S. companies—who, incidentally, can now order, receive, and pay for the product entirely by satellite.

Companies have launched international government relations programs precisely because they are affected by such measures. The emergence of worldwide markets and communications means that decisions reached in Washington, Brussels, or Tokyo can have major and immediate impacts anywhere—as the Microsoft Corporation discovered when it was forced to negotiate consent orders relating to its competitive practices with both the U.S. Department of Justice and the European Union *simultaneously*.

Nor is international government relations confined to businesses. The AFL–CIO has been active internationally for decades. Environmental organizations like Greenpeace also operate around the globe. The willingness and capability of such groups to influence the policies of countries other than their own is growing rapidly, precisely because what happens *any*where influences what happens *every*where.

International government relations means different things to different interest groups. To some, it may simply mean hiring a lawyer in another country to influence a regulation. To others, it may mean comprehensive programs in several countries. Still others may concern themselves only with certain of the UN's affiliates or with one of the regional trade organizations. A relatively few companies engage not only in government relations but in broad-gauge public affairs programs to demonstrate a role as concerned corporate citizens in the countries in which they have significant operations or markets.

Lobbying abroad is still an emerging, and occasionally awkward, effort for government relations professionals who learned their craft in the United States. The system of government is different in most other countries, as usually are the structures, the processes, and the rules. Applying principles learned at home may lead Americans into treacherous quicksand in another culture and political environment. Many of the tactics and techniques available to government relations practitioners in the United States, such as direct lobbying, political action, and the use of associations, coalitions, and the media, may have different applications in other countries and organizations. Other tactics, like grassroots lobbying, may work in some places but be completely inappropriate elsewhere.

International government relations is a relatively new craft for most American companies. The 1996 survey of corporate public affairs found that 65 percent of companies have international business units, but only 40 percent have a "developed" or "highly developed" international public affairs capability—somewhat more among manufacturers, less among nonmanufacturing companies. Public affairs personnel have a lead or advisory role in only 38 percent of these companies. In most of the remainder, management makes decisions without benefit of public affairs input. Since international government relations is an expanding function, these numbers will probably change over time.[1]

Broadly speaking, there are two arenas of international government relations. One is the governments of individual countries. The other is the array of regional or global organizations comprising those national governments.

An entire volume would be required to do justice to the complexities of international government relations. This chapter has three limited goals:

1. To outline important considerations about lobbying in other countries, particularly those with parliamentary systems.
2. To describe the process of government relations in the European Union, the world's most important international organization.
3. To summarize some important government relations principles.

GOVERNMENT RELATIONS IN OTHER COUNTRIES

The practice of government relations is different outside the United States because governments are structured and operate differently, and because they are based on cultural and social value systems that may not closely resemble ours. The systems of government and national politics, as well as the nature of public values, all have critical implications for the lobbying process.[2]

Let's begin with the system of government. Some countries in Latin America and elsewhere have forms of government modeled, more or less, after that of the United States, in which the powers of government are divided between the legislative and executive branches. But the prevalent pattern throughout the industrialized world—including European states, as well as Canada and Japan—is parliamentary government (sometimes also called cabinet government) in which government powers are undivided. Parliamentary government evolved in Great Britain, the paradigm for most of the world's democracies. Although no two parliamentary systems are exactly alike (any more than the structures of the fifty state governments are) there are similarities and patterns.

Parliamentary Government

Every country in the world has a head of state and a head of government. In the United States the president is both, but in parliamentary governments the positions are separate. In a few countries, the head of state is still a hereditary monarch—the emperor of Japan, the kings of Belgium and Spain, the queen of Great Britain. In a few others, members of the British Commonwealth, the queen's representative (in Canada, for example, the governor-general) fills this role. Everywhere else, the head of state is the president, usually elected by the parliament. The head of state in most countries plays a largely ceremonial role, but in some countries, like France and Russia, the office has real power; the president is elected by the voters in the latter two states.

In parliamentary democracies, the voters elect the members of at least the lower house of the national legislature—sometimes through single- or multi-member districts, sometimes through systems of proportional representation in which political parties win seats according to their relative percentages of the vote, sometimes through a combination of these techniques.

If one party obtains a majority of the lower house, it wins the right to form the government. In multiparty countries, often no single party has a majority, and the largest party must try to form a coalition with others to gain a majority. Occasionally, two large coalitions try to get a majority, and the head of state then gets to decide which to ask first to form a government.

The head of the majority party, or the largest party in a coalition, usually becomes prime minister, the head of government. (An unusual innovation was recently instituted in Israel where the prime minister is elected separately from the members of the Knesset, giving rise to the possibility that the prime minister may not always be a member of the parliamentary majority party.)

The prime minister then chooses the ministers to head the various ministries (equivalent to departments or major agencies) and who make up the cabinet. In parliamentary coalitions, the selection of cabinet members is a key element in the negotiation of the coalition. The prime ministers and cabinet ministers are almost always members of parliament; a minister who leaves parliament also leaves the cabinet. (In parliamentary countries, the cabinet is called "the government," a narrower usage of the term than in the United States.)

A principal point of difference with the U.S. system, therefore, is that the executive leaders of the government are also the legislative leaders. It is as if the head of the majority party in our House of Representatives automatically became president.

Another difference, compared to the American system, is that the two houses of parliament are not coequal. There is usually an upper house with severely limited powers; in Great Britain, it is the House of Lords; in France and Canada, the Senate. Most of the power lies in the lower house, and it is that body that is usually meant by references to "parliament." The upper body typically functions as a mechanism to slow down or, rarely, to veto certain publicly controversial measures that the government is trying to ram through.

The cabinet is a far more important institution of parliamentary government than it is in the United States, where its role is essentially advisory to the president. The cabinet collectively makes governmental policy and decides what legislation may be introduced in parliament; virtually no legislation of any consequence is seriously considered that has not been proposed by the cabinet.

The significance of this for government relations is that lobbying focuses not on key legislators or parliamentary committees but on the cabinet and the senior members of the bureaucracy.

The Structure of the State

It is also important to know whether the government system is a *unitary* or a *federal* state. Germany with its Länder and Canada with its provinces are examples of federal systems in which the subdivisions have powers like those of the fifty American states, if not even greater ones, as the Canadian provinces do. In a unitary state, virtually all power lies in the national government, as it does in Britain, France, and Japan; local government bodies may be elected and have administrative authority, but they take policy direction from the national ministries.

The division of powers in federal systems is not a clear-cut distinction anywhere, any more than it is in the United States. Some functions of government are clearly divided in federal systems, others are mixed. When the members of the Oakland Board of Education approved the teaching of Black English in local schools in 1997, they clearly had the power to do so (although the California legislature could have overruled them). The U.S. Department of Education had no say on the policy, but it immediately made clear that Oakland need not look to Washington to fund the program. Problems like these arise all the time in federal systems. On the other hand, if the local authorities in Marseilles want to teach Arabic in the public schools, the policy decision will be made by the Ministry of Education in Paris.

Federalism always produces stress. The jockeying that goes on between Washington and the states over who has the power to do what is modest compared to the constant tensions between the Canadian provinces and the government in Ottawa. Quebec's constant threats to secede are only the most extreme problem. Manitoba wants to abandon the mandatory expense of translating all government documents into French because it has hardly any French Canadians. Alberta wants control of its own energy sources. The Maritime Provinces want more help from Ottawa to save commercial fishing jobs, even though the cost may be greater than the economic value of the industry. The addition of the five eastern Länder when Germany reunified produced not only financial difficulties but federal strains as well. Other countries with a federal system of government have their own sets of problems.

This is not a mere academic concern for government relations advocates. If a medical group wants to influence the regulation of health insurance reimbursements, it needs to know where health policy is made. A company that wants to sell a new kind of firearm to Italian local police forces has to learn whether the police have authority to purchase the new weapons or if the company must first convince the authorities in Rome.

National Politics

Political systems may vary even more than the country's political structure. A company considering operations in another country wants to know how stable politics are there. Is democracy secure or is there a colonel somewhere plotting a barracks coup? Even in countries where democratic institutions are not in danger, how stable is the government? Coalition governments, like those that characterize Italy, must constantly worry about losing their parliamentary majority in a vote of confidence. Germany's three-party governing coalition does not have these fears, but even two-party systems may be vulnerable if the government's majority is thin and subject to defections or vacancies. The British Conservative government operated under such a cloud for several years before it was defeated in the spring of 1997.

Parliaments are elected for a fixed term, typically five years, but prime ministers can dissolve parliament at any time and call new elections—which they often do when they believe their party is in the best position to win a new majority. (Political leaders have also been known to guess wrong, as French President Chirac did in 1997.) In Britain, new elections are usually called no more than four years into the parliament's term; hanging on to the end, as the Conservatives did, in the vain hope that their popularity would improve, was as exceptional as it was futile.

If the cabinet loses a vote of confidence, the government falls; and a new one must be assembled, unless the prime minister chooses to call new elections. Governments collapse when they no longer command a majority in parliament. This can happen for several reasons: if one of the parties withdraws from a coalition; or if the governing party's majority is lost through defections to another party; or if the opposition wins enough seats in special elections. Japan's Liberal Democrats lost power for a time when several of its factions split off to form new parties.

Votes of confidence are routine in parliaments. Normally, the government prevails; when it does not, it falls. Once in a while, the outgoing prime minister is asked by the head of state to try to form a new cabinet; but usually someone else is invited to do so, unless new elections are called.

The political rules may occasionally change, or at least appear to change. After Japan's Liberal Democratic Party (actually a conservative party dominated by business interests) lost its majority in the Diet, other cabinets governed Japan for a time. Eventually, the Liberal Democrats formed a coalition with the Socialists, first under a Socialist prime minister, then under a Liberal Democrat. Meanwhile, a new electoral system took effect, replacing the old multimember districts. In the 1996 elections, half the new members of the Diet were elected from single-member districts, half from party lists by proportional representation. The Liberal Democrats narrowly failed to win a majority and were forced into another coalition government. Whether the new system will have any effect on the way Japan makes public policy, and the way interest groups and their lobbyists operate, remains to be seen. Skeptics believe the "reforms" have the substance of clouds, and that the keiretsu (major industrial corporations), the rural agricultural interests, and the complex and powerful bureaucracy will continue as the nation's dominant forces, as they have since the end of World War II.

Other political changes have real significance for interest groups. Canada's Progressive Conservative Party had long been the ally of the nation's business community until the government fell in 1993. In perhaps the worst calamity to befall a modern political party, the Conservatives lost not just their majority, but 150 of the 152 seats they had held in the 295-member House of Commons. The Liberal Party gained a large majority and formed the new government, with three other parties dividing most of the remaining seats. Interest groups that had been allied with the Progressive Conservatives suddenly found themselves politically friendless and had to scramble to build relationships with the new cabinet. (The Progressive Conservatives gained some seats in the 1997 elections, but the Liberals retained their majority.)

Political ground rules matter to lobbyists. Are political campaigns publicly funded, privately financed, or a combination of both? If public, what formula distributes funds to the political parties or candidates? If private, are contributions broad based, or does one interest group tend to predominate as the keiretsu do in Japan? If the latter, what is the impact on the balance among interest groups in public policy debates? Is political spending limited or not? Is lobbying regulated? How extensively?

The Political Culture

Every culture has its own value system that colors the governmental and political processes. These public values are worth some study by interest groups based in a different political culture. Here are a few examples:

- In the Scandinavian states, the prevailing ideology is social democracy; differences among the parties tend to center on debates about whether to expand the welfare state or trim it slightly—but certainly not to abandon it.

- The Japanese culture influences individuals to derive their satisfactions primarily from the achievements of a larger organization of which they are part, a very different set of cultural values from that of the United States, and one that has significantly influenced Japan's economic growth and resistance to institutional and social change.

- Germans have largely bought labor peace at the price of acceding to most of the social and economic objectives of the unions, including mandatory representation on corporate boards of directors and some of the most costly employee benefits in the world. The results—rising unemployment and declining productivity—have almost halted economic growth at a time when Germany needs all the resources it can muster to rebuild the economies of the states that once made up East Germany.

- Canada's problems exist, in part, because of the continuing dispute between English and French Canadians, but also because "economic forces flow largely north–south while legal jurisdiction is east–west."[3]

All these generalizations are admittedly broad, but it is essential to remember that all societies have characteristics that are reflected in their national politics and the character of public policy debates. Together with the governmental and political systems, they are major determinants of what interest group advocates can do and how and where they must go about doing it.

INTERNATIONAL ORGANIZATIONS

Interest groups lobby international organizations, first to affect international laws and regulations (of which there are a growing number) and second to affect the laws of many individual countries at a single step. Once an international organization has adopted a policy or a set of standards, individual national governments very frequently incorporate it into their own bodies of laws and regulations. In a sense, influencing policies one country at a time is lobbying at retail. By working through international organizations, interest groups can engage in wholesale lobbying.

For that reason, the United Nations and its complex of affiliated global organizations (listed in the appendix) are of increasing importance to many American interest groups. The new World Trade Organization is the focus of considerable attention by U.S. companies, but it is far from the only one such group which American business interests have a stake. The agribusiness industry concerns itself with the work of the Food and Agricultural Organization, pharmaceutical manufacturers with the World Health Organization, and airlines with the International Civil Aviation Organization. Other interest groups may be involved with such global intergovernment organizations as the United Nations Educational, Scientific, and Cultural Organization (UNESCO) or with the International Labor Organization. In all these organizations, decisions are made by negotiations among member governments through which private-sector groups must work to influence political decisions. Interest groups operating in these international bodies are called NGOs (for nongovernment organizations). All the international organizations have full-time secretariats, often very large ones, and they are open in varying degrees to substantive input from NGOs.

The North American Free Trade Agreement (NAFTA) is only the most recent example of *regional* treaties designed to reduce trade barriers and further economic integration among their member countries. Other important treaties are found in Asia (ASEAN and APEC), and in Latin America (Mercosur). Of course, the largest and most advanced of them all is the European Union.

THE EUROPEAN UNION

The importance of America and Europe to each other is vast, by any measure. Americans fought two wars to preserve the integrity of Europe and were ready to fight another if it came to that. Our cultural and political heritage is still essentially European. Most Americans are of European descent, although that will change by the middle of the twenty-first century. Like the United States, the nations of Europe are all democracies.[4]

Europe's population is about 370 million, compared to 260 million Americans. Europeans live closer together than we do; population density is 380 per square mile in Europe, 70 in the United States. Europe's economy (gross domestic product) is nearly $7 trillion; ours about $6 trillion. Unemployment rates and government deficits are higher in Europe, in large part because of expensive "cradle-to-grave" social policies that are prevalent in most European countries. Nearly a fifth of U.S. exports go to Europe, and a similar percentage of Europe's exports come here. When American companies and individuals invest abroad, it is primarily in Europe; and most European direct foreign investment is in the United States.

Europe is also America's principal economic rival and competitor, as symbolized by a single example: Worldwide commercial aircraft manufacturing is dominated today by only two companies—Boeing and Airbus, a consortium of European companies. The importance of Europe and the United States to each other is also illustrated by the mergers and other economic combinations taking place between American and European companies—the pharmaceutical and telecommunications industries provide many examples.

Europe was once merely the name of a continent stretching from the Atlantic to the Urals. Today, the word means an open, fully integrated market economy much like ours, that negotiates trade agreements as if it were a single country. Europe also means a complex of institutions with governmental and quasi-governmental powers over the economies and much of the social policies of fifteen countries, and eventually perhaps as many as twenty-five or thirty. Not since the demise of the Hanseatic League, the largest of the merchant guilds that dominated Europe in the Middle Ages, has there been a single organization with the multinational economic power exercised by the European Union.

The European Union is a unique government structure; there is nothing quite like it anywhere else in the world. No other regional organization comes close to it in economic integration. In some policy areas, the EU makes law that is binding on its national governments; in other areas, it sets policies these governments must implement; and in still others it merely makes recommendations. Its policy-making processes are as unique and fluid as its internal structure and membership, all of which change every few years as new organic treaties are negotiated.

Virtually all of this is alien to the American legislative process, and yet the EU is the most important focus for most Americans involved in international government relations.

The roots of European integration lie in the wars that raged across the continent for centuries. Following the end of World War II, political leaders, particularly in France and Germany, decided that if there were to be an end to these conflicts it would come about only if the economies of European nations became so intertwined that future wars would be impossible. Their goal was a continental economy modeled after that of the United States but painted on a multinational canvas.

For the most part, the economic objectives have been achieved:

- A free trade area within which tariffs and other trade barriers have been eliminated that is now being extended to financial services. In addition to EU members, this European Economic Area also includes Norway, Iceland, and to some extent Switzerland.
- A customs union, with a common tariff schedule toward imports from countries outside the EU. Turkey also participates in the customs union.
- A common market, eliminating most (but not quite all) internal barriers to the free movement of capital, goods, services, and people.

Subsequently, the EU's objectives came to include social policies, finances and a common currency, justice and internal security, European citizenship, foreign policy, and perhaps ultimately some form of political unity. Justice, internal security, and foreign policy are still largely the province of individual national governments but there is increasing coordination among them.

Starting in 1951 with the coal and steel industries of Germany, France, Italy, Belgium, the Netherlands, and Luxembourg, what is now the European Union has come to encompass the entire economies and societies of fifteen countries. The original six have been joined at various times by Denmark, Sweden, Great Britain, Ireland, Spain, Portugal, Greece, Austria, and Finland. Cyprus and several countries of central and eastern Europe are likely to be admitted in the near future. Virtually all the other former satellite states of the Soviet empire have expressed interest in joining, as has Turkey. Norway and Switzerland have so far declined to join.

European Institutions

The institutions of the EU have little parallel anywhere else except for the Parliament, the only popularly elected body. Unlike the other EU institutions, which are structured by nationality, the Parliament is organized by political groups, of which the largest are the Party of European Socialists and the center-right European People's Party. The 626 MEPs (Members of the European Parliament) are directly elected by the voters of their countries for five-year terms; the next elections will be held in June 1999. The Parliament's power is limited, but it has been given more legislative authority in recent years.

The Parliament must approve the EU budget and the appointment of the commissioners and the Commission's president. Parliament also has the power to force the entire Commission to resign, but has never exercised it.

The other key bodies besides the Parliament are the Commission; the Council of the European Union (formerly the Council of Ministers and still better known by that name); and the European Council, comprising the heads of government (prime ministers) of the fifteen countries as well as the French president and the president of the Commission. Despite the similarity of names, the two councils should not be confused with each other. The differences were clearer before the name of the former Council of Ministers was changed; its members are the equivalent of cabinet officers in the United States and change according to the subject matter under discussion.

The role of the European Commission approximates that of the executive branch elsewhere, but some of its functions are judicial, legislative, and administrative. In some ways, it resembles a parliamentary cabinet, but so does the Council of Ministers. Comprising twenty commissioners selected by the national governments, the Commission is headed by a president, selected by the heads of the member states subject to ratification by the parliament. The current president is Jacques Santer, former prime minister of Luxembourg, who succeeded Jacques Delors in 1995. Delors, a Frenchman, was regarded as one of the most influential presidents the Commission has had. The larger countries (Britain, Germany, France, Spain, and Italy) at present appoint two commissioners each, the smaller states one each, but this is likely to change in a few years. The commissioners are all former top civil servants or political leaders in their own countries, but all are supposed to act on behalf of the EU, not their home countries. Like MEPs, commissioners serve five-year terms.

Each commissioner oversees one or more "directorates-general" (DGs), the equivalent of a government department or ministry, each headed by a director-general. The directors-general are civil servants; the commissioners play the political role. One DG is responsible for agriculture, another for competition policy, a third for environmental matters, and so on. The EU attracts some of the best civil servants in Europe, in part because of high compensation levels.

Headquartered in Brussels, the commission has a staff of about sixteen thousand, not a huge number considering its breadth of responsibilities, especially since a fifth of them are translators (there are eleven official languages). The EU's budget is about $100 billion, more than half of which comes from the value-added tax (VAT), a form of sales tax collected by the member states that is levied at every stage of production and distribution.

All legislation begins with the Commission. In addition, it can sue in European courts not only individuals and companies for violations of EU rules, but also any of the national governments.

The EU Legislative Process

Legislation originating within the appropriate DG must be approved by the commissioners. It is then proposed simultaneously to the Parliament and the Council of Ministers. Like national ministries or U.S. government agencies, each DG has its own interest and point of view. The issues each pursues may be different, and very possibly at odds with those of another DG. The DG concerned with agricultural issues will look at issues quite differently than the one concerned with reducing trade barriers.

As in the United States, the earlier the stage at which lobbying input occurs, the greater its impact is likely to be. Lobbying that provides new or additional information has significant impact. Pressure lobbying, on the other hand, is likely to be resisted and resented.

Information is the prized commodity in EU lobbying, especially at the Commission level. Having the connections to learn about ideas for potential legislation while they are still gestating and to obtain early drafts of working papers are valuable skills in a Brussels lobbyist, perhaps even more so than in the United States, because the Commission and its staff are sometimes less open about what they are considering. "It's generally the case in the U.S. that what is public is public, and you can get it," said a lobbyist who works both sides of the Atlantic. "In Brussels, it's much less of a clear line between what is correct to give to the private sector and what isn't. [It's] really a matter of who you know."[5] Others disagree. A lobbyist who represented his company in Brussels for several years told the author, "there were opportunities to access their policy process at some unique points in the formative stages that one could hardly imagine existing here."

Once a proposal has gone from a DG to the commissioner who oversees it, interest group discussions of political factors become more appropriate, first with the commissioners' staffs and then with the officials themselves. Other commissioners may also get involved at this point. For example, a proposal relating to competition policy within the transportation industry is likely to involve at least two commissioners. Even where only a single commissioner is involved, lobbying opportunities are widespread. Most Commission decisions require what is called "consensus" but which is really unanimity. While a couple of friendly commissioners have the ability to kill a proposal, they are unlikely to do so often, lest the commissioner sponsoring the measure take revenge later on one of their issues. However, objections among commissioners can help create a climate in which amendments can be made.

After the Commission has proposed a legislative measure, the Council of Ministers takes it up. The Council is not really a single body. If the measure deals with education, the Council consists of the education ministers of each country; the agricultural ministers consider farm legislation, and so on. Continuity is provided by the Council's Committee of Permanent Representatives ("Coreper"), with a staff of two thousand, headquartered in Brussels. The Council must be unanimous if it wants to amend a Commission proposal. Passage of issues without change needs only a "qualified majority," based on a system of weighted voting, ranging from ten votes each for Britain, France, Italy, and Germany, down to two votes for Luxembourg.

Weighted voting currently has a total of eighty-seven votes, with sixty-two constituting a qualified majority. A "blocking majority" of at least twenty-five votes cast by five or more countries can delay a decision for a time so that negotiations can take place—an opportunity for lobbyists to shape the final product. Tax legislation and amendments to the EU's enabling treaties require a unanimous decision. (This system may change when new members are admitted.)

Lobbying opportunities exist on the Coreper staff, with the ministers themselves, and in their home countries. Significant interest groups, which are likely to have their own sets of relationships within the national parliaments and cabinets of the fifteen, can use them to influence the positions of the ministers concerned with the issue on the Council.

The Parliament also plays a role in this process, though a far smaller one than in national governments. It considers Commission proposals in various legislative committees and then in the full body. What it does with them depends on the rather arcane points of law on which they were based. ("Law" in this case refers to the various treaties that govern the EU. The most recent of these are the Maastricht Treaty which took effect in 1993, and the Amsterdam Treaty of June 1997.)

If the proposal falls under the "consultation procedure," the Parliament has the right to give the Council of Ministers its opinion once. If it falls under the "cooperation procedure," Parliament can offer its opinion twice; in between, the Council adopts a position to which the second opinion can react. The third procedure, called "co-decision," will be used often under the Amsterdam Treaty. Co-decision enables the Parliament to exercise a veto on legislation if it cannot work out an agreement with the Council of Ministers.

MEPs have fragmented schedules. One week a month is spent in Strasbourg, one week back home, and two weeks in committee meetings and other business in Brussels. The greatest opportunities to meet with them personally occurs while they are in Brussels.

Because the Parliament is an elected body, its members are more likely to consider lobbying appeals based on political considerations, including those affecting their home countries, than are officials at the lofty Commission. On the other hand, MEPs are products of national parliamentary systems and owe their positions to the national party organizations that elected them, not to interest groups. In any event, issues are at a rather advanced stage by the time they get to the Parliament—or, for that matter, to the Council of Ministers—and so lobbying opportunities for affecting legislation at this stage are considerably fewer.

The European Council consists of the prime ministers of each country (plus the President of France, who is the only European head of state with significant governmental authority). Generally meeting twice a year for top-level planning, it also has responsibility for common foreign and security policy. Though not part of the legislative process, it has the political power to break legislative stalemates, but is unlikely to intervene except on the weightiest of issues.

Types of Legislation

Legislative proposals from the Commission begin with a "green paper" that lays out a problem, discusses options, and invites comments. The issue then proceeds to a statement of policy published as a "white paper" and then to specific legislation.

The final product of the legislative process can take one of three forms:

- *Regulations* are laws that apply to the member states. They take effect immediately, have the force of law, and can be enforced in the European court system.

- *Directives* also apply to the member governments. They are mandatory in terms of the objectives to be accomplished but leave up to each country the manner in which objectives are to be achieved, usually over several years. Regulations and directives are roughly comparable to the laws passed by Congress and the state legislatures.

- *Decisions* may apply to anyone—governments, companies, or individuals—and are binding on those to whom they are addressed. Because they are most commonly used for implementation and enforcement of the law, they compare approximately to the rules and regulations issued by federal and state agencies in the United States.

The Rationale of the EU's Legislative Process

This entire extraordinarily intricate system is constructed as it is because the European Union is not a national state in the way that, say, Germany, Denmark, or the United States is. In a sense, it is comparable to the system that existed in this country under the Articles of Confederation before the former thirteen colonies adopted the U.S. Constitution and ceded most of their sovereignty to the federal government. But the EU is not a federal government, at least not yet. It has many government powers, but it exists on the sufferance of its member countries. For example, Britain exempted itself for a time from EU social policies; it was as though Pennsylvania could say, as it cannot, that federal labor laws do not apply to it.

The American Civil War established the principle that states cannot secede without the permission of the federal government. That is not true in Europe. In theory any country can opt out by abrogating the various treaties that underlie the EU, although in practice the economic ties that have been built over the last five decades would produce excruciating pain for any country that tried to depart.

Thus the entire complex legislative structure in Europe emphasizes *consultative* procedures to a far greater extent than the American system. When Congress was considering welfare reform legislation in 1996, it sought out the views of the state governors and accepted much of what they had to say. But legally it had no need to do so; Congress does not need permission from the states to enact federal law. This is not true in Europe. The operating legislative principles of the EU are consultation and consensus, not majority rule.

That is also the reason the system includes two other bodies not discussed above: the Committee of Regions, comprising local and regional representatives from within the member countries; and the Economic and Social Committee, comprising interest groups for agriculture, business, labor, consumers, and so on. Both committees have statutory authority to offer opinions to the Commission and the Council of Ministers.

Lobbying in Europe

The Economic and Social Committee provides a formal mechanism for interest groups to express their views on legislation, but informal contacts on the part of lobbyists are far more extensive, pervasive, and effective.[6]

Lobbying has the same two functions in the EU it has in the United States: to obtain unpublished intelligence about potential legislation and to communicate to officials information about the impact legislative proposals would have. However, those functions are carried out in somewhat different ways in Europe. Although considerable emphasis is placed on "transparency"—openness would be the American term—Eurocrats are less prone to discussing early legislative ideas in public or freely distributing working papers or other information about them to the press and the public.

This situation creates opportunities for lobbyists with the skill or the contacts to ferret out intelligence and drafts. Similarly, lobbying in the EU is expected to be substantive; providing policymakers and their staffs with information they might otherwise lack can have great impact. Lobbyists know how and where to find the intelligence their clients want and have the personal relationships to get it. They also know what kinds of information people in the DGs are likely to welcome and when is the best time in the process to give it to them.

On the other hand, lobbying tactics that are commonplace in the United States—for instance, trying to put pressure on one of the Commissioners from political leaders from her or his home country, or flying in an American CEO to lobby (and impress) an EU official—can easily backfire. The precept that the Commission represents the interests of Europe rather than those of the member countries, let alone interest groups, often creates resistance to forms of persuasion and pressure that American lobbyists are accustomed to applying. Subtlety is prized more than direct tactics. Grassroots lobbying, for example, may or may not have some impact with members of the Parliament, but it certainly will not impress the Commission. American lobbyists who used tactics that are accepted and effective in the United States developed a reputation for being pushy and boorish in the early years, an image that has taken some time to live down and change.

Some government relations tools—issues research, issues management, the identification of emerging issues, and legislative tracking—are applicable today. Organizations like the AmCham EU Committee (described later) and some individual companies have been using such techniques for several years. It is the tactics of persuasion, leverage, and pressure where care must be exercised.

What *does* work, however, is support from one or more national governments. Interest groups with operations or memberships in several countries will generally work to build support for their positions at the national level before approaching the Commission and other EU institutions.

Notwithstanding their preference for subtlety and indirection, when European interest groups choose to be overt, they can be very overt indeed—as

European farmers, transport workers, and truckers have shown when thousands of demonstrators or strikers pour into the streets of Paris, Rome, or Bonn to stop a legislative proposal dead in its tracks.

If the EU's legislative process eventually evolves into one that closely resembles those in national parliaments, a wider range of lobbying tactics may become applicable. For now, though, that is years away.

Lobbying Regulation

Lobbying and conflict-of-interest laws in Europe are not at all what they are in the United States. Until 1996, there was no code applicable to MEPs, even though they are permitted outside employment and other forms of income. New rules of Parliament now require its members and personal staff to declare the sources of all outside professional and paid activities but not their financial value. Although they are expected to refuse gifts or payments (including loaned staff) that might influence their votes, there are no penalties for violations.

Some new rules are also applicable to lobbyists on a quasi-voluntary basis. Anyone who wants to obtain passes for regular entry to the Parliament buildings and offices may choose to register and obtain a badge stating his or her name and employers. The lobbyist must also agree to comply with a code of conduct that will not be adopted until late 1997 at the earliest. The only penalty is loss of the badge.

MEPs obviously lobby each other, as legislators do everywhere, but the reason the new rules are so innocuous is that MEPs consider themselves above self-dealing and conflicts of interest. It is inconceivable that Americans would accept such a rationale on the part of lawmakers or other public officials. None of this mattered when the Parliament's legislative powers amounted to little, but the trend toward enlarging its ability to shape legislation changes that. A couple of juicy scandals in the EU sooner or later will undoubtedly alter the legalities there.

The only existing standards for lobbyists are voluntary codes adopted in 1994 by a group of Brussels lobbying firms and by the Parliament in 1996. Under these codes, lobbyists may not sell Commission documents for profit, should declare whom they represent and avoid conflicts of interest, should not offer inducements to Commission officials to obtain documents, and so on. It is possible that these voluntary codes may become the basis for whatever the Parliament ultimately adopts. Even then, a code applicable to the Parliament would not necessarily apply to lobbying before either the Commission or the Council of Ministers unless they choose to require it. At the moment, they have nothing in place to regulate lobbying.

Choosing a Lobbyist

Lobbying was a growth industry in the EU for many years. The corps of Brussels lobbyists once numbered a few hundred, then thousands, then it may have approached the size of the Washington lobbying corps. Today, the number appears to have stabilized. Some U.S. multinational companies have reduced their public affairs presence, and many American lobbying firms have cut back their operations or gone out of business. Still, lobbyists and lobbying organizations are not in short supply.

A company or other interest group that needs representation in Brussels has exactly the same options it has in Washington. It can work through an association, retain a local law firm or public affairs consulting organization, open its own office, or use a combination of these.

If the company's issues are largely shared with others in its industry, it will probably choose to work through an association. If it has its own unique group of issues that are relatively limited in scope or number, retaining an on-site lobbying firm that knows its way around Brussels may be the cost-effective approach. If it wants to stay continuously on top of a large group of significant issues, it will open its own office.

The analogy with considerations about Washington government relations offices is almost exact. Should the company put one of its own executives, who knows the company, in Brussels and let the individual learn the ways of the EU; or should it hire someone who understands how the EU operates and teach him or her about the company? Considering the purpose of having a Brussels office, the latter approach is probably more effective, but many companies have decided the question the other way and with considerable success.

An additional question for U.S. companies that decide to open their own offices is whether they should staffed by Americans or by Europeans. Some companies opt for the best of all worlds by putting two top people in the Brussels office—an American executive who knows how the company operates and a European who can work the corridors of the EU's institutions.

The Role of Associations

Associations representing various interest groups are prevalent in Europe, if not to the same extent as in the United States. In Brussels, some associations have developed substantial influence, particularly those representing business.

An umbrella association is UNICE—the Union of Industrial and Employers' Confederations of Europe—whose members are both national business associations and multinational companies; the latter participate though an allied organization, the European Enterprise Group, which includes some European subsidiaries of American companies. UNICE analyzes EU legislation and provides policy makers with position papers on issues affecting multiple industries. (Individual industry associations focus, as in the United States, on issues affecting their members only.)

Another important organization is the European Round Table of Industrialists (ERT) whose members are the chief executives of forty to fifty multinational corporations headquartered in Europe. (Companies based in the United States are not invited to join the ERT.) It resembles the Business Roundtable in the United States in this regard, but where BRT members lobby on business legislation, the ERT focuses on strategic issues affecting the European economy and economic integration as a whole. ERT members are chosen for their political influence and use it individually and collectively, rather than through lobbyists, both with the Commission and member governments at the highest levels.[7]

Another organization of growing importance represents U.S. companies operating in Europe—the EU Committee of the American Chamber of Commerce in Belgium. American companies have long had a major presence in Europe. Some (like CPC International, the food manufacturer) have had European operations since the early decades of the twentieth century. Others established operations more recently, as European economic integration was taking shape, to assure their ability to do business throughout the EU. Because U.S. multinational corporations are always sensitive, in Europe and elsewhere, to charges that they are "foreigners," members of the EU Committee like to describe themselves as "European companies of American parentage."[8]

The fact that public opinion surveys indicate that many Europeans actually believe a number of these companies (IBM, for instance) are in fact European demonstrates how effective their public affairs programs have been. A European visitor to New York several years ago was heard to express pleasure that she could buy such "European" products as Colgate toothpaste and Knorr soups, both in fact made by subsidiaries of U.S. corporations.

Such companies were among the earliest to develop capabilities to lobby the EU and to learn, perhaps the hard way, that American-style lobbying is often the wrong way to do things in Brussels. "At the same time, however, the companies and the EU Committee introduced a number of American lobbying techniques—providing detailed input, creating legislative tracking programs—to the Brussels policymaking process."[9] The EU Committee acts as the umbrella group for U.S.-based companies, just as UNICE does for European business.

Just as European interest groups work through member governments, so the EU Committee (as well as individual American companies) has access to the diplomatic resources of the United States, in this case through the U.S. Mission to the European Union, headed by an ambassador who often has strong political connections in Washington. (Stuart E. Eizenstat, a high-ranking official of the Carter and Clinton administrations, held the post for several years during the early 1990s.)

Many associations in Brussels represent individual European industries— or, more precisely, are federations of national trade associations that speak for their industries in their own countries. The federation can address EU institutions while the national associations that make it up muster support among the EU's member governments.

A number of major U.S. trade associations also maintain Brussels offices, partly to deal with EU institutions directly and partly for ready access to the U.S. Mission. U.S. trade associations also need to maintain excellent working relationships with their European counterparts, who inevitably have greater influence with the EU. Keeping the European groups on the same side as the American associations is a prerequisite to getting almost anything accomplished.

New Policies and Institutions

The structure of the European Union is in perpetual transition. Every few years, the members negotiate new treaties that generally expand the scope and goals of the EU. Legislatively, the trend is in the direction of slowly giving more powers to the Parliament, while the Commission seems to be evolving more into an administrative and regulatory body.

The Maastricht and Amsterdam treaties made a number of important changes, the following among them:

- European citizenship was created for the first time. Europeans now travel on European passports rather than those of individual countries. (Travel within Europe is largely as free as it is in the United States.) Europeans can vote and run for office in local (but not national) elections wherever they reside; an Italian living in Munich can be elected to the city council there, but not to the Bundestag.

- Merger of European monetary systems is scheduled to begin in 1999, with a new currency, the *euro*, replacing at least some national currencies in consumer transactions in 2002. A European central bank (comparable to the U.S. Federal Reserve) will replace its national counterparts in participating countries.

- The Parliament's powers have been expanded, and further political changes will be negotiated before the next wave of new members is admitted in the early years of the new century. These will alter the size and composition of the Commission and voting procedures in the Council of Ministers. The Amsterdam Treaty broadened public access to EU official documents. It also instituted disciplinary procedures and personal legal remedies should any member country violate fundamental rights and freedoms. Amsterdam also provided for strengthened coordination among the members with respect to foreign affairs, immigration, and the administration of justice.

Europe's Future Course

Where the European Union goes from here is a matter of considerable debate. One school of thought believes that Europe needs time to digest and accommodate all the changes that have occurred, particularly if the EU is to continue its geographic expansion by admitting the new democracies of central and eastern Europe.

An ongoing problem is the EU's enormously expensive program of agricultural price supports that produced huge, unmarketable surpluses of commodities like wine, butter, and cheese. Although some changes have been made, farmers (who have far more political influence in European countries than they do in the

United States) have prevented the national governments from supporting serious market reforms and major cuts in farm subsidies In 1994, the agricultural program consumed 50 percent of the EU's budget; and even after the changes, it will cost 47 percent in 1999 according to the EU's own projections.

Still another continuing problem is the economic development of Europe's poorer regions, ranging from the five Länder added to Germany with the assimilation of East Germany to entire countries like Greece and Portugal. The EU's probable expansion eastward will add new candidates for economic development.

A burning issue will arise out of the planned monetary union. Because of the fiscal discipline that the new financial system imposes, European countries will be forced to scale back their expensive but popular social welfare programs. This has the potential to produce political uproar almost everywhere.

The second body of thought advocates continued rapid integration, not only of the European economy but of society. There has always been a substantial number of Europeans who dream not just of integration but of eventual political unification—a United States of Europe. It is easy to envision that the early decades of the twenty-first century will produce a European Union of twenty-five to thirty countries with close to a billion people who speak two dozen different languages. On the one hand, realists say that unifying them into a single federal republic requires not just vision but a leap of faith. On the other hand, few "realists" fifty years ago could have imagined that European integration would ever come as far as it has in such a comparatively short period of time.

SOME PRINCIPLES OF INTERNATIONAL GOVERNMENT RELATIONS

Interest group advocates faced with a need to affect the public policy process outside the United States want immediately to know how lobbying is done in this or that country, this international organization or that one.

American lobbyists venturing into Latin America find at least superficial familiarities. Democracy exists in almost all of them, however tenuously. In most of these countries, the executive branch is separate from the legislature, as it is here. Major countries like Brazil and Mexico are federal states. So far so good. But who really makes policy? Who are the prime lobbying targets? Which interest groups have significant influence? Despite the existence (or return) of democratic institutions, is there still a general somewhere who has to be dealt with? Is the process reasonably honest or basically corrupt by U.S. standards?

The answers vary from country to country: Chile still has its generals. A recent president of Brazil was forced from office over corruption scandals. A disgraced former Mexican president lives in exile. The most powerful interest group in Colombia is the illegal drug cartel. Other countries, from Argentina north to Costa Rica, appear to be stable and reasonably honest democracies; and Mexico is groping toward an open multiparty system.

The situation is quite different in the major industrial countries, even though all are staunch democracies. When the lobbyist ventures north to Canada, west to Japan, or east to Europe, the very structures of government, the processes of public policymaking (and hence of lobbying), are basically unfamiliar. Americans find it hard to understand a democratically elected government where the parliament has little of genuine importance to say about the details of legislation.

In these countries, the cabinet controls not only the introduction of legislation but its fate and progress. Parliaments do have committees and may debate bills, but they usually have little or no power to affect legislation. Party loyalty is usually strong, often intense; and the opposition will frequently attack the government's proposals as the devil's spawn while the majority defends them as almost divinely inspired. But all this political thunder is rumbled solely for the benefit of the voters, to build a case for the next election. If members of the government's party disagree with its legislative proposals, they can say so in caucuses (or occasionally even in public), but strict party discipline keeps them in line. The majority has the votes or it would not be the majority—a very different situation from the one found in Congress and the state legislatures, where party loyalty among members is weak because their sails are filled by other winds.

Policy in parliamentary systems is developed in the ministries. Proposals work their way up through senior civil servants to the political leadership at the ministerial level. In some countries, this process may be moderately open. In others, it is closed, even secret. The ability to pierce these barriers is the reason lobbyists are paid: They obtain intelligence about evolving legislation at the earliest possible point and then provide the appropriate kind of feedback to influence the shape and fate of the issue.

In addition to the ministries, the secretariats of political parties are generally more useful points of access to advocates than they are in the United States. The parties often have staff specialists on a number of major issues whom public officials tend to trust more than they do the civil service, which lacks loyalty to any political party.

The lobbying path typically progresses in all these countries from the bureaucracy where the legislation arises, through top career officials, to the minister's office, and eventually to the full cabinet. Major legislation is usually discussed and debated by the cabinet. The rules of cabinet debate vary from country to country, but the cabinet must approve significant proposals before they are placed before parliament. By the time they are announced to the public and reach the elected lawmakers, bills are usually in their final form. Parliaments can theoretically amend legislation; but in most countries major changes are uncommon. Therefore, lobbyists who wait until parliament has received a bill have delayed to the eleventh hour and have probably not done their homework in the ministries and with the cabinet.

The role of civil servants in parliamentary systems is hard to overstate. They are "the permanent government," serving the ministries and cabinet regardless of party. In many countries, the cabinet minister does little more than outline the broad strokes of legislation. The bureaucracy's role goes well beyond mere drafting. Frequently, most of the key decisions about the measure's content are made by career officials whose positions and prospects may be little influenced by elected politicians but greatly affected by their superiors and their ability to work the system.

As in the United States, lobbyists in these countries may be employed by individual companies, by trade and business associations, or by other interest groups. Alternatively, they may be hired guns—freelance advocates with law firms or legislative consulting firms. In every country, their skill is the ability to penetrate official curtains to learn what their employers or clients need to know, communicate that information to their principals, and then reverse the flow of information to influence the legislation's final form (or to kill it, if that is the objective). Of course, interest groups often have their own legislative initiatives, and then lobbyists must persuade the ministries and the cabinet to adopt them.

This is why good lobbyists so often have backgrounds in government. They know how the system works and where the pressure points are. French and British business executives, civil servants, and lawmakers share common university backgrounds to a remarkable degree. In no country, however, are the relationships between the bureaucracy and interest groups, especially those of business, more intricately developed than in Japan, where they may be a veritable spider's web of professional, social, personal, and sometimes family ties. A common career path for a Japanese bureaucrat leaving the civil service is to move for a time into a leadership post with an important trade association and later into a top position with one of the country's great corporations, maintaining all the while close relationships with those still in the ministry of which he was part.

Lobbying in international organizations more closely resembles advocacy in parliamentary states than in the American system. The secretariats of the European Union, the United Nations, and the World Trade Organization, for example, have much to say about how policies are shaped—and especially about the detailed provisions that are often the matters about which interest groups are most concerned. Once good relationships are established, staff experts are likely to be willing to exchange useful information, data, and draft documents.

The political decisions, however, are made by negotiation among the member governments. Interest groups must be able to work through them, and their ability to do that may be very dependent on the state of national politics at the moment. American business lobbyists have generally found U.S. negotiators willing to advance and defend their positions, regardless of which party controls the White House. Few environmental organizations could make the same statement during Republican administrations, however, any more than pro-life groups can when the Democrats are in power. British industries have sometimes had difficulties when the Labour Party controlled the government; it remains to be seen how

British business will fare under Tony Blair's "New Labour" government. Privately owned enterprises in France under Socialist rule sometimes found their interests subordinated to those of state-owned companies.

Not only are modes and styles of direct lobbying in international organizations often different, but the other familiar tools of government relations, as practiced in the United States, may or may not be applicable elsewhere. Issues research and tracking tools, and perhaps technology, are generally transferable; other tactics not necessarily so, as illustrated by the following:

- Americans, accustomed to relying on vigorous and assertive trade associations, will be disappointed in Britain by the weaknesses of associations there, satisfied by the influence of German associations, and very possibly overwhelmed by the power and exclusiveness of associations in Japan. In a contest for the title of the world's most powerful business association, the Japan Federation of Economic Organizations (better known as Keidanren) would be a prime contender.

- The ability, even the willingness, to create broad-spectrum coalitions of diverse interest groups is shaped not only by the relationships that have existed among them in the past but also by cultural characteristics. From time to time, some European industries have been willing to make common cause with consumer groups on certain issues. On the other hand, few Japanese business executives could even conceive of such a coalition.

- Similarly, grassroots lobbying cuts across the cultural grain in many countries. The French would take to the streets and man the barricades before they would consider an organized letter-writing campaign.

- The ability to use public relations and mass communications tactics also varies. Public opinion polls are increasingly prevalent in most countries. The press is vigorous and independent in some countries, docile in others. The electronic media are sometimes state owned and may or may not be willing to express an independent voice.

- The political process is equally diverse. Campaigns are publicly funded in Britain and Germany, privately financed in Italy and Japan. Some political parties, including Canada's Liberal Party and the German Christian Democrats, are allied with a relatively broad range of interest groups. In contrast, Britain's Labour Party was, at least until very recently, exactly that—the party of the unions. The Liberal Democrats in Japan are essentially the party of big business and rural interests. Political parties and the cabinets they support (or oppose) are stable in Germany, France, and Britain. Since the break-up of Italy's Christian Democrats, the country's political parties are fragmented and in constant turmoil. Multiple parties and coalition governments are commonplace in the Scandinavian countries. Canadian politics seem to be in transition from a two-party system to one of multiple parties.

The capability of interest groups and their lobbyists to apply familiar tactics in advancing their viewpoints depends substantially on a wide range of factors and circumstances, depending on the country or the international organization in question. That is why the governmental and political environment has to be studied and understood before any lobbying effort is undertaken.

Notwithstanding this range of national and organizational diversity, lobbyists everywhere share a universal objective: to learn what is happening at the earliest possible time and to influence the final outcome so that it comes as close as possible to the interest group's purposes and objectives.

NOTES

1. James E. Post and Jennifer J. Griffin, *The State of Corporate Public Affairs: 1996 Survey Results* (Washington, D.C.: Foundation for Public Affairs, 1997), Figs. 10.1–10.8.

2. Much of the framework for this discussion is based on material in W. T. Stanbury, *Business–Government Relations in Canada: Grappling with Leviathan* (Toronto: Methuen, 1986).

3. Ibid., p. 24.

4. There is an extensive and growing body of literature about government relations in the European Union. Works by Dr. Maria Green Cowles, cited in the bibliography, cover aspects of the subject extensively. Those looking for good summaries are referred to the following: Bureau of National Affairs, Inc., "Lobbying in The European Union," *Daily Report for Executives*, July 28, 1994; Delegation of the European Commission in the United States, *The European Union and the United States in the 1990s* (Washington, D.C.: The Delegation, 1996) [earlier editions of this publication, revised every few years, have had other titles]; Klaus-Dieter Borchardt, *European Integration: The Origins and Growth of the European Union*, 4th ed. (Luxembourg: Office for Official Publications of the European Communities, 1995).

5. *Wall Street Journal*, April 14, 1995.

6. Europeans associate "lobbying" with unsavory or illegal actions and dislike the word perhaps even more than Americans do. Still, it describes the process. The author tenders apologies to those who may be offended by its use here.

7. Maria Green Cowles, "The European Round Table of Industrialists," in *European Casebook on Business Alliances*, ed. Justin Greenwood, Case 16 (London: Prentice-Hall, 1995); see also Luca Lanzalaco, "Constructing Political Unity by Combining Organizations: UNICE as a European Peak Association," in idem, Case 18.

8. Maria Green Cowles, "The EU Committee of AmCham: The Powerful Voice of American Firms in Brussels," *Journal of European Public Policy* 3(3) 1996.

9. Ibid.

Chapter 11

Using Associations

Round up the usual suspects.
> —Julius J. Epstein and Philip G. Epstein, *Casablanca*

Leveraging government relations capabilities to a higher level of influence through an alliance creates a synergy that can exceed the effectiveness of its components. Multiplying influence through membership in trade associations and other membership organizations is one way to do this. Joining with other organizations in an ad hoc issues coalition is another. Each is an important instrument of government relations success.

The dictionary defines *alliance* as "a bond or connection between families, states, parties or individuals; an association to further the common interests of the members." *Coalition* is defined in turn as "a temporary alliance." One might talk about an alliance of companies or an alliance of environmental organizations—but a coalition of business, labor, and consumer groups since such a group is more likely to be temporary and oriented toward a particular problem or issue. Trade and other business associations are really permanent alliances.

We deal with associations in this chapter.[1] Coalitions are the subject of Chapter 12.

Trade and business associations serve a wide variety of purposes for their members' companies, but representing the interests of their industries with governments at all levels is the most important. For many firms, trade associations are their principal lobbies, sometimes their only ones.

These groups range from the national giants—*umbrella associations* like the U.S. Chamber of Commerce, National Association of Manufacturers, and the Business Roundtable—to local chambers of commerce in communities across the nation. They also include the national, state, and local associations that represent specific industries and professions with lawmakers and government officials on behalf of the members who pay their dues. These members are sometimes individuals but more often companies. (In general, the memberships of professional associations or societies are usually individuals; trade associations are almost always made up of companies.)

There are thousands of such groups at the national level and probably tens of thousands at state and local levels. An individual company may belong to several associations or to several dozen. Indeed, the largest companies may belong to hundreds.

Trade associations are a principal means through which American corporations relate to one another, to governments, and to the public. In the area of government relations particularly, trade association participation can be a highly cost-effective means of achieving a company's public policy objectives. Indeed, trade associations are probably the first lines of both defense and offense for most companies.

A point not often recognized is the distinction between an association's *opponents* and its *competitors*. Groups with potentially overlapping memberships compete with each other for dues dollars, and therefore for prestige points, even though they are often (but not always) allied in their legislative aims. For instance, the AFL–CIO opposes the National Association of Manufacturers and the Chamber of Commerce on many legislative issues, but it does not compete with them economically because there is no common constituency. The Chamber and the NAM are rivals for dues precisely because there is a substantial commonality of membership.

Competing associations are usually allies but sometimes opponents. When competitors share positions on issues, they vie for leadership and effectiveness. When their positions are opposed, they fight to protect the interests of a distinctive membership element but also for organizational self-interest.

Merger pressures are common in industries or movements with multiple associations, more so in this period of corporate downsizing and cost control. Food retailers and wholesalers, for instance, are represented by a number of associations, and efforts to merge some of them are a constant in the industry— sometimes successful, often not. The question for the individual member is how it can best be represented, but there is rarely a unanimous view among members. Associations themselves, both elected leaders and staff, have a broad sense of organizational identity and deep streaks of self-protectiveness.

Some companies are wary of trade-association participation because of antitrust concerns. A few companies decline to attend certain meetings or even to join at all. Actually, a well-run association has little problem complying with the law, particularly if an attorney is present at key meetings. The law is both clearcut and well established with respect to trade association activities. Such groups have wide latitude in the government relations area particularly.[2]

ASSOCIATIONS AND THEIR LEGISLATIVE POSITIONS

In Washington and in the states, some of the most skilled and sophisticated lobbyists are those on the staffs of various associations. They know the fine points of direct lobbying and apply them with diligence, often with ingenuity. They have constructed programs to mobilize their members politically and to generate copious and informed legislative communications. They can build effective coalitions, and they know how to influence a variety of publics to support their associations' positions. And the result is quite often victory.

But sometimes they lose. Perhaps they were fighting an issue whose time, very simply, had come. Perhaps the other side had utilized government relations tactics with even greater effectiveness than they. Or perhaps they were using outstanding abilities to implement a politically deficient position.

Issue positions in associations are adopted by committees and boards of directors, some of whom—like the financial executive described in an earlier chapter—confuse what they want with what can be done. In business associations particularly, what members commonly want is to keep the government out of their operations, but taking that posture in an association committee is hardly the same thing as getting it past all the hurdles of the legislative process. In associations, ideology is rarely the handmaiden of legislative success.

The great strength of associations is their size and homogeneity. Their great weakness is their size and diversity.

When public officials hear from an association on an issue, they know they are receiving the views of an entire industry or profession. For this reason, an association can speak with a voice of considerable power, especially if it is backed by tactics that produce voluminous mail and political communications. There may, of course, be a dissident member here or there who expresses a minority point of view that may or may not receive much consideration, but the association's input tends to carry the weight of its members' opinions. How much weight depends on the economic size and political clout of the association's constituency.

What often weakens the effectiveness of associations is the diversity of views its members hold on any given issue and the almost universal impulse among associations for a consensus.

Virtually all associations utilize a committee system to develop issue positions. If the number of issues affecting the membership is few, there may be only a single public policy committee; if it is many, there may be several such committees and perhaps a structure of subcommittees as well. Issues are typically brought to the committee by the association staff, which has done the kind of issues research described in earlier chapters.

The committee examines proposed bills (or regulations), debates the pros and cons, and reaches a decision. If there is unanimity, well and good. But if not, it is unusual for the decision to be made by motion and vote, with a majority carrying the day. Instead, the discussion that ensues will try to find a consensus that everyone can live with. The result is generally an association position at the lowest common denominator of membership opinion. The problem is that such a position may not have any connection with political realities.

If the staff has a streak of boldness and has done its homework, it might explain that the position the committee wants to take will never be accepted by legislators. Or one of the more politically sophisticated committee members may make the same point. Absent that input, the members may approve a position that everyone can live with, even if it is irrelevant to the options lawmakers are considering. The position goes up to the board of directors, which duly adopts it, and why not? After all, "our legislative experts" have recommended it.

The upshot of all this is that the association has neutralized its own ability to affect the legislation by taking a position that lacks credibility, with the result that it may suffer a defeat and find itself accepting an unpleasant new law, both of which were completely unnecessary.

Had the committee, the board, and the staff been a bit less eager to mollify the recalcitrant, they might have taken time to consider what the public problem was that gave rise to the issue and which alternatives might resolve the issue in a less onerous way.

Actually, a great many associations with competent staff people do not let this kind of situation develop. Good staff people provide leadership, not just minutes of meetings. But some staffers are cowed by their members and let bad situations ripen into disaster.

A few such incidents eventually lead at least some of the members to wonder if the association is as effective as it ought to be and if they are getting their money's worth out of their memberships.

EVALUATING ASSOCIATION EFFECTIVENESS

Associations are one of the most valuable and efficient resources available to companies. They can also be a great way to waste money. Both trade association dues and even more costly executive time are squandered if the company does not take steps to assure that the goals, priorities, and performance of its trade associations meet the company's established needs.

Coupled with their potential for effectiveness is their generally modest cost—often less than the cost of adding a professional to staff. However, dues may be only a small percentage of a company's real cost of association membership. The real cost is executive time. This is especially true of associations whose individual annual dues may be only a few thousand dollars or less.

It is important to calculate all the costs and all the benefits of the individual company's association memberships. The latter are measured by the extent to which each association fulfills the company's goals and priorities—not whether the association is doing a good job for its industry but how well it is performing for the individual member-company, which is not at all the same thing.

In the view of companies such as Exxon, Hershey Foods, Imperial Oil, and Matsushita, the critical concept is *value*, and value is a cost–benefit relationship.

Analyzing the Real Costs of Association Participation

Many businesses take their trade associations for granted. They tend to leave policy development to the staff or to a committee of association experts on which the company may or may not be effectively represented. While they are often acutely conscious of the dues they pay, companies seldom calculate the real costs of membership, which go well beyond mere dues. Firms that have not established written goals and purposes for their memberships have no way to evaluate whether they are getting true value.

What does it cost a company each time an executive spends a day on association activity? That day may be spent attending a meeting, traveling to the meeting, or doing anything else directly related to his or her involvement with the association. These expenses can be measured. The measurement formula should include personnel costs, office overhead, and travel expense. Taking all such costs into account, it costs, on the average, between 1.5 and 2.5 percent of an executive's salary to attend a single overnight meeting.

If that executive is moderately active, he or she attends several board and committee meetings annually, as well as occasional seminars, the annual convention, and other functions. At a conservative estimate, the executive probably incurs the equivalent of six overnight trips a year in connection with association business and events.

On top of that, considerable time may be spent on the telephone, in correspondence, and reading association-related documents. Add all that in, and the aggregate costs to a member company come to somewhere between 11 and 15 percent of the executive's salary.

Since even a moderately active company will have several executives involved in an association, attending meetings of its board and committees, conferences and conventions, and so on, a subtotal of real costs may well be in the annual range of $50,000 to $60,000—to which must then be added dues, any special assessments and fees, and so forth.

For associations with low dues levels (under $10,000), the ratio of time costs to dues is quite high. But even those companies that pay their associations large annual dues ($50,000 to $100,000 or even more) may find their total real membership costs are twice what they believe.

The critical issue for the member-company at this point is, "What are we getting for all that money?"

Evaluating Benefits and Value

Companies often include contributions to nonprofit organizations on the same budgetary line-item as association membership dues. This may produce (or stem from) a mistaken belief among some managers that these groups are essentially alike. Not only is this untrue; it leads to misleading thinking about how to evaluate the expenditure.

The nonprofit recipients commonly include local and national charities—United Way, universities, certain foundations, and so forth. We call such institutions "caregivers." Donors support them because they are worthy causes or enhance the community in which their business is located, but they do not expect to receive specific benefits from them.

Trade and business associations and professional societies are different. Companies and individuals join them to obtain certain concrete benefits—to receive economic services, informative publications, the ability to attend useful meetings, and so forth. These associations are not caregivers. They are "bacon bringers," and the bacon we are especially concerned with here is their government relations and political programs.

The association's rasher of bacon should include direct and grassroots lobbying, relevant political activities, and the other tactics discussed in this book. The bottom line, however, is the overall quality of the bacon. Is the association delivering for its members on its issues, particularly on its top-priority issues?

Corporate executives often assess their trade group with the comment that "the association does a good job for the industry." This may be true, but it obscures a more critical issue. The question should not only be whether the association is doing a good job for its industry but how well it is doing for the individual company paying the bills. On any given issue, the interests of the company may or may not be identical with those of the industry as a whole. The distinction has to be made if the association's value is to be correctly evaluated.

Many managers regard their associations as they would some caregiver pleading for the donation of some executive time. "Look," said one in a typical remark, "we pay our dues, we have a seat on the board of directors, and we go to the annual convention. What more do you want? We can't spare the man-hours to put people on every committee."

The point this executive overlooks is that his company belongs to each association for important business objectives. If his company is to stay in the association, it must be sure that those goals are being met. If the group is not meeting the company's goals, then steps should be taken either to cure that condition or to reassess the value of membership in the trade association in the first place.

What is generally not appreciated is the extent to which an individual company can shape the goals, policies, and performance of its associations. Moreover, individual companies can exercise influence far beyond what might be expected from their size and share of market, often typical measures of association influence.

To maximize the benefits of its association memberships, the member company should formulate a set of goals for each trade association to which it belongs. Then it should become deeply involved in the association's affairs, striving to achieve and maintain positions of leadership and influence over objectives, policies, and priorities. Finally, the association's performance must be evaluated—not only against the group's own goals but also against those of the company.

How to Evaluate an Association

The process should begin with a close review of each trade association to which the company belongs. This review should take place at least annually and consist of two parts: (1) Evaluating the objectives and performance of the trade association; and (2) evaluating the role and effectiveness of the company within the association.

Company Goals for the Association

Individuals and companies join associations for a variety of reasons, of which government relations support may be only one. Others generally include information and education, trade relations with customers and suppliers, group insurance programs and other economic benefits, industrywide public relations programs, contact opportunities, and just good fellowship with peers and colleagues.

Step 1 *Analyze the respective roles of the association and the member-company and understand the relationship.* What business is the association in? The head of a drug industry association is neither a pharmaceutical manufacturer nor a druggist. It is his or her job to look after the needs of the membership, but he or she also has an association to run. Revenues must be raised, programs planned and conducted, and a budget maintained. The association must serve the industry it represents, but it also has its own needs and objectives of survival and prosperity quite apart from those of its membership. As an economic institution, it must do both—just as any business must take care of its customers while also managing its own affairs.

For the members, the critical issue is whether the association is meeting their needs while also meeting its own or pursuing an independent agenda devoted to its own aggrandizement. Says a former staff member of a large, well-known national business group, "I left when I realized that the association's only real purpose was the betterment of the executives on the top floor." Much of the blame for this kind of situation has to be placed at the doorstep of the members who not only failed to cure the condition but unquestioningly went on paying dues year after year to support it.

Step 2 *Calculate the real costs of company membership in the association.* First, list the *direct* outlays: dues, special assessments, contributions to the association's foundation, and the like.

Next, list the executives active in the association, and estimate their daily cost to the company including salary, benefits, secretarial and other staff support, and office overhead.

Third, ask them to approximate the number of days each spent during the past year on association activities, including not only committee and board meetings, educational conferences, conventions, and the like but also telephone, correspondence, and meeting preparation time. Add in meeting registration fees, travel costs (including travel time), and entertainment.

Multiply the daily cost by the number of days—by individual for a reasonably precise number; by average cost and number of days for a rougher approximation. This is the *indirect* cost.

The total of both direct and indirect expense is the *real cost* of membership in that association.

Step 3 *Prepare a list of the company's basic objectives in belonging to the association.* Why does the company belong? For government relations information and services? News of developments within or affecting the industry? Executive education? Statistical and economic surveys and services? Industry standard-setting? Trade relations with suppliers, customers, and competitors? Industrywide promotion and marketing? Group insurance and similar benefits? Other specific benefits from attendance at conventions, conferences, and committee meetings?

Within such major categories, list the priority goals the company wants the association to meet within a finite and reasonable time, perhaps a year: passage, defeat, or amendment of specific legislation or regulations; expansion of a particular educational tool or economic service; development of a new insurance or group discount benefit, and so on.

The association represents the industry as a whole. If the industry's needs have a high priority to the individual company, so does the trade association. That priority should be reflected in the intensity of the company's participation within the association. (The converse is also true; if the association is not especially important to the company, perhaps it is not worth belonging at all.)

In the case of government relations objectives, the company's goals for the association should be extracted from its overall lobbying aims as determined in its needs analysis (see Chapters 3 and 4). After all, trade associations are a vehicle for achieving lobbying objectives, and the whole purpose of analyzing and monitoring association performance, at least in the area of government relations, is to make sure the vehicle is traveling the right road toward the member's desired destination.

The list of major purposes should not need to be altered frequently although it should be reviewed at least annually. The list of goals under each major purpose should also be updated as often. Of course, the matters on both lists should be realistic and fall within the association's purview.

The company should maintain close relationships with association leadership and staff to ensure that it is represented on every association policy body bearing on the company's priorities, working within those bodies to make sure company objectives are reflected in association policies and programs. The member-company's representatives should understand that they are accountable as part of their job performance reviews for effective lobbying of the association so that the company's objectives become an integral part of association policies and program.

Note that even when the association's goals match those of most of its members, it is still important to be sure that the individual member's priorities are fully reflected. If the company's needs are primarily legislative, while most of the association's other members are more concerned with education and training, there clearly is not a good fit.

Step 4 Evaluate the association's performance. Is the association delivering for the member-company on top-priority matters? If so, thank it and reward it, perhaps with a voluntary increase in that year's dues. But if the association is not performing, consider why and what can be done about the situation.

A few companies assess trade association performance from time to time. Even fewer do it regularly and systematically. One way to undertake such an analysis is to retain a consultant knowledgeable about both association management and corporate public affairs to undertake an audit of the association's effectiveness from the member-company's point of view. Another approach is to survey the company's executives who receive services from the association or who are active in it.

Some companies have queried a panel of such managers about goals and performance for each association to which the firm belongs. The advantage of this approach is that these executives usually know what the associations are doing and what benefits they are deriving. The disadvantage is that they often have a loyalty to the association and an emotional vested interest in it that can cloud objectivity. Because these attitudes can hamper an objective analysis, the consultant approach should be considered, either in lieu of the panel survey or perhaps in tandem with it.

The kinds of questions a survey or audit should pose include the following:

- Is the trade association staff competent in all the dimensions of government relations and public affairs? Are the legislative positions and strategies politically and substantively sound? How well are nonpublic affairs objectives being met?

- Is the association staff led or member led? Neither is inherently good or bad, but a staff-led association to which the members provide only lip service rather than strong backing for the staff is in trouble. Should such an association encounter serious difficulties—for example, financial problems or a loss on a major issue—few leaders are likely to champion its cause in the face of membership anger. A staff-led association to which members feel little emotional attachment will have problems with membership involvement in areas like a grassroots lobbying program. The staff may also lack the ability to cope with a dissident faction within the association.

- Does the staff have the resources to do what the members demand of it, or is it left to cope as best it can? Is the staff backed up with formal objectives, programs, budgets, timetables, and the like? How is it held accountable? For that matter, how are the elected leaders held accountable? (Hardly any are; as volunteer leaders, their benefits are largely psychological and their sanctions virtually nonexistent—unless accountability is required by the companies that pay them and whom they represent.)

- What about competitive trade groups? Competition strengthens companies, but it weakens associations and dilutes their effectiveness. In government relations particularly, public officials expect an industry to speak with a single voice on pertinent issues. When there are multiple voices (particularly when they convey conflicting messages), the industry's ability to achieve its goals is severely reduced.

- Does the association take an ideological or a pragmatic approach to its mission? Every organization needs to have a point of view, but highly ideological business associations tend to be partisan and muscle bound and have difficulty negotiating. They can also attract needless hostility from those with whom they have to deal. Some major organizations have been criticized for preferring to retain a highly polarized position instead of being willing to compromise and thereby help shape the legislative nuances. Such groups must take what wins they can achieve on a relatively small number of black-or-white issues; their influence is little felt in the gray areas where most legislation is shaped.

- Is the association flexible and able to move quickly as the legislative situation changes? Do staff lobbyists have authority to negotiate deals on the spot if circumstances require? Sometimes the association has to be agile, able to modify its stands and negotiate positions and amendments on the spot. As a general rule, associations with large numbers of members find it more difficult to resolve competing interests than more narrowly based ones. A position often represents a consensus that can fall apart when a decision has to be made on a crucial amendment.

Evaluating the Company as Member Once the survey or audit results are in hand, they can be validated by an informal check with a few other members of the association to see if their experiences and observations are parallel. (If not, the study methodology should be re-examined.)

The next step is to interpret the conclusions in the light of the member-company's role in the association. This is another area in which an expert consultant can be helpful, particularly in the development of the remedial action plan that should logically flow out of the Step 5 analysis that follows.

In a sense, trade associations are only as good as their staffs and elected leadership. But in a deeper sense, they are really only as good as their membership wants them to be. A vital aspect of this is the question of how active and involved the members are.

Step 5 *Evaluate the effectiveness of the company as a member of the association.* Assuring that the association's goals and priorities closely parallel the member-company's is an important strategy for the achievement of company objectives. It will not happen simply by writing a letter, even from one chief executive to another, and leaving it at that. The strategy works only if the company takes pains to involve its people deeply on all the relevant committees and the board, making an intense, ongoing effort to influence, if not actually dominate, association decisions.

Contrary to what many executives believe, this is not a power limited to the largest companies in the association. Any company can do it if it knows how to go about it and where to invest the executive time. There is a great myth about trade association participation and governance.

The *myth* is that the largest members run the association, indeed that their very size in the industry entitles them to dominate the association almost by divine right. The *truth* is that regardless of company size, involvement and achievement in associations lead to influence—and influence is power.

There is an unfortunate converse to this situation—the tendency of many association members to take free rides on the coattails of the largest members. It is not only that the smaller company believes it must concede association leadership to the larger but that in many cases the "smalls" are actually happy to do so. Their reasoning is that the "bigs" have more resources to work with and that, after all, the interests of both are identical, another myth.

From issue to issue, companies in any single industry may have common interests; else, why belong to trade associations? But their common interests do not extend to their competition in the marketplace. The "bigs" have larger market share and wish to maintain it; the "smalls" want to take it from them. And even companies of similar size have different business needs, plans, and objectives.

Companies that content themselves with the role of free riders in their trade associations concede to their competitors a powerful instrument to achieve individual goals and priorities.

Here are criteria that can be used to evaluate the effectiveness of the member-company's trade association participation:

- Is the company achieving the benefits it wants, as determined in Step 3 previously mentioned? Do these benefits equal or exceed in value the real cost of membership, as calculated in Step 2? If the answer is negative to either question and yet the Step 4 analysis indicates a strong and healthy association, then there are deficiencies in the company's involvement.
- Is the company represented on the board of directors? Do its executives serve on the committees whose actions bear on the company's aims for the association?

Equally important, what is the *quality* of the company's representation on these groups? Quality of representation demands this level of commitment:

- Being prepared for the meeting, not only in terms of the association's agenda but also armed with goals advancing the company's aims with respect to that committee—indeed, communicating with the staff and committee chairperson in advance to help shape the agenda.
- Effectively participating in the meeting—contributing meaningfully to the discussion on behalf of both the association's and the company's agendas.
- Staying in close touch with the staff after the meeting to insure that decisions on matters important to the company are followed through—and where appropriate, volunteering to aid in implementation.

Effective committee participation involves contributing to the achievement of the association's aims as well as the company's. The extremes of committee behavior need to be avoided: Dominating the discussion produces hostility, but sitting silently throughout produces nothing.

Equally critical to the effectiveness of the company's participation in the association is the identity of its principal representative on the association's board of directors. In many companies, it is the chief executive officer of the operating company or of the parent corporation. In others, it is often the senior public affairs executive.

Usually, it should be neither, but rather a top manager in the area most closely affected by the association's programs and activities. All too often, though, this responsibility is inappropriately delegated—sometimes down, sometimes up.

In the case of downward delegation, a lower-level manager or staff assistant is sent to the association's meetings. "Don't make any decisions," he or she is instructed. "Just take notes and brief us on what takes place." What sometimes happens, however, is that an important discussion occurs on a key policy issue. A decision is then made without the company's input and sometimes to its dismay.

Upward delegation may be almost as bad. Many associations insist that the seats on the board be held only by the chief executives of member-companies. This assures a certain amount of prestige for the association. Since CEOs seldom have the time to be intimately involved in trade association affairs, the practice tends to result in a staff-dominated association. Moreover, while chief executives come to the board meeting briefed by their operating people, they often possess very little understanding of the underlying issues. Should the staff, or an unusually informed peer, bring up a deep issue for a policy determination, the decision may be made without really meaningful company participation.

The optimum "ambassador" from the company to the association should be the highest-ranking executive whose operations will be directly affected by association actions.

Dues for this association should be in her or his budget, not some corporate catchall line item. Liaison with the association should be a responsibility included in this executive's job description, and part of the individual's personal annual performance review should include accountability to top management for the performance of the association on both association and company objectives.

This will, of course, require considerable involvement in association affairs on the part of these executives—time and effort they may be reluctant to invest unless true accountability to superiors exists. But if the trade association is not important enough to invest the money and managerial time required to assure that the association performs for the company, then the association is probably not worth belonging to in the first place.

Member-companies should regard their trade association memberships as ongoing investments made to achieve specific company objectives. Like any other investment, performance must be constantly monitored to assure adequate payoff.

Maximizing the value derived from a trade association does not require the company to sacrifice its right to take independent action on issues when, despite its best efforts, the association's position is not in the company's interest. Acting independently of the association on certain matters has its risks, but it can also have benefits. The member may be embarrassed within the industry if it loses after going its own way, but even such a situation can be played politically to enhance the firm's long-term position within the association. Win or lose, it is always an embarrassment to an association to be seen publicly as having a divided membership. The association may be willing to take steps to placate an aggressive member it otherwise might have disdained. The association may be even more willing to do so should the member-company's minority position prevail in the public arena.

THE ASSOCIATION'S STAKE

The trade association and its staff executives have an interest at least as great as those of its members in assuring that its goals and performance meet both collective and individual member needs. The association's members are not only its owners but also its clients and must be treated as such if the association is to continue receiving their "business."

For that reason, if the member-company is unhappy with what it is getting from its association, the association executive should be too. Either the association is not giving the company what it needs—or the company has not made a substantial effort to influence the work of the association—or, most likely, both.

If either party believes it is not winning full value from the relationship, both are losing. The development of a "win–win" strategy requires a mutual assessment and understanding of the other's needs. It is in the trade association's interest to pursue a marketing strategy intended to satisfy the needs of each of its "clients" as fully as possible.

NOTES

1. The material in this chapter is treated in more detail in Charles S. Mack, *The Executive's Handbook of Trade and Business Associations* (Westport, Conn.: Quorum Books, 1991).

2. See, for example, George D. Webster, *The Law of Associations* (New York: Matthew Bender & Co., 1986).

Chapter 12

Using Coalitions

In all bodies, those who will lead, must also, in a considerable degree, follow. They must conform their propositions to the taste, talent and disposition of those whom they wish to conduct.

—Edmund Burke

Coalitions are becoming an increasingly popular tool among a wide variety of interest groups. They can raise the profile of what otherwise might seem a parochial issue and provide a means to multiply the voices and resources available for advocacy. They can offer an opportunity to expose an issue position to minds with a different point of view, so that the position and the arguments used to advance it are well refined before being put before policymakers and the public. They can enhance the respectability and credibility of a group's issue position by attracting a number of allies, sometimes unusual ones. They broaden the sources of information and the number of people available for direct and grassroots lobbying. They are a channel for outreach and communications, so that one interest group can establish a relationship with another with which it may normally have little in common.

Coalitions are, most commonly, temporary assemblages of different interest groups that come together to accomplish a limited objective. That objective may be a legislative issue, an initiative or referendum, or some other public policy goal. Coalitions are also being increasingly used to affect political campaigns.

Coalitions are most prevalent within interest group sectors—bringing together various environmental organizations, for instance, or clusters of labor unions or sets of companies and business associations. But coalitions can be especially effective when they cross sector lines, to join business interests with consumer and minority groups, for example, or with labor and environmental organizations.

Coalitions are harder to establish and maintain than associations. Associations are permanent organizations of more-or-less likeminded members; once established and staffed, they develop their own forward momentum. Coalitions, on the other hand, are ad hoc groups, frequently comprising organizations with a limited, sometimes single objective. Both their diversity and their temporary nature make them harder to establish and sustain.

On the other hand, coalitions have simpler structures. There are no bylaws to be drawn up, no office space to be leased, no antitrust lawyer to sit in on meetings if the coalition is diverse enough. There is seldom even need for staff. Budgets are straightforward and goal directed, with no need for overhead expense. Coalitions typically set a specific objective, accomplish it, and then disband.

On rare occasions, the objective turns out to be an enduring one, and the coalition persists for some time. It may even hire a staff and take office space. Eventually, the coalition may be transformed into an association. This is not a typical development, but it has been known to happen. An example is the Emergency Committee on American Trade, formed in 1967 as a coalition of multinational corporations to achieve a specific international trade objective. After the issue had gone its way, ECAT's member-companies decided they needed a permanent organization to represent their common interests on future issues. ECAT became permanent, but never changed its name. The original emergency disappeared, but ECAT continues.

Among like-minded groups, coalitions are quite common. Environmental, consumer, civil rights, labor, and agricultural organizations (and many other categories of interest groups) come together within their interest group sectors with relative ease on issues of mutual concern. So do business groups on many issues. Indeed, coalitions of diverse companies and associations are an increasingly common mechanism to manage broad issues in Washington and many state capitals as well.

Less common are coalitions that cross sector lines. Clearly, however, when interest groups that do not normally find themselves on the same side of the fence can come together on an issue in a mutually supportive relationship, the credibility of the position they advocate is multiplied substantially. A business group may disagree with the League of Women Voters on public financing of elections but be able to ally with it to promote international trade. A company or trade association interested in protecting domestic industries threatened by imports from other countries can broaden its effectiveness through an alliance with the AFL–CIO.

However, the fact that the groups have opposed each other on other issues sometimes makes it difficult for them to leap emotional boundaries. Coalitions of this type must be organized and managed with extraordinary care and tenderness. It is easier if the parties involved keep in mind that they are not getting married but only dating, and only for as long as everyone benefits. The more diverse the coalition, the harder it is to put, and keep, it together—but the greater its public credibility.

Coalitions can engage in a variety of forms of government relations. They may consult with each other on legislative tactics and strategy, perhaps dividing the burdens of research, intelligence collection, and direct lobbying, while coordinating with each other on utilization of their separate grassroots systems. Or they may choose to lobby legislators together because of the credibility and dramatic value of having, say, advocates from a labor union and a trade association pay a joint visit to the lawmaker. Coalitions often jointly undertake activities in the areas of press communications, issue advertising, and other forms of public relations.

Coalitions frequently form in states that utilize referenda and initiatives. A Massachusetts ballot measure to impose a mandatory deposit on soft drink and beer containers brought together coalitions of environmental and consumer groups on one side, and grocery retailers, beverage bottlers, and labor unions on the other.

Coalitions were an important political factor in a number of congressional campaigns in the 1996 elections. Labor unions, consumer groups, pro-choice organizations, and environmental interest groups joined forces in a number of races, for the most part to elect Democratic candidates. Helping their Republican opponents was a group of national business associations that called itself, simply, "The Coalition." Often cooperating with The Coalition, but not part of it, were various social conservative groups, notably the Christian Coalition (not a coalition at all, of course, but a permanent association).

CREATING AND MANAGING COALITIONS

The first step on the part of a company seeking to create and mobilize a coalition is to identify potential members. A good technique was suggested by Edward A. Grefe.[1] Instead of the usual classification of groups as either friends or foes, Grefe suggests a refinement:

Family Employees, shareholders, retirees, spouses.

Friends Customers and suppliers and others with an economic relationship to the company.

Strangers Groups that might be interested in the issues if they know of the measure and understand its impact. Grefe includes here academics, the press, and leaders in communities in which the company has operations. Additional coalition candidates could be minority, environmental, and consumer organizations, charitable groups, local clergy, and government officials—indeed, any organization that believes or can be convinced it has a stake in the outcome of the issue. (Another name sometimes used for highly diverse ad hoc alliances is "third-party" coalitions.)

"The family should share an emotional interest," Grefe wrote, "the friends an economic interest, the strangers an intellectual interest. At least that should be the beginning point of approaching one or more of these groups to become involved in the coalition being formed."

Potential allies should be identified from among those the issue would affect: Who gains? Who loses? Who might have an interest that they might not be aware of? For example, the latter category might include local officials and merchants if an issue would have a significant impact in the community in which a facility is located. So might interest groups whose economic interest is not directly involved but where there is an underlying principle that bridges to another issue that does affect those groups.

Thinking as broadly as possible, even using group brain-storming, may be useful to develop as large a list as possible of potential allies. Consultants are available who can aid in ally development and also advise on other phases of coalition management.

Recruitment

The second step is recruitment of these potential allies. This is still another of those points in the government relations process where CEO support is so important. CEO-to-CEO communications are much likelier to gain both attention and a successful recruit than solicitations further down the table of organization.

Whoever makes the contact, however, it is important to explain the issue in terms of its effect on the potential ally and frame it from the ally's point of view. An altruistic tone should be avoided. The group sponsoring the coalition should state forthrightly its own self-interest while appealing to that of the organization being solicited. Candor, persuasiveness, and empathy are all essentials here, especially when contacting groups outside the categories of friends and family. Write the kind of letter you would find persuasive if you, as a business executive, were to receive an invitation from another group to join a coalition.

Letters are rarely sufficient, however. Letters should be preceded by an introductory telephone call, from the writer if he or she knows or has some credibility with the person being invited; if not, then by an intermediary or "honest broker" who has a relationship with both groups. The writer should then follow up with a personal call.

If the group being solicited to join the coalition should decline the honor, it is worthwhile to try to get a commitment of neutrality, thereby at least denying the other side a recruit.

Or the group may be sympathetic but, for one reason or another, unwilling to participate in the coalition. However, its leaders—and other community opinion makers—may be willing to speak out on their own or get in touch with lawmakers whom they know well. Mobilizing particularly influential people in the community, called "grass-*tops* programs," is a logical extension of local coalition activity and is carried out in similar ways.

The third step is to call a meeting of the invitees for an initial discussion of the stake of the participants in the issue, its importance for each, and the position the coalition will take. This last point is ticklish. If the issue is clearcut, the logical position should be obvious to everyone. But many issues are complex. The impact of the measure on Group X may be ambiguous to it for one reason or another. Group Y may be concerned with only part of the bill. Group Z may like one section of the bill and dislike another. The priority of the issue also may differ from group to group.

These matters must be discussed and resolved in a completely amicable and understanding manner, or there is likely to be no coalition at all. If one member tries to push its position down the throats of the others, it may end up sitting at the conference table alone.

Coalition Structure

Step four involves deciding the structure of the coalition. A chairman is needed to provide coordinating functions—calling meetings, taking minutes, assuring that assigned responsibilities are carried out, and maintaining communications among the members between meetings. It is reasonable to expect that the organization putting the coalition together should fill this role. On the other hand, there may be good reasons why the leader should be someone else, to share the glory with another coalition member whose ego warrants stroking, for example, or because another participant would have more external credibility as a spokesperson.

If the issue is complex and important enough, then coordination and staff needs may require bringing in a manager. This could well be an executive from one of the coalition's members. But it might be preferable to retain someone independent, perhaps a consultant specializing in coalition management.[2]

The allocation of coalition costs is another potentially touchy point. On the one hand, nonbusiness members of the coalition are unlikely to have the economic resources of the corporate members. On the other, many of the nonbusiness groups may be sensitive to appearances of being "bought." Careful and diplomatic handling of this question is important.

If the coalition is large enough, a small steering committee, empowered to make decisions, will be necessary. The organizing sponsor (and perhaps financial "angel") will certainly want to be part of this leadership group.

However questions of leadership and funding are handled, the company or organization bringing the coalition together has a major stake in the outcome of the issue and should be careful to retain a controlling interest.

Step five relates to division of tasks and functions. Once the structure, funding, and positions of the coalition have been determined, it needs to develop and carry out a government relations plan as any single organization or company would—particularly the research and analysis, direct lobbying, and grassroots phases. The difference is that these functions will probably be divided up and apportioned among coalition members in some rational manner. Grassroots activities are typically among a coalition's greatest strengths, and the more diverse the coalition the greater its ability to generate public pressure on lawmakers.

Coordination and Communications

It is important for the coalition's leadership to identify who can be depended on to perform and who may be shaky, and to handle the division of labor thoroughly but also sensitively.[3] Some members may have an unrealistically high opinion of their own influence, skills, and knowledge. Others, regardless of their competence, may be willing to do certain tasks but have no interest in others.

Considerations like these explain why coalitions are usually harder to manage than any other kind of government relations structure. Diplomacy is always an ingredient in effective leadership, and the guidance of coalitions requires exceptional skills in this area.

The sixth step involves the critical elements of negotiation and compromise, important in any lobbying campaign, and particularly hazardous points for coalitions. Some members will be willing to yield on points that others consider crucial. The very timing of negotiation and compromise may become highly controversial within the coalition.

One business coalition opposing a state environmental measure successfully held off enactment for ten years. As proponents began to succeed in building momentum, it became clear to some coalition members that a credible alternative was needed. The nature of the alternative became hotly controversial within the coalition, and a weak choice at the level of the lowest common denominator was ultimately made to keep the coalition from disintegrating. Despite vigorous pursuit of the alternative, it never achieved sufficient credibility, and the coalition was ultimately defeated by its adversaries—consumer groups and environmentalists operating through their own coalition.

Preserving the business coalition was important, for reasons that went well beyond the legislation, but the price ultimately paid to do so—defeat on what turned out to be a very expensive issue—was higher than the coalition's value to a major segment of its members.

Sensitivity to the needs of coalition members is important, but so is leadership. Vigorous leadership willing to risk consensus to achieve the larger goal is essential to coalition success. Although this observation may seem at odds with the earlier comment about the importance of diplomacy, it is more important to win than to avoid stepping on toes. Skilled leaders are deft at managing varied, often argumentative constituencies to accomplish the greater goal.

Step seven involves public communications. One of the great strengths of coalitions is their ability to enhance public credibility, and the more diverse the coalition the greater its credibility is likely to be. But that does not mean that every participating group should speak out publicly on the coalition's behalf. On the contrary, in most cases a single spokesperson should be designated, possibly the chair, possibly not. The ideal spokesperson should be articulate, knowledgeable on the issue, and committed to the coalition's good. That individual should also be someone with the greatest possible credibility—seldom an executive with the company or other organization that brought the coalition into being. A minority group leader, an environmentalist, a former public official, a schoolteacher, a show business personality—these are all examples of spokespeople who can add to the credibility of the cause.

Television and radio interviews, including talk show appearances, or issue advertisements are good ways to utilize such people. A direct-mail campaign, utilizing a letter signed by a well known public figure, can be an effective mechanism. Press releases and interviews (including meetings with newspaper editorial boards), public speeches, op-ed columns, and letters to the editor are all useful devices. Community and alternative newspapers may be helpful in reaching special audiences. A bulletin board or a chat room on the Internet may also be an effective outreach medium. (See Chapter 15.)

The key point is the coalition's capability to build public support for its legislative position through its diversity.

PRESERVING COALITIONS OVER TIME

Some legislative issues are resolved within a short time. Others drag on for years. Between crises, the coalition has to be maintained, the members stroked and kept motivated and informed. This is not easy during periods when attention may be distracted by other, more immediate concerns; but unless it is done carefully and systematically, the coalition will not be there when its existence and effective operation are most needed. Personal and organizational relationships, awareness of the individual and shared stake, and motivation must be maintained. Unless there is a permanent staff, in all likelihood the company or group that initiated the coalition's founding will also need to accept responsibility for its continued care and feeding during the quiet periods that are typical of long-term issues.

Even if the legislative issue is resolved within a short time, a related one may materialize in a few years. Initiatives and referenda often recur on the same or similar subjects. There will be another political campaign in two years. The coalition may disband for a time, but it is important to maintain communications and relationships among its members so that it can be easily reassembled when the need arises.

The complexity of coalition management may make it tempting to shun its use. But that means forgoing the use of an exceptionally valuable tactic, one that multiplies leverage, increases the forces able to advance the organizer's position, and enhances credibility with the public and lawmakers. Using coalitions means enlisting allies, and allies can make the difference between victory and defeat.

Sleeping with strange bedfellows may be uncomfortable, but it is far better than sleeping alone.

NOTES

1. Edward A. Grefe. "Creating Winning Coalitions," *Public Affairs Challenge*, Fall 1983.

2. For an analysis of the potential pitfalls in selecting such consultants, see Mary Ann Pires, "Initiating and Renewing Advocacy Group Contacts," *Impact*, December 1987.

3. Ten principles of coalition management are discussed in Anne Wexler, "Coalition-Building: How to Make It Work for You Now and in the Future," *Public Affairs Review*, 1982.

Chapter 13

Grassroots Lobbying

GLENDOWER: I can call spirits from the vasty deep.
HOTSPUR: Why, so can I, or so can any man,
But will they come when you do call for them?
—Shakespeare, *Henry IV, Part I*

With all the skills the most talented lobbyists can bring to bear, there is one thing they cannot do for most of the legislators they cultivate, and that is vote for them. Like everyone else, lobbyists vote where they live. To almost every legislator, therefore, the lobbyist is someone else's constituent.

In each legislator's eyes, the wants and needs of her or his own constituents are paramount. Satisfying them is key to the legislator's "bottom line"— reelection. Legislators are elected to represent their constituencies' best interests, but in practice that often means responding not just to the opinions of the electorate as a whole but particularly to the views of vocal, well-organized, and active local groups.

Such groups tend to be more influential than the average citizen because, on the issues that concern them, they care more deeply than most other people do. The public at large may not share the views of the National Rifle Association, for instance, but it will not be a tenth as expressive about gun control as are local gun owners. "You just have a ton of grief in your district if you don't vote with them," said an Illinois congressman after a House vote on a gun issue. "They really turn up the heat locally. You just don't want to spend every district appearance talking about that one vote."

In consequence, lubricating the frictions and stress points of local interest groups becomes the almost daily task of every elected official. As the late Senator Everett McKinley Dirksen used to say, "The oil can is mightier than the sword." Another Dirksenism also applies: "When I feel the heat, I see the light."

It is that principle that underpins grassroots lobbying. By mobilizing informed local members of an organization—or the employees, retirees, and shareholders of a company—lobbyists extend, multiply, and reinforce their efforts in every legislative district into which they can reach. Provided some understanding of the issues is reflected, one hundred calls, visits, or letters from back home provide substantial and impressive support for the position the direct lobbyist is urging a legislator to adopt. Communications from 500 constituents are overwhelming, even for a member of Congress representing more than half a million people.

Grassroots lobbying is no longer merely a supplement to direct advocacy but a major tactic whose use is exploding. Estimates of the amounts spent on grassroots activities at federal and state levels, both in house and by outside consultants and vendors, increased from $470 million in 1991–1992 to $790 million in 1993–1994.[1]

This is true whether the lawmaker is a U.S. senator or representative or a state or local legislator. "All politics is local," former House Speaker Thomas P. O'Neill liked to say. So is the most effective government relations.

From the elected official's viewpoint, the grassroots communications that mean the most are those that come spontaneously from constituents. Mail or telephone calls that are clearly personal expressions of opinion, even if stimulated by an interest group, are also quite influential. Communications that have obviously been manufactured, perhaps by a specialized telemarketing firm, from citizens who obviously have little idea what they are talking about, fall into a third category, called not grassroots but "astroturf," and little attention is paid them. Preprinted or otherwise identical letters or postcards have a different name, "trash."

An effective grassroots lobbying program *educates* its participants about the legislative process, *informs* them about the issues affecting them as members or stakeholders of the interest group, and *motivates* them to direct their own personal communications to the legislators who represent them in Washington or the state capital. A superior program goes even further, to aid them in cultivating their lawmakers personally, so when they communicate on the issues, they are not faceless entities but individuals personally acquainted with and known to the legislator. Best of all are those who participate in politics and are known as people who have helped candidates get into public office and then helped them stay there. That subject is treated in Chapter 16.

Grassroots programs can operate through members (or employees and other stakeholders), either as a network of individuals or in teams. *Individuals* in a grassroots network can be encouraged to write or call legislators on key issues. *Teams* can be used to make visits to legislators and engage in other group activities on major issues, while still communicating as individuals on issues of lesser importance.

The advantage of the individual network is that it involves less training and can potentially get more people involved since less effort is needed from any one of them than would be required of members of an active team. Computerization also makes this approach quite easy to manage. A disadvantage is that it is often difficult to learn if requested legislative communications have actually been made.

The advantage of the team approach is that personal visits generally make much more impact on the legislator. The disadvantage is that more training, organization, and other staff preparations are necessary, as are fairly substantial time commitments on the part of team members. Actually, all the activities a team may engage in can also be carried out by individuals—and often will be once team members become comfortable with the process. At the beginning though, it is less fearsome for most people to go in a group to sit down for the first time with a mighty member of Congress or state senator.

ESTABLISHING A GRASSROOTS NETWORK

Some interest groups can get a grassroots program started more easily than others, simply because of the nature of the organization.

Individual membership organizations, such as professional societies and some labor unions, have the easiest time because they are in direct and frequent contact with those they want to participate. Their members often know first hand how legislation affects them, and if the impact is substantial, they may be eager to get involved. Medical professionals and schoolteachers fall into this category. Interest groups like environmental organizations or cause groups are in an exceptionally strong position because their members tend to be unusually motivated from the start. In many cases, local chapters can be the instrument for direct motivation and training, a considerably more effective technique than a stand-alone manual.

Most groups of this sort encourage all their members to participate, and a substantial share often do. Very large groups sometimes limit the number of members asked to participate, partly because of cost and partly to avoid overkill. Several thousand letters from their members are not likely to have a greater effect on a legislator than several hundred; a vast number of telephone calls overwhelms legislative offices; and if they recur frequently from a particular interest group, they can generate anger. Some of the largest individual membership organizations utilize only a portion of their members for a different reason. For instance, AARP's membership is so large and diverse that it cannot always control what they all might say and do. AARP therefore makes use of only a small percentage of its vast membership and carefully selects them to assure that it gets the effect it wants.

Organizations that use selection criteria make a point of knowing which members have a record of local political connections or involvement, perhaps including participation in the associations' political action committees or other indications of political awareness. These groups will also take political geography into account so that, if possible, they have a cadre in every state legislative and congressional district. If that is not possible, priority will be given to those districts represented by legislators who sit on committees important to the organizations' legislative agendas.

Individual companies have a different problem. They have diverse groups of stakeholders, few of whom are likely to have a pre-existing motivation to participate in a grassroots program. They must be informed about the need and motivated to participate. Their willingness to do so may depend to a great extent on their attitude toward the company and its management. A company with a long history of good relations with its stakeholders will get a much better response than one that has been downsizing, cutting costs right and left, laying off employees, and slashing dividends. High morale and good personal relationships with top executives are factors that will get a grassroots program off to a strong start.

Corporate stakeholders who should be considered for grassroots recruitment include both "family" and "friends":

- Managers and executives

- Professional employees, such as in-house accountants and attorneys, economists, scientists and engineers, human relations and public affairs staff people, and computer personnel

- Sales and marketing personnel (who have the advantage, typically, of being based in a variety of locations rather than at the company's headquarters)

- Other employees, including administrative assistants, who work closely with the above categories and are likely to share their values. Most companies do not want to enlist blue-collar employees, especially if they are unionized; on certain issues, though, especially those that could affect their jobs, incomes, or benefits, their involvement may be worth considering.

- Retired employees from the above categories

- Individual shareholders (it is pointless to solicit institutional investors)

- In the "friends" group are executives of major customers or suppliers—including such vendors of services as advertising and public relations agencies, consultants, and law firms, as well as suppliers of raw materials, components, and similar materials.

- Spouses and other adult family members of all the above "friends and family." Their involvement can at least double the number of grassroots program participants.

Small and mid-sized companies may want to target everyone in these categories. Larger firms can use this universal approach or can segment recruitment, using much the same political criteria as large individual membership associations. Keep in mind that *any* employee, not just executives, may be politically involved or at least know key legislators or officials: A blue-collar worker may be a town mayor; a secretary may be a state or local legislator; a clerk may have a family or neighborhood relationship with an important political party official.

Decentralized, multidivisional corporations may find themselves in a different predicament. It may be difficult getting personnel associated with the defense contracting division to understand or care about the issues faced by the consumer widget unit. Each of those operations may have to develop its own grassroots program, separate from the others, but countenanced and coordinated at the corporate level.

Trade associations have the most difficult time establishing grassroots programs. Because their members are companies, not individuals, their first problem is persuading each of their corporate members to develop its own program. Before the association can even think about motivating individual grassroots participants, it must motivate its member companies to take part in the program, and to do so on a basis reasonably consistent with other corporate programs within the industry.

Every association has a prime contact within each member company. It is one thing if the prime contact is the chief executive or a senior officer. It is something else again if the prime contact is a middle-level operating manager who may or may not have the interest and the influence to persuade top management to become involved. If the company has already established a grassroots network, either on its own initiative or at the behest of another association, it probably is willing to use the network on the second association's issues if they are sufficiently important to the company.

THE IMPORTANCE OF SUPPORT FROM THE TOP

Any program that involves individual business firms has to begin with a strong statement of support from the company's chief executive officer. (Obviously, this is not relevant to individual membership organizations.) Without such an endorsement, it is pointless to proceed any further. If the CEO will not lend support, no one else in the company will believe the program is important to the business and be willing to give it time. A written statement endorsing the program is the minimum level of CEO support. Even better are demonstrations of the chief executive's willingness to participate by frequent communications to elected officials; reproducing those communications in company publications sets a good example for everyone else.

Supportive chief executives understand that the only way to lower the high costs of government regulation is, first, to elect officials who believe that market-oriented remedies to public problems are preferable to government mandates and, second, to help them apply that principle issue by issue, through direct and grassroots lobbying. They also understand that elected officials are as responsive to their constituents as successful companies are to their customers.

Many times, the impetus to begin a program is a crisis issue on which all possible weapons must be brought to bear. Nonetheless, embarking on a grassroots program should be a strategic, long-term decision; a strong grassroots capability will add to the company's arsenal on future issues, as well as the immediate one. Properly managed, it can be integrated not only with direct lobbying but also with coalition activities, the political action committee and political participation efforts, community and public relations, and other public affairs programs. It is also a means of improving employee morale and esprit de corps.

THE ELEMENTS OF GRASSROOTS PROGRAMS

Once the CEO has blessed the grassroots program in principle, the next step should be to prepare and distribute a policy statement that incorporates the CEO's endorsement and authorizes employees to take the time to participate in legislative contacts and perhaps also in coalition activities. Some companies even make these contacts a part of employees' job descriptions and appraise annual performance accordingly.

Planning and Budgeting

A manager must be designated to design and execute the plan and to manage the program thereafter. One of that individual's first tasks should be the development of a well thought out plan and budget.

An early decision that must be made is the focus of the program. Should it try to enlist as many of the company's stakeholders as possible wherever they may live, or is it better to concentrate on geographic areas represented by specific legislators who sit on legislative committees with jurisdiction over the company's key issues? It may be possible to do both, developing the targeted approach in the program's first phase and working to broaden it later on.

Other elements of the program should also be planned out, including recruitment techniques, training, ongoing motivation, and issue and program communications. How the program is to be coordinated with other government relations and public affairs activities should also be part of the plan.

In preparing the budget, consider the following likely costs:

- Staff time
- Travel
- Telephone and computer costs (perhaps including program management software)
- Communications and publications
- Training
- Legislative conference costs (meetings, meals, perhaps speaker fees, and participant travel)
- Recognition programs and awards

Motivation and Recruitment

Recruitment of volunteers for a company's grassroots network has to be predicated on an understanding of motivations. Some people volunteer because they have a high degree of loyalty to the company and want to be helpful. Others are interested in politics and legislation and find the program a way to learn and do more. Still others enjoy being at the "cutting edge" of something new. And some see involvement as a way to network within the company or make new friends. Various studies of corporate grassroots participation have also found that the higher individuals rank in the company or the more shares stockholders own the more likely they are to participate. (Given the breadth of stock ownership today, an appeal to individual shareholders is likely to reach employees in even the most subordinate positions.)

Individual business owners, on the other hand, are more likely to participate in an association's grassroots program if they perceive an economic stake in an issue, regardless of the size of their firms. The National Federation of Independent Business, the U.S. Chamber of Commerce, and the National Association of Manufacturers have had considerable success in mobilizing these people. Small business executives respond to legislative alerts more or less in proportion to their perception of the importance of the issue to their businesses. That implies the need to be selective and to prioritize.

Other associations that have made extensive use of grassroots lobbying include the Chemical Manufacturers Association, the Edison Electric Institute, the American Nursing Association, the National Restaurant Association, the Independent Insurance Agents of America, the National Association of Life Underwriters, the National Rifle Association, and the AARP. Individual companies with widespread programs include Philip Morris, RJR, WMX Technologies, TRW, and Browning Ferris Industries. Virtually every labor union and environmental organization makes extensive use of membership grassroots lobbying; the National Education Association and the Sierra Club are considered two of the most effective.

Depending on the program's focus (targeted or broad based), a list of potential recruits should be compiled, people who then will be requested to participate. The essential word here is *requested*. Even within a company, individuals cannot realistically be commanded to engage in a program of this sort. The principle that "when you have them by the throat, their hearts and minds will follow," may possibly produce results in the short term, but after a while, it breeds only resentment and foot-dragging. (Compulsion is not remotely possible, of course, in association programs.) The exception to this principle is those personnel who have been assigned political and community relations responsibilities as part of their jobs.

The essential beginning is a solicitation letter from the chief executive. The letter should invite participation in an important cause, utilizing the power of citizen communications to persuade elected officials to adopt sound and sensible public policies (however the group or company wishes to define such policies) and to help the company. The letter should make clear whether the network will seek to influence legislation at the federal, state, or local levels, or some combination of them.

The letter should also explain that the cause is important, that the effort requested will not be burdensome, and that clear information on the issues will be provided often so that participants in the network will be able to communicate intelligently with their legislators. The network should be given a special name, for example, "XYZ Corporation's Grassroots Democracy Council." A special letterhead can be designed for use in newsletters and action appeals to help promote personal identification with the network. (See the sample letter on page 195.)

While it is useful to describe the kinds of issues grassroots network participants will be asked to write their legislators about, it is best not to ask for action in the initial recruitment letter. But do ask for the pledge: a form (with a postage-paid envelope, of course) that the individual signs, agreeing to be a participant—perhaps for a limited time (such as two years, the length of most legislative terms) so that the participant does not feel that he or she is volunteering for a life sentence. Invitations to re-enlist can always be extended later.

A letter by itself will not draw an enormous response rate. That rate can be significantly increased, though, by follow-up visits or telephone calls from a peer to reduce the hesitation and uncertainty many people will feel about participating in a program that may involve unfamiliar activity. The follow-up call is an opportunity to provide answers to questions, encouragement, and a general increase in comfort level.

Often, this follow-up comes from the administrator of the grassroots program, but an alternative approach might be to establish a solicitation committee, broadly representative of all those being solicited. Ideal members of such a committee would be individuals highly regarded among their peers.

Wherever possible, it is valuable to supplement the written invitation and follow-up calls with a solicitation meeting at which the cordial but low-key invitation to join is reiterated, explanations of what is involved are given, and opportunities are provided for questions and discussions.

The list of individuals agreeing to participate should be computerized, including name and address; local, state, and federal legislative district numbers; political contacts and activity; particular issue interests and sensitivities; and other useful data. All this information can be requested on the return-mail form; note that legislative district identification may need to be researched by staff since many people do not know the districts in which they live. It is important to think through ahead of time what other kinds of helpful data could be requested without arousing concerns about invasion of privacy.

Training and Orientation

Unless they have considerable familiarity with politics and government, most members of the grassroots network will need information about the governmental process (legislative, executive, and regulatory), striking a balance between what the individual has to know and how much all but the most committed are actually likely to read. A booklet could be specially written for network members, but it may be possible (and certainly cheaper) to obtain supplies of educational publications prepared for this purpose by Congress and most state legislatures. Groups such as the League of Women Voters are also good sources. The National Association of Manufacturers has published a useful guide to employee grassroots involvement.

XYZ CORPORATION
Bigtown, New Ohio
Office of the Chairman

Mr. Thomas H. Jensen
515 Cedar Street
North Bigtown, New Ohio

Dear Tom:

This is a cordial invitation to you to join in an important new civic endeavor that XYZ is sponsoring. We're calling it the Grassroots Democracy Council, and it's a program to enlist active members of the XYZ community in an effort to communicate with our federal and state legislators more effectively than we ever have before.

There are many issues before Congress and the New Ohio Legislature that affect us in a variety of ways: as business people, as investors and shareholders, and as taxpayers and citizens. Too often, we have failed to let our legislators know what we think about those issues while they're still making up their own minds. They have an obligation to represent us, true, but we also have an obligation to share our views and experiences with them.

Because I know how active you and some of our other retirees have always been in the community, I'm inviting you to be a part of this new civic campaign. What we're asking you to do is express your willingness to write or call five lawmakers to tell them your thoughts on particular issues when circumstances warrant.

These five are New Ohio's two United States Senators, the Representative from North Bigtown's Congressional district, and your state senator and assemblyman.

To help keep you, and the other participating retirees, employees, and shareholders completely informed on the issues, we're beginning a special newsletter, *The Insider's Report*, that will be prepared from material provided by our state and federal lobbyists and trade associations and sent only to members of the Grassroots Democracy Council. It will not only discuss the issues that we think are important but also cover issues that you and other Council members have a special interest in; just let us know.

Then, from time to time, we'll be in touch to let you know when you might write or call these legislators to have the greatest impact on important issues.

Please sign and return the enclosed card to let me know if you're willing to be part of this exciting new program. Incidentally, there's space on the form for you to indicate, if you care to, how well you know these and other legislators. That would be very helpful information to us in managing this program effectively.

Tom, I do hope you'll join us in this important effort. My best to Dorothy—who might also enjoy being part of this!

Sincerely,

Harvey Howard
Chairman & CEO

P.S. We're having a meeting on Thursday, the 14th, at 5:30 in the employee cafeteria to explain this program and answer any questions you and the other invitees may have. Senator Seymour Solon will also be there to discuss how our laws are made. Can you and Dorothy join us?

This material could also be included in a training manual or handbook that gives pointers on how to communicate with legislators and how to develop relationships with them and their staffs, as well as basic information about the company or industry (sales, employment, and other data). If this material is published in looseleaf format, it can easily be updated with sections reserved for federal, state, and local government directories, issue fact sheets, action appeals, and similar materials.

Alternative media for training and orientation are specially prepared video-tapes or self-study computer diskettes. Some combination of these could also be distributed on the company's intranet, if it has one.

Orientation seminars should be considered for program participants if their locations make that feasible. In the case of employees and other company stakeholders, such a seminar could be held in a company facility during the lunch hour or immediately after office hours. Because much of the essential information is complex, it may be worthwhile arranging a series of one- or two-hour seminars. Ample time should be built into the schedule to answer questions and improve participants' comfort level. Role-playing exercises are both educational and fun.

The seminar should be led by the senior government relations or public affairs executive of the sponsoring company or organization, assisted perhaps by lobbyists or others on the staff. Seminars in company facilities permit much of the material to be localized. Including the local federal or state legislator as a guest speaker will increase the appeal of the seminar and boost attendance. Having a legislator provide the briefing on how laws are made and influenced not only lends authority to the seminar but also provides the legislator with a welcome opportunity to speak to a group of constituents.

To avoid overloading participants with more information than most are likely to be able to absorb at one time, detailed issue briefings are not a good addition to the orientation seminar, although thumbnail descriptions of a small number of issues may be useful. A packet of position papers can be provided for later reading.

The orientation seminar should be renewed at least annually—not only for new network participants but also as a refresher for veterans.

Communicating to the Network

The time to begin communication with network participants on the issues is *not* when an issue has heated up to the point that an urgent action appeal is needed. Participants need advance information about the issue and how it affects them and the company. They also need time to absorb the information. Good communications increase interest and cooperation and build a sense of civic legitimacy about communicating with lawmakers.

A special newsletter targeted, or even restricted, to grassroots participants is a cost-effective medium to convey news about key issues. Profiles of participants and success stories make good feature articles. Distribution by broadcast fax or e-mail assures prompt delivery and saves money compared to use of the mails. A well-designed newsletter with a special logo enhances the appeal of the program, and can be sent as an e-mail attachment. E-mail facilitates two-way communications, and replies should be actively encouraged so that grassroots network members get into the feedback habit relating to actions they have taken and responses from individual legislators they have contacted.

In addition to newsletters, other ways to provide legislative information include issue fact sheets, position papers, and special action appeals. Personalized letters are always an effective technique to provide or request information and particularly to express thanks for action taken. Even if you use a mail-merge program to produce letters, try to personalize them in some way. Be sure to avoid the use of computer codes or labels on envelopes.

Communications should be consistent and frequent. If a newsletter is started, it should not be dropped after an issue or two. Recipients should be kept informed and up to date as often as needed, but if six months go by without receiving anything, they may well assume the network is defunct or that they are no longer part of it. Some communication should go out at least bimonthly to maintain interest and involvement, more often when there is much news. Old information is as stale in a newsletter as in a newspaper.

Information about the issues must always be factual and reasonably objective. Giving participants only propaganda puts them at a disadvantage in discussing the issue with lawmakers. There is nothing wrong with presenting the organization's point of view, but respect for those in the grassroots network requires that the position of the other side also be fairly presented. One way to do this is in the form of rebuttal arguments:

1. "Our bill would achieve the following . . ."
2. "Opponents argue that the bill is not needed because . . ."
3. "However, they fail to realize that . . ."

Worth considering is an annual poll of network members, inviting them to suggest information that could be included in the newsletter on issues of particular interest to them. For example, employees who are working parents might express interest in child care legislation; retirees might want to know about health issues; shareholders might be concerned about a new tax bill. Even if such issues are not ones in which the company is involved, it should be no great effort to include information on them in the newsletter from time to time, thereby further contributing to a sense of personal involvement.

Action Appeals

The payoff for its investment in developing and maintaining the network comes when the sponsoring company or organization needs grassroots support on its issues. Not every issue lends itself to grassroots appeals. An issue with emotional aspects will produce a better response than a very technical one. (And even if it is technical, avoid burdening network members or legislators with extensive scientific or economic data. If that information is truly necessary, it can be delivered by lobbyists.)

The time for an action appeal may arrive when a bill reaches a crucial stage of consideration by a legislative committee or comes up for floor debate and voting or goes to some other critical point. The appeal for action can take either of two forms.

The General Alert "Now that the bill is scheduled for legislative action, you may wish to inform your legislator what you think." The network participant, having been well briefed in past communications, is encouraged to express his or her own views. Not all who write will necessarily endorse the position of the grassroots network's sponsor, but the vast majority will—and the fairness of the sponsoring company or organization is underscored by the few who do not. (See the example on page 199.)

The Specific Appeal This is the more common approach. It requests network participants to get in touch with their legislators and convey as their own personal views those of the organization: "Tell Senator X why you think he should vote for S. 1234. Here are some arguments you can use (in your own words) to express your opinion."

Note the essential elements of the specific appeal:

1. Whom to write or call and how to reach them.
2. The name of the issue and bill number.
3. The position to be expressed on the issue.
4. Talking points to be used, in the writer's (or caller's) own words—backed up where possible with personal experiences that can lend substantial credibility to the message.

All this information can be communicated in computerized personal letters to network participants. (See the example on page 200.) Software programs readily available permit coding of legislative or congressional districts and names and addresses of legislators so the personalized letter can also tell the recipient specifically whom he or she needs to contact and how to reach him or her. Such programs also allow the sender to contact selected segments of the network by manipulating almost any number of variables.

Let's suppose that a company wants to generate mail from its grassroots network to the members of a legislative committee before it votes on a particular bill. Assuming the variable data have been correctly programmed and coded, a number of different, highly personalized versions of the letter to the network are possible:

1. The name and address of the particular legislator representing that specific recipient.
2. Different versions of the letter, depending on whether the legislator's position on the bill is pro, con, or unknown.

3. Still different versions to employees, managers, retirees, and shareholders—and to any desired subgroups among them—suggesting different motivating arguments.

4. Different versions yet, depending on whether the constituent is known to have a relationship with legislator.

5. Exclusion of grassroots participants whose legislators are not on the committee—or another version of the letter suggesting that lawmakers be asked to lobby their colleagues who *are* on the committee.

6. Different signatures on different letter versions, depending on whose name will have the most impact.

XYZ CORPORATION
Bigtown, New Ohio

Office of the Vice President—Public Affairs

Mr. Thomas H. Jensen
515 Cedar Street
North Bigtown, New Ohio

Dear Tom:

For the past several months, *The Insider's Report* has been telling you about H.R. 1234, the bill to increase import duties on a number of raw materials imported from Europe. This would increase the cost we pay for one of our essential raw materials, black wicker chips, that we can obtain only from European sources.

The sponsors of this bill believe that the United States has to take steps to force the Europeans to open up more of their markets to American products, and that the only effective way to negotiate is to make it harder for European Union exports to sell in this country. The bill raises trade barriers on about 20 commodities to do this.

Opponents of H.R. 1234, including XYZ, believe trade barriers of this kind are a bad way to negotiate—that raising barriers is no way to remove them. Of course, you're familiar from the newsletter with the other arguments opponents have used, including our own concern about what this bill would do to our production costs and the resulting impact on our domestic markets.

The House Commerce Committee is scheduled to consider H.R. 1234 on February 24. As you know, Congressman Warren Wisdom from your district, is an influential member of this committee.

Whatever your personal views may be on this bill, now would be the best time to share them with Congressman Wisdom. (If you'd care to send me a copy, I'd enjoy seeing whatever you may say to Representative Wisdom—and also his reply to you.)

My thanks and best wishes.

Sincerely,

Marvin Miller
Vice President

NATIONAL MANGLERS ASSOCIATION
Washington, DC

TO: Mr. Harris Fellowes
             Clench Mangler Industries, Inc.
             Windward, Minneconsin

FROM: Wendell Philpotte, Executive Vice President

This is an urgent appeal for your help with Congressman Stephen Statute in connection with H.R. 1234, the raw material import tax. The House Commerce Committee has scheduled a vote on this bill for February 24, and Rep. Statute remains uncommitted.

Please make these points to him, putting the following in your own words:

1. Recognize that the sponsors of this bill are well-intentioned in their desire to take constructive action against the trade barriers erected by the Europeans.

2. However, the import restrictions that H.R.1234 would impose in terms of higher duties on raw materials are not a workable negotiating tactic with the Europeans.

3. American companies like Clench Manglers will be hurt because of the cost increases H.R. 1234 will impose. (Document this damage with specific facts and numbers.)

4. These increased costs will eventually be passed on to consumers, raising prices and adding to domestic inflation.

5. Thus, it is ultimately the American consumer, not the Europeans, who will be penalized by this bill.

6. A better approach would be to allow U.S. trade negotiators to work out an effective arrangement in their discussions with their European counterparts.

The sooner you can write Congressman Statute, the better. Please be sure to let us have a copy of your letter and whatever reply you may receive.

Many thanks for your help on this. If this bill should be approved by the Commerce Committee, we will probably ask you and other members of NMA's Legislative Action Teams to visit the Congressman and his colleagues to lobby him in person on this issue.

It is not likely that every mailing will be this complex—but computers can provide this kind of flexibility and more.

Some organizations enclose a postage-paid postcard to be returned when grassroots participants have sent the letter to legislators or ask for blind copies of correspondence, so that they will know which legislators are being written (and, of course, see who in the network is actually working).

Follow-Up and Feedback   Most legislators will respond with a note of acknowledgment. This letter may say only that the legislator will take the writer's views into account in deciding how to vote—or it may say that the legislator is already inclined to a particular position. If network participants get information of this latter type, encourage them to pass it along; the organization's direct lobbyists may find it helpful intelligence.

A note of thanks should always be sent to each network participant who the organization knows has gotten in touch with his legislator. Either this note or the newsletter should tell the network as promptly as possible what the outcome was once the issue has been decided.

Expressions of thanks from the constituent to legislators if their votes were favorable should be strongly encouraged. It may also be appropriate in some cases to send a tactful note if the lawmaker's vote was adverse: "I was disappointed to see that you voted against S. 123."

Feedback to network participants is as important as it is to legislators, and valuable to maintain interest and morale. Recognition from a manager or a peer will encourage them to be even more effective in the future.

To be credible, grassroots communications have to demonstrate an understanding of what the issue is about and how it would affect the constituent. This is where the value of keeping network participants well informed as issues develop pays off in *quality* messages. Legislators don't expect constituents to be issue experts, but an uninformed or canned message will obviously not have a fraction of the impact of a call or letter from individuals who know what the issue is about and how they will be affected.

Motivation and Recognition

A lawn needs water, sunshine, and a little fertilizer to stay healthy. Grassroots programs need nutrients too. Grassroots network participants must be recognized for what they have achieved. Sooner or later, the novelty of participation wears off, which is one of the reasons so many grassroots programs wither after a time. Personal recognition and motivation help retain program participants and encourage new ones to join.

The most important form of motivation is continued vocal support from the chief executive and all levels of management, including conspicuous examples of personal participation by executives at all levels.

Personal recognition is also an important motivator. In addition to letters of thanks for their efforts, participants should be recognized with certificates, plaques, or modest gifts. Lapel pins provide not only recognition but walking advertisements for the program throughout the company. Employees who have been especially effective can be profiled in company publications or publicized by press releases to their local newspapers. High achievers can also be given cash awards or extra vacation time. Similar kinds of recognition should be developed for retirees, suppliers, customers, and other participants.

Another way to motivate participants is to give them a voice in the program—for instance, by providing them opportunities to evaluate the program and propose improvements or by soliciting their opinions on issues and proposed positions.

It is unfortunate but true, however, that positive messages are not always the most effective motivation. Constituencies are hard to arouse in noncrisis situations and hard to keep aroused once a crisis has apparently passed. Fear of loss is a greater stimulus to action than the promise of gain. The danger that a job or public entitlement will be taken away is a more powerful motivator than the possibility of lower taxes or higher pay.

Grassroots motivation needs constant tending at a very personal level. Program participants must be reminded as frequently as necessary of their personal stakes in the issue and why they need to act—and continue acting.

Risky Techniques

Still another approach to grassroots lobbying involves solicitation by specialized telemarketing firms retained by an interest group to promote mass communications to legislators from their constituents on a particular issue. Because it produces legislative communications that may not really reflect grassroots opinion, it is called "astroturf" (no doubt, unfairly to the company that manufactures the synthetic for sports fields).

Using such sources as organizational membership lists or industrial or community directories, the telemarketer calls names within targeted legislative districts to explain the issue and how the individual would be affected by it, more often than not in prejudicial language. The consultant then seeks permission to send a telegram or a mailgram in the individual's name to his or her legislator, at the same time also soliciting pertinent personal or business details that can be used to individualize the communication.

Astroturf can generate large amounts of legislative mail in a short time on a given issue. Of course, the approach must be both genuine and memorable enough that the citizen will confirm his interest in the issue if the legislator should inquire about it.

The technique is both expensive and risky. One incident caused an uproar while Congress was debating telecommunications deregulation. A substantial percentage of constituents' telegrams generated by an astroturf marketer were discovered to be fraudulent—sent without the permission of the people whose names were on them. The company that had hired the astroturf firm was deeply embarrassed, and its legislative cause was seriously damaged.

Two other means of facilitating constituent contacts to lawmakers are technically related to astroturf but less susceptible to misuse. *Third-party calling* (also called "direct connects" or "telephone patchthroughs") also starts with a telemarketing survey to identify constituents sympathetic to the sponsoring interest group's legislative position. Once identified, the constituent is immediately connected with the lawmaker's office to talk directly to a staff aide, if not to the legislator personally. *Interactive kiosks* are special booths at an association conference where people can use a telephone or computer to send issue messages to legislators.

Devices all too commonly used in promoting legislative mail by some organizations are the preprinted, identical letter or mailgram, postcard, or signed petition—all of which should be shunned. The purpose of a grassroots program is to engender individual involvement and numerous personal messages to legislators, not to demonstrate how many identical pellets can be fired out of the organization's legislative shotgun. Most legislators are turned off by these techniques, and some even have been known to use them against an organization.

Petitions may have some value with local officials on strictly local issues, for example, a town zoning matter. They should be avoided for other uses. Legislators realize that most people will sign any worthwhile-appearing petition. That, after all, is how most legislative candidates get on the ballot.

TIPS ON COMPUTERIZED COMMUNICATIONS

- To maximize response rates, seek a personalized appearance to letters. Use letter-quality printers such as laser or ink-jet printers. Dot-matrix printers are dead give-aways that a computer was used; and besides, their output looks dreadful.

- Addresses should be printed directly on envelopes. Avoid labels. Omit computer codes.

- Personalize the salutation. "Dear Mr. Jones," *not* "Dear Friend" or "Dear Colleague." "Dear Tom" is better yet—but only if the signer knows the recipient. (Even in this age of gregarious familiarity, many people are irritated by being "first-named" by someone they don't know.)

- The body of the letter should also appear as much as possible as a personal letter. Content should also be personalized, but do it naturally. Shun language like "you and your neighbors on White Street in Hometown"; you are not selling magazine subscriptions. For the same reason, avoid headline- and flash-type effects.

- If there are too many letters to sign personally, use a software program that prints emulated signatures. Use a color printer for this purpose so that signature will appear in blue (or whatever color you usually use). There have long been machines on the market that reproduce a signature on each letter, but they are expensive.

ESTABLISHING A LEGISLATIVE ACTION TEAM

A second tier of a grassroots system is the Legislative Action Team— individuals working to help influence public policy through *personal* visits with targeted legislators.

Recruitment and Training

Team members are recruited in much the same way as those in the individual grassroots network. However, because team members will be communicating with legislators in person rather than by mail, their selection should be made with added care. Team members need outgoing, persuasive personalities and a keen sensitivity to the political and legislative process. Remember that these are people who will be representing the company or organization when they meet with legislators.

Selection should begin by identifying those legislators whose views and actions are critical to the company or association: legislative leaders and the chairmen and members of key committees. Team members should then be sought in those congressional or state or local legislative districts represented by the targeted legislators.

Invitations to participate should utilize the same approach as the individual network, particularly including a letter from the CEO. Because team members are being asked to devote much more time than are participants in the individual network, they need that much more personal attention at all phases.

Training needs to be thorough—a seminar is important, backed up by a manual of legislative information and issue fact sheets or position papers. Team members need to understand not just the broad outline of legislative procedure, but also the finer details and political background. They also need to know a great deal about the issues because they will be questioned about them during their meetings with legislators and staffs.

Organization and Communications

The team will require staff support and coordination from the sponsoring group or company. Working as part of the organization's government relations staff, coordinators will be responsible for

1. Organizing the team and assuring adequate membership on an ongoing basis
2. Keeping team members well informed about the status of the issues on which they are focusing, as well as pertinent political developments
3. Mobilizing them for action as required by legislative needs
4. Assisting in planning and implementing major meetings and functions of the teams or, if necessary, carrying out the organization of such events directly

Personal recognition is important. The team organization should be provided its own letterhead for internal communications to and among the members. (Communications to legislators and government officials should always be on each member's own personal or business stationery.) Some organizations may want to create state teams, and each of these should have its own letterhead, including the names of its officers.

An awards program for distinguished achievement should be considered, using the same kind of techniques discussed above.

Communications to legislative action teams must provide several different kinds of news:

- Issue briefings and legislative news, similar to that provided the members of the individual network but probably on a more frequent basis—as often as weekly during heated legislative periods—and by telephone, fax, or e-mail when crises arise
- Information about relevant political matters such as shifts in legislative committee chairmanships or memberships
- News of forthcoming team events
- Recognition of achievements of individual team members

Team Events

A major purpose of the legislative action teams is to show strength, concern, and involvement on major issues on the part of either the sponsoring organization and its members or the sponsoring company and its stakeholders. The team should concentrate on a fairly small number of top-priority issues, perhaps only one if its importance is overriding.

The most effective use of team members will be visits to legislators in their offices in Washington or at the state capital, to make the case for their company's or organization's position on the issues. Properly briefed (and usually accompanied) by the group's lobbyists, team members "from back home" can make an impressive, occasionally overwhelming, impact on the legislators they visit, particularly if the lawmakers know that the team members will continue to be involved and will watch carefully what happens on the issue and how each legislator votes in committee and on the floor.

These visits can be of two kinds. One is almost a mass rally (if the organization's membership is large enough to produce such an event) in which hundreds, perhaps even thousands of people, often adorned with slogans on political-style buttons or wearing distinctive clothing, descend on the capital for an annual visit to press their case on their vital issues. The second, more valuable type, is a series of frequent, quieter visits by small groups to lobby their legislators personally.

These visits, of whichever kind, must be organized in the closest consultation with the organization's lobbyists on the scene. The whole objective is to back up their efforts on the issues with demonstrations of grassroots concern and strength, not to shunt the lobbyists aside.

Variations on these visits at the capital can also take place back in the districts. Congress and the legislatures of the larger states are now in virtually year-round sessions, but members are usually home a day or two a week at even the busiest times; more during recesses. Satellite conferencing is a way for the team to discuss issues with a member of Congress stuck in Washington or a distant state capital. Members of local legislative bodies are generally even more accessible.

Supplementing team visits are other useful events or functions.

Annual Legislative Dinners or Receptions Lawmakers (and often their staffs) from particular states or regions are invited to break bread or bend elbows with team members. Team members can help promote attendance among legislators by follow-up notes or calls after the formal invitations from the sponsoring organization.

The value of these events, particularly receptions, is the opportunity they provide for extensive socializing and, of course, lobbying. Speeches and receptions tend to be a poor mixers so if a few brief talks are needed—as perhaps at an awards event to which legislators are invited—a sit-down meal is the better medium. Socializing is difficult at dinners, but these can be preceded by receptions, thus providing the best of both worlds.

Such events must be scheduled long in advance because they are increasingly popular among interest groups, and legislators' social calendars are generally overflowing.

Be careful to organize these events so as to comply with applicable federal or state laws. For instance, for members of Congress to attend legally, they must be recipients of an award (based perhaps on their voting records) or meet another of the gift-ban criteria.

Plant, Store, or Facility Visits by Legislators These can be quite useful, especially when used to demonstrate the effect a particular bill would have on operations. Legislators also welcome the chance to meet employees, whether or not they get to speak. If a talk is to be given, a few well-planted questions and comments can help underscore the position the organization wants the lawmaker to adopt.

Such visits need not be limited to legislators. Other elected officials and regulators may find it helpful to visit an operation in order to observe the potential effects of a proposed law or regulation.

Annual Legislative Conferences for Team Members These provide another opportunity for issue briefings and meetings with legislators and can be coordinated with a dinner or reception. The conference agenda can include a mix of staff reports on issues, panels of legislators and regulators, speeches by top elected officials, and so on.

Team members should make every effort to get as close to their legislators as possible: visiting them, contributing to and participating in their campaigns, and doing whatever is legitimately possible to build not just constituent relationships but personal friendships.

It is important to express thanks whenever legislators vote as the constituent recommended. When they do not, a very low-key note of reproach may also be appropriate to let them know they are being watched—but threats or other angry (and therefore antagonistic) statements should always be avoided.

COORDINATION WITH RELATED PROGRAMS

Grassroots programs should be coordinated or integrated with political participation and community affairs programs, as well as with direct lobbying. Contributors to the organization's political action committee are a prime source of recruits for the grassroots program, and vice versa.

If employees or members are actively involved in a variety of civic organizations and causes, the contacts they develop through community participation can be a strong asset in their grassroots lobbying efforts and in coalitions as well. For example, if a bill would have a substantial impact on a company's local investments and employment, local officials should be enlisted to aid in lobbying appropriate lawmakers on the issue.

Similarly, if a program to promote employee political activity exists, its participants already know top political and elected personalities. Their ability to constitute an effective lobbying force is already in place.

Conversely, if a political participation program does not exist, the grassroots program provides both ample evidence why one is desirable and the potential base to start it up.

ESSENTIAL PRINCIPLES

In sum, the key points about all effective grassroots programs are these:

- Individuals must be motivated and recruited to participate.
- They must be mobilized and trained in techniques of legislative communication.
- Issues communications to participants should be frequent, factual, and objective.
- Grassroots messages to legislators must reflect some understanding of the issues to be credible.
- Appeals to action must be specific and clear as to issue messages, action needed, and action targets.
- Grassroots, political action, and community relations programs should be closely coordinated.
- Participants need frequent feedback to assure them of the value and effectiveness of their efforts.
- Participants should be encouraged to provide their own feedback to program managers on responses from legislators.

Finally, bear in mind the restrictions described in Chapter 8 on federal tax deductions for grassroots programs. Check to see what applicable state laws may apply.

NOTE

1. Ron Faucheaux, "The Grassroots Explosion," *Campaigns & Elections*, December/January 1995.

Chapter 14

Political Action

Money is the mother's milk of politics.

—Jesse Unruh

But my intention being to write something of use to those who understand, it appears to me more proper to go to the real truth of the matter than to its imagination; and many have imagined republics and principalities which have never been seen or known to exist in reality; for how we live is so far removed from how we ought to live, that he who abandons what is done for what ought to be done, will rather bring about his own ruin than his preservation.

—Machiavelli

Jesse Unruh understood the role of money in the political and public policy process as well as any politician in America. State Treasurer of California at the time of his death in 1987, he mobilized his counterparts in other states to wield great power with Wall Street merchants of public bonds. But it was in an earlier role, as Speaker of the California Assembly, that Unruh organized political fund-raising to a high art. By centralizing in his office both fund-raising and disbursements, he bolstered Democratic majorities in the Assembly and made both lobbyists and his fellow lawmakers extraordinarily dependent on his leadership. In his day, he was arguably the most powerful state legislator in America.

With the huge amounts of money Unruh raised from lobbyists, interest groups, and other contributors, he poured record sums into winning key legislative districts, often spending more on Assembly contests than was being spent on some congressional races.

Political campaigns in the United States depend almost entirely on funds raised from the private sector. (Although a few state and local campaigns are financed with public money, as is the presidential race, the vast majority are still privately funded by voluntary contributions.) Much of this money comes from friendly individuals, but a great deal of it has always been raised, one way or another, from interest groups keenly concerned about both pending public policy issues and the candidates running for the offices empowered to decide them.

Campaigns have become an expensive business. As recently as the early 1970s, $100 thousand or less would finance almost any race for the U.S. House of Representatives. But spending soared in the 1980s and 1990s. By 1988, party spending was up to $500 to $800 thousand for each House seat, with several House campaigns costing $1.5 million. In the 1996 election, any seriously contested House seat cost each of the candidates $1 million or more, and several topped $2 million. In the most expensive 1996 House campaign, House Speaker Newt Gingrich and his Democratic opponent spent $9 million between them, more than the cost of most Senate contests. (In Gingrich's case, some of his reported expenditures probably included contributions to other House GOP candidates, a practice of congressional leaders in both parties.)

Total House campaign expenditures were $478 million in 1996, double the amount spent in 1988, and an 18 percent increase since 1994.

Campaign spending for U.S. Senate seats totaled $288 million in 1996. That actually was a decrease from 1994 when the most expensive Senate campaign in history was waged—$30 million by the losing candidate in California, $14 million by the winner. No 1996 campaign approached that total, but a number were in the $15–20-million range. Even in the smaller states, nonincumbents must raise several million dollars to be competitive.

One reason 1996 Senate spending was comparatively modest was the lack of races in several big states like California, Pennsylvania, and New York. That will not be true in 1998, and spending on Senate campaigns is likely to soar once again that year.

Amounts spent in 1996 by Senate and House candidates do not include another $100 million spent by candidates who lost in the primaries. An additional $623 million was spent by political party committees, plus $267 million in soft-money outlays. Interest groups spent almost $11 million in independent expenditures.

The presidential campaigns spent $81 million in privately raised funds, on top of $150 million from the taxpayer-financed Presidential Campaign Fund.

Spending at the state level plus soft-money expenditures that need not be reported probably bring the grand total of 1996 campaign costs to about $3 billion. That number will undoubtedly continue to rise if there is no change in the law.

Because there is such a vast amount of public hand-wringing about the size and growth of campaign spending, it is worthwhile to put such numbers into perspective. Far less is spent on political campaigns than on marketing consumer products; surely, the election of candidates to public office is worth at least as much to American society as advertising for beer or antacids. Moreover, campaign costs are only a small fraction of the sums legislators must appropriate to fund even a modest government program.

Nonetheless, the political appetite for funds is insatiable. A New York Democratic activist spoke for both parties when he said, "Candidates look at money the way Mark Twain regarded bourbon. Too much is never enough." Although both parties profess a desire to limit expenses, neither is willing to practice unilateral disarmament. Until recently, it seemed that only stringent campaign finance legislation could put a ceiling on political spending, but even that is now in doubt as interest groups become major players in their own right through advocacy advertising and independent expenditures.

How all that money is used is another, oft-told story. This chapter discusses political finance from the donor's point of view:

- *Who* contributes
- *Why* interest groups give to political candidates and organizations
- *How* they give
- *What else* they do to influence the political process

WHO GIVES

Many political contributors—but far from all—are lobbyists or people who give because one interest group or another stimulated their donation. Many other people give for ideological reasons: 94 percent of contributors say they give to candidates who think as they do on issues they consider important, according a January 1997 survey.[1] Large majorities also contribute in part because it would benefit their business interests and in part because "it is important for average Americans to be involved in the political process." Half think their political access opportunities improve by giving, but more than 40 percent believe they neither gain nor lose access by giving.

They attribute different motivations to others, however. Almost 80 percent say they are bothered "by political contributions from companies that do business with the government or are regulated by Congress or a government agency."

Most contributors in the survey give only to their own party's candidates. Fewer than 5 percent give to candidates of both parties. The total contributions of each of these people averaged more than $3,000.

The demographics of these contributors are interesting. Almost all are white. Two-thirds have college degrees and household incomes of more than $50,000; about a fourth have incomes over $150,000. Nearly 60 percent describe themselves as conservative, and almost 70 percent voted Republican for both President and Congress in the 1996 elections.

WHY GROUPS GIVE

It needs to be said at the outset what political contributions *do not* buy: legislative votes. Paying a public official for a favorable vote or decision is an act of corruption, completely illegal everywhere. No sane lobbyist offers bribes or other illegal payments, and public officials would be not only mortally offended by an attempt but likely to report the matter immediately to the nearest prosecutor. On those rare occasions when political influence and decisions are bought and paid for, the resulting investigations, prosecutions, and trials are front-page news stories for months. Neither lawmakers nor lobbyists enjoy having their careers terminated by jail sentences.

Preferential business and investment deals and dubious contributions to a campaign or pet cause in return for improper favors are more common. President Clinton and his wife have spent almost their entire time in the White House under investigation for possible transgressions of this sort. Although Lyndon Johnson's only visible income during nearly forty years in public life was his official salary, by the time he left the presidency he and his wife owned a chain of radio stations. House Speaker Jim Wright, a Democrat, was forced to resign and a Republican successor, Newt Gingrich, was reprimanded and fined by his colleagues because of questionable political activities.

The entire area of political ethics is colored in shades of gray. It is clearly illegal for someone to say to a governor, "Make sure my company gets that highway contract, and I'll throw a lot of business to your wife's company." But if a friend happens to mention to that same official, "I invested a little money in Gizmo Corporation last week and expect to make a lot from it," is that wrong if she seeks no favor in return for the stock tip? Even if it is, is it illegal?

Political contributions are quite different, provided there is no explicit quid pro quo. There are legal—and ethically legitimate—reasons for political giving:

1. To help elect officials favorable to an individual's or interest group's viewpoint on issue positions—and oppose candidates who are not
2. To gain and enhance access to elected officials
3. To express appreciation for their favorable positions and actions

In the historical course of events, acting successfully for the first reason has automatically achieved the second. Legislators and other officials look more fondly on those who have helped elect them than on those who didn't. Access has always flowed to those who were there from the beginning, as well as to those who helped along the way.

With the growth of legislative careerism, these two motivations have tended to drift a bit apart. Lobbyists can hardly be personally active in the district campaigns of all the legislators with whom they deal and wish to thank, but they can assist by contributing funds; and since campaigns have gotten so expensive, the funds are increasingly needed and solicited, and their donors made welcome. (It is not easy to separate cause from effect. Part of the reason campaigns have gotten so expensive is that so much more money has become readily available to fund them.)

There are differing views among government relations practitioners about whom to support and why. One school of thought tends to be ideological: "We need lawmakers who share our basic philosophy. More important than access is their basic commitment to our point of view. Senator Omega may be an important leader, but he is not in tune with us on the issues. We should support his election opponent who is, and who would vote with us more than 10 or 20 percent of the time. We have to take the long view and work to elect legislators who share our views even if that means antagonizing some incumbents until we can defeat them at the polls."

Another view is heavily pragmatic, tilting more to the importance of contributing to gain access and appreciation. Not surprising, lobbyists tend, more often than not, to fall in this group. Their argument goes something like this: "Everybody wants to see Senator Alpha on the issues, but he and his legislative staff have only so much time. Preference is going to go to important supporters, political and financial. Gaining timely access and a sympathetic ear is not only legitimate, it's essential; we can't present our views if we can't get in the door. Moreover, if he's been helpful to us on the issues that are important to us, we have to be helpful to him when he needs it, and that means financially supporting his reelection campaign."

"We also have to contribute to his colleague, Senator Beta. She is more neutral than supportive on our issues, but she chairs the committee most important to us, and we have to have her good will and access to the committee staff which she controls. We can't risk antagonizing her by supporting her opponent."

Some lobbyists fear retribution if they don't give. Public officials can be quite aggressive in their fund-raising requests. A U.S. Senator, after all, must raise something like $15,000 to $20,000 every week of a six-year term to finance the next reelection campaign. Interest groups often contribute, not to gain access but because they are afraid they may lose it.

A former representative, chairman of the committee that raises funds for Democratic House candidates, used to call business groups that he thought were not giving enough to Democrats. His message was essentially this: "Don't expect to be able to get an appointment with committee chairman X if we don't get your contribution." Republicans were equally forceful when they took control of Congress.

Challenged about these assertions, some officials have been known to respond, "If they didn't give, it wouldn't make any difference, but they don't know that." As President Clinton said about contributors, "What they get from me . . . is a respectful hearing if they have some concern about the issues. . . . But nobody buys a guaranteed result, nor should they ever."[2] Most lobbyists view such statements skeptically; politicians want and need the money too much. San Francisco Mayor Willie Brown, a fund-raiser in the Unruh tradition, sardonically asked a business group once, "Why buy a legislator when you can rent one?" The audience roared with appreciative, if rueful, laughter.

An association executive was involved in a series of small fund-raising meetings with another well-known elected official. At each session, the executive reported, the official asked what the industry's problems were in the agencies reporting to him. As each matter was outlined, he would dispense his decisions: "Yes, you can have that." "No, I've got problems with what you ask." "Let me look into that one and see what we can do." As each group left, its contribution was discreetly handed to a staff aide. Not all elected officials are quite as open about the arrangement as this one.

Many legislators dislike the chase for dollars. They think they have to spend too much time raising money, and some have chosen not to run again because of it.

Which philosophy is correct? In practice, motivations for contributing must be mixed. Only an interest group more interested in ideological purity than in winning can ignore the need for access and good will. But groups willing to totally sacrifice long-range interests for today's issues are not so much pragmatic as cynical.

Some organizations have written political contributions criteria stating what their mix is. One company's political action committee guidelines state that 75 percent of its funds will go to candidates "who have demonstrated a clear business orientation in their public positions," with no more than 25 percent allocated to access support.

This is a rational principle. If interest groups neglect to help elect candidates sympathetic to their points of view, they will always have difficulty getting their positions adopted by philosophically hostile lawmakers. Giving only for access on today's issues, however, undercuts their long-term legislative agendas.

Many lobbyists and executives will counter with the words of John Maynard Keynes, "in the very long run we are all dead"—that long-range thinking is all very well, but meanwhile there is S. 1234 that must be defeated this year. That is why incumbents receive far more money, in the main, than their challengers— and therefore why it is a rare election when fewer than 90 percent of incumbents are reelected. In 1996, House incumbents collected three times as much money as their challengers; Senate incumbents got 60 percent of the contributions (but a record number of open-seat campaigns probably held that percentage down). Interest groups that want to bring about change in the composition of federal or state legislatures therefore tend to focus most of their efforts on open-seat contests (i.e., those in which no incumbent is running), where the chances of victory are greater and where there is no one to antagonize.

It has not been common for interest groups to make the massive effort against incumbents that labor and environmental organizations did in 1996; their successes were not numerous, and it remains to be seen how much legislative vengeance the Republican majority exacts and whether the effort will be repeated in future elections.

Planning and Organization

Political contributors who give more than occasionally should operate with a written strategy and plan. An interest group that contributes without a plan will almost inevitably be giving only to acquire access, and probably not very effectively at that. Whether money is given through individual contributions, a political action committee, soft dollars, or independent expenditures, it is important to decide in advance why the group is giving, what kinds of short- and long-term objectives it has, and how it plans to proceed.

Such a plan should begin with a brief mission statement that sets forth the purpose of the political contributions program. Will it give primarily for access, or will the focus be on electing like-minded candidates? If the latter, will it give to nonincumbents? Helping candidates in districts without an incumbent running for reelection is one thing, but what about support for challengers to incumbents? Even programs with a strong philosophic bent often have reservations about giving to friendly candidates running against incumbents with long memories. This is usually the point at which long-range ideological objectives bump up against short-term situations. It is never comfortable to be courageous, but it is easier if the problem has been considered in principle before it actually arises.

A strategy and plan should follow, implementing the mission statement in more detail, and guiding operational decisions: Will the program operate at the federal level, in one or more states, or both? Is there a desirable ratio between contributions to incumbents and those to nonincumbents, to philosophic giving as opposed to access donations, to Republicans rather than Democrats, to members of important committees instead of legislators representing company facilities? Will candidates be interviewed prior to contribution decisions, and what kinds of questions should they be asked? Will contributions be made in primaries as well as general elections? Will they made only during campaigns, or also afterward to help retire candidates' debts? Will contributions go only to candidates or to political committees as well?

Because political and legislative circumstances change, short-term goals and tactics in the more detailed plan should be updated each election cycle, a two-year period. Obviously, a sound plan requires a sound budget that then should be adhered to. Of course, in any political campaign critical situations arise that require deviations from the plan, but if there are too many of these "emergencies," maybe there is something wrong with the plan or, more likely, the way it is being executed.

Why bother with all this planning? Without a predetermined guide to decision making, interest groups are at the mercy of political fund-raisers, making decisions off the cuff and sometimes regretting them. The story, not at all uncommon, is told of the corporate chief executive who happened to sit next to a prominent official on an airplane trip. When the CEO got back to the office, he told his staff to make a $10,000 soft-money contribution to the politician's pet political committee. Was it a worthy contribution? Did it meet the company's political goals? Who knows, least of all the CEO who was talked into a seat-of-the-pants decision by a persuasive political salesman.

HOW GROUPS GIVE

At least nine devices are currently used by interest groups to provide political support to favored candidates and parties, some of them overlapping in practice:

1. Individual contributions
2. Bundling
3. Political action committees
4. Conduits
5. In-kind contributions
6. Independent expenditures
7. Direct corporate and union contributions
8. Soft money
9. Advocacy advertising

Individual Contributions

Despite the rise of political action committees and public financing, contributions from individuals remain the backbone of political funding. Most contributions are made in presidential campaign years. The number of people who give to political candidates, parties, and interest group political action committees is probably about 25 million. Funds raised directly from individuals or from PACs financed by individual contributions are called "hard dollars," to distinguish them from "soft money," described later.

Historically, individual giving was dominated by large contributors, "fat cats" in political parlance. As late as 1972, before federal campaign finance limits were tightened, some individual contributions to both the McGovern and Nixon campaigns reached the upper six-digit range, and a few exceeded $1 million.

This pattern changed as a result of two developments: stricter regulation of campaign finance, triggered by the Watergate affair, and the rise of direct-mail solicitations.

Political Reforms

Federal election statutes were substantially rewritten in the 1970s by a series of laws and court decisions. The changes were these:

- Limits were established on individual political contributions in federal elections (allowing spouses to give equal amounts):
- $1,000 per candidate per election (with primaries, runoffs, and general elections each considered separately)
- $5,000 annually to a PAC or to a state or local party committee supporting federal candidates

- $20,000 annually to a national party committee
- $25,000 annually in total contributions to any or all of the above
- Contributions in cash over $100 were disallowed, and political candidates and committees were required to identify contributors giving over $200 by name, address, occupation, and place of business
- Public financing of presidential campaigns was instituted, funded by the income tax checkoff
- Regulation of political action committees, campaign expenditures, and reporting requirements was increased
- The Federal Election Commission (FEC) was established to regulate the process and to receive reports on campaign receipts and expenditures

In 1976, the Supreme Court decided its landmark case on campaign finance, *Buckley v. Valeo*, in which it upheld limits on contributions to the campaigns of national parties and candidates for federal office. However, the Court overturned most limitations on expenditures (except where public financing has been accepted) on the ground that they were unconstitutional restrictions on rights of political free speech. An exception was made for candidates who may spend unlimited amounts of their personal funds on their own campaigns. Disclosure requirements and public financing were both upheld.

The *Buckley* decision resulted in an increase in the number of congressional campaigns by wealthy candidates since they can finance virtually their entire campaign out of their own pockets, while their less well off opponents must raise money in the small amounts permitted by law.

The Supreme Court decision also resulted in major changes in many state campaign finance laws. As a result, individual contributions are limited in about half the states. Limits vary widely. Disclosure of both contributions and expenditures is required in all states.

At the federal level, individuals are free to raise money voluntarily on behalf of favored candidates and parties although they must report their expenses if they go over certain limits; there may be state limits as well. In general, companies and other interest groups can also encourage individual contributions to candidates and political committees (including PACs). However, solicitation activities and costs are regulated both at the federal level and in some states as well.

Direct Mail and Telemarketing

Actually preceding the political reforms was the development of direct mail solicitations to targeted mailing lists. Begun in the 1950s primarily by the Republican Party, direct mail financing was an important factor in Barry Goldwater's 1964 presidential bid. Eight years later, Democrat George McGovern also used direct mail with great financial success, actually tripling Goldwater's collections.

Over the years, Republican committees and conservative groups became much more attentive to the development of direct mail technology and utilization than their Democratic and liberal counterparts and therefore invariably raised far more money nationally through this approach. Not until the 1980s, when they had the policies and programs of Ronald Reagan to rail against, did Democratic committees and liberal groups begin to raise significant sums, but they still do less well than Republican and conservative solicitations. Direct mail appeals are also being utilized with increasing frequency and effectiveness in state and local campaigns.

Issues and ideology play a substantial role in persuading an individual citizen to mail a check to a political cause. Republicans solicitations have relied heavily on strong conservative, antigovernment appeals, even during the Reagan and Bush presidencies. Similarly, McGovern's successful financial appeals centered on vehement opposition to the Vietnam War.

Telemarketing for political purposes is a logical outgrowth of direct mail appeals. Using computerized lists, telemarketers aggressively and successfully solicit funds for candidates, parties, and interest groups.

Whether for political parties, candidates, or interest groups, two factors must be present to achieve substantial fund-raising results from direct mail and telemarketing:

1. A cause (ideology, issue, or personality) about which people feel quite strongly and emotionally
2. A substantial, highly targeted list of individuals likely to be highly responsive to the cause underlying the fund-raising appeal

Examples of such causes include the abortion and gun-control issues (both pro and con), an immensely unpopular war, threatened loss of an important economic benefit (such as Social Security), environmental issues, and so forth. Jesse Jackson, whose 1988 campaign started on the proverbial shoestring, was raising substantial amounts of money through direct mail by the end of his campaign as a result of the strong emotional appeal he was able to generate among certain groups. On the other hand, Ross Perot, who personally financed his 1992 presidential campaign, did poorly four years later when his Reform Party sought to raise money through fund-raising drives (presumably because people saw little reason to give to a billionaire's pet project).

Negative appeals are often exceptionally effective. Liberal organizations raised fortunes during the 1980s by attacking President Ronald Reagan and his policies, just as conservative groups have placed Senator Edward Kennedy in the honored role of whipping boy over an even longer period.

Bundling

Some groups like to show substantial political support for a candidate or party by collecting a number of checks from individuals and presenting them as a package to the recipient. Thus, the group might solicit checks for $250 from each of two hundred individuals, thereby enabling it to gain credit for $50,000 in contributions—a total that would be illegal if presented as a single PAC contribution.

This process is called "bundling" (with no relationship to the quaint colonial-era courtship practice of the same name). The only real requirement is that the bundler must register with the FEC as an agent for the candidate(s) on whose behalf the funds are collected. Despite this modest regulatory burden, bundling is not a widespread practice, although a feminist PAC, Emily's List, has utilized it. On the whole, it is easier to get people to contribute to a PAC, and they can do so in larger individual amounts. Still, should PACs ever be banned, bundling could become the vehicle of choice for interest group political fund-raising.

Political Action Committees

No other fund-raising technique has proven as successful or as controversial as the political action committee. Invented by organized labor and often the subject of bitter business criticism, the PAC was finally seized upon by business groups that greatly expanded its political utilization. Today, it is business-sponsored PACs that receive the most criticism, though for reasons that are obscure since union and corporate PACs operate in much the same way. On several occasions, Congress has tried unsuccessfully to curtail or even abolish federal PACs, but it has never succeeded.

Today, thousands of PACs participate in federal elections under the sponsorship of individual companies, labor unions, various kinds of associations, and cause groups. There are also PACs that are unaffiliated with any sponsor. Numerous PACs also operate at the state level.

The first PAC, the Committee on Political Education (COPE) was created by the CIO after Congress prohibited direct political contributions by labor unions in federal elections in 1943. The first business PAC arrived two decades later, the Business–Industry Political Action Committee (BIPAC). Corporate PACs have mushroomed since 1975 when they were authorized by the FEC in its Sun Oil Company decision.

What do PACs look like? Here is a profile of the average corporate federal PAC, based on a BIPAC survey after the 1996 elections:[3]

- Total raised: $222,615
- Frequency of solicitation: 56 percent solicit annually, 27 percent biannually, 17 percent irregularly
- Participation: 32 percent of the employees solicited contributed. 16 percent of the PACs solicited below the managerial level. Fewer than 10 percent solicited shareholders
- Total givers: 1,092
- Average amount given: $225
- Number of candidates supported: ninety-seven

- Average political contribution: $1,003 to House candidates, $1,610 to Senate candidates. 60 percent of the PACs gave to political party committees; the average among these was $21,382

- Distribution: 38 percent of contributions went to nonincumbents, 72 percent to incumbents

- Some 40 percent gave soft money to political parties (average contribution: $67,085); 25 percent gave an average of $24,906 to interest groups

- About 75 percent of the PACs had written criteria for candidate support

PACs are not particularly democratic in deciding who gets their money. A different survey, conducted in 1996 among 260 companies, found that in only 16 percent did PAC members at large make the candidate support decisions. In over half, those decisions were made by headquarters public affairs executives or by Washington office staff. Senior management picked the recipients in a fifth of the companies.[4]

Labor PACs make decisions in much the same way. They are far fewer in number than those of business, but rank among the very largest in receipts and expenditures.

How PACs Operate

Political action committees are voluntary organizations established to collect contributions from classes of individuals for the purpose of making contributions to political parties and candidates or using the money in other ways to influence elections. Their underlying theory is that by aggregating relatively small donations from a large number of contributors the sponsor can maximize the political effect of the money: A single contribution of $1,000 has greater impact than 100 donations of $10 each. The corporation or other organizational sponsor of the PAC can pay its administrative and solicitation costs. Unconnected PACs—that is, those with no organizational sponsor—must pay their own expenses.

PACs seeking to influence elections for president and Congress are regulated by the FEC. Federal PACs can accept up to $5,000 annually from any individual ($10,000 from a married couple). There is no limit to total PAC collections; and although some take in millions, the vast majority are far smaller. In 1996, the number of federal PACs was a bit over 4,000, about the same number as in 1986.

Each PAC is required to have a treasurer who signs the checks and the reports required by the FEC or its state equivalent. Being treasurer of a PAC (or of a candidate's committee) is not an honorary position; this is the individual the government comes after if errors or irregularities are found in the reports.

Corporate PACs are largely limited to soliciting management personnel and shareholders and their families, although they can solicit contributions from other employees twice a year. Similarly, labor PACs raise their funds mainly from union members, although they too are allowed to solicit corporate managers up to twice annually. Few if any do.

PACs affiliated with such individual membership associations as medical societies and teachers' groups are among the most successful. Trade association PACs have a harder time, since the association's members are mainly corporations, and corporations are not allowed to contribute to federal PACs. Trade association PACs may solicit corporate executives, employees, and shareholders once a year, only with the member-company's permission, and only if no other PAC has been given permission that year. These PACs are usually most successful in industries where member-companies do not have their own PACs, but many companies do not permit any associations to solicit corporate executives at all. These legal restrictions are generally less confining at the state level, but as a practical matter no association can solicit corporate personnel if the member-company does not allow it.

Unconnected PACs typically promote either a political philosophy (such as a liberal or conservative agenda) or work in such special fields as women's rights, abortion (pro-life or pro-choice), and the like. BIPAC, one of the oldest political action committees (founded in 1963), is an example of an unconnected PAC. It is an ideological organization in that its mission is the election of pro-business candidates to Congress. Unconnected PACs can solicit any U.S. citizen at any time.

Contributions to a PAC must, by law, be wholly voluntary and without promises of economic incentives or threats of reprisal. While guidelines can be suggested, no minimum contribution may be specified.

PACs may contribute up to $5,000 per election to a candidate, a total of $10,000 for a typical cycle of primary and general election. They can also give to other PACs (up to $5,000 per year) and to political party committees (up to $15,000 per year). PACs can also make independent expenditures (those wholly uncoordinated with a candidate or party) without limit. Nor is there a limit on the total dollars they can contribute.

What the government giveth with the right hand, it taketh away with the left. Although organizations are permitted to pay the administrative costs of their PACs, those costs are not tax deductible. Moreover, individuals' political contributions—whether to PACs, parties, or candidates—have not been tax deductible since the Tax Reform Act of 1986.

Most states permit PACs. Although there are wide variations in regulations and tax status, state PACs can generally operate with more flexibility than those involved in federal elections. For example, in states that permit corporate and union political contributions, companies and unions can usually contribute directly to a state PAC, a process that simplifies both fund-raising and administration.

Notwithstanding the complexities, PACs at all levels provide companies and other interest groups with the opportunity to become involved in the political process, reward their friends, and work to elect candidates sympathetic to their causes and interests. These are not small advantages for any organization involved in the government relations process. Although they are cumbersome, particularly at the federal level, by their very nature PACs involve their contributors in the political process and thereby provide a useful tie-in and incentive to their grassroots legislative participation as well.

Some organizations, however, prefer to avoid the organizational and political problems of a PAC, finding it easier to decline all requests for political contributions.

PAC Guidelines

Several organizations, both in Washington and the states, provide members and supporters with useful information about how to organize a political action committee. These resource groups can provide handbooks, sample letters and brochures, solicitor training manuals, and similar materials. (See National Resource Organizations in the Appendix.) Before starting a PAC, expert legal advice should be obtained to be sure that all requirements are met.

Based on the experiences of a number of organizations, here are some pointers on the process.

PACs have to be *organized from the top down*. Like grassroots and other government relations programs, strong endorsements and leadership from chief executives are critical to success, both in getting started and in maintaining the process. Without that continuing support, the PAC either will not get under way at all or will falter and fail in a year or two. This is true of both companies and membership organizations.

In the case of the latter, the PAC must be strongly endorsed and backed, not only by the chief staff executive but by the chief elected officer and board of directors as well; association chief elected officers generally serve only a year or two, so it is important that the PAC have the backing of the group's board of directors.

The first corporate meetings to promote the PAC should take place between the CEO and top officers and operating unit executives. The CEO should express enthusiastic support for the PAC and ask that the others do the same among their subordinates. In the case of unions, associations, and other membership groups, these first meetings should enlist vigorous backing from the board and other influential members.

The initial announcement to employees should also come from the chief executive of the corporation or, if more appropriate, the chief executive of the operating unit. In membership groups, this letter should be over the signatures of both the chief staff executive and the chief elected officer, assuming they are not the same individual (as they are in labor unions and a few other groups).

Solicitation also needs to begin from the top down. In companies, solicitation of funds should start with senior executives and then, with their support, move down into the ranks of middle management. In membership groups, it is best to begin with the influentials—directors and larger members. (Spouses can also be solicited, thereby doubling the potential revenue base.) Solicitation letters should be separate from but quickly follow the CEO's letter and include an informational brochure. Where possible and appropriate, small group meetings should be announced to explain and promote the PAC. These meetings should be opened by a senior executive who, after introductory remarks, turns the program over to the local solicitor and perhaps even leaves the room to avoid any hint of pressure. The most effective solicitation efforts are decentralized and localized. Local solicitors should be peers, well known and highly regarded.

Solicitation appeals should both emphasize the importance of political support to the company's legislative goals and point out the importance to the country and the community of electing candidates who share contributors' points of view. As in any other sales appeal, personal enthusiasm, commitment, and communications skills are important. (Promotional films and video tapes that can help are available from several resource groups.)

For both legal and public relations reasons, any hint of coercion must be avoided. It should be made clear that there are no economic rewards for giving, no penalties for not giving. Confidentiality should be assured to the maximum extent possible, consistent with legal reporting requirements and with contribution collection techniques (such as payroll deductions). This does not preclude incentives, though. Lapel pins, medallions, honorary membership in special clubs, or invitations to special PAC dinners and other events are all useful incentives, possibly tied to levels of giving.

General PAC contribution guidelines should be discussed, perhaps as a percentage of salary, but a minimum contribution may not legally be specified. Payroll deductions are legal and widely used.

Special PAC fund-raising events can supplement (but not substitute for) individual solicitations: for example, golf or tennis tournaments, picnics or dinners, sports outings, casino nights, and the like.

An ongoing communications program is important. Contributors should be individually thanked by the solicitors (not their superiors), and special thanks and recognition should be given the solicitors. Contributors should also be kept posted as to fund-raising progress and should be told about PAC disbursement policies and recipients. Reports (annual or more frequent), newsletters, and CEO letters are possible elements in such a program.

Disbursements should be made in accordance with a written policy and determined by a steering (or candidate evaluation) committee broadly representative of contributors, not just senior managers and government relations executives. Contributors should be asked for their suggestions as to recipients; after all, it is their money. Some PACs encourage contributors to be part of the check-presentation process.

PAC checks—and indeed any political contributions—should be presented in person if at all possible. Some candidates resent the time this takes, particularly in the middle of a campaign; but a contributor of a substantial sum ($500

or more) certainly should have a chance to chat with the candidate about issues and problems. For legal reasons, contributions should never be made on
government property.

Contributions are most needed and appreciated early in a campaign when
they can be put to best use. (It is hard to plan for the intelligent use of money
that does not arrive until a few weeks prior to the election—which does not
mean that candidates won't enthusiastically welcome money at *any* time.) This
is not always easy since many PAC contributions do not start coming in until
the general election campaign. One solution is to carry over a portion of PAC
funds to the next election cycle to facilitate some early giving. However, getting early contributions will not keep candidates from asking again if they
need the money.

PACs can engage in other activities besides direct contributions to candidates and parties. Labor PACs for many years have used their funds to organize voter registration drives, particularly in neighborhoods and communities
likely to support labor's favored candidates. Money can also be spent for candidate training, public opinion polls, consultant expenses, voter information,
and a variety of programs beneficial to the candidates supported by the PAC.
PACs can also use their funds for in-kind contributions and to make independent expenditures.

Conduits

Conduits are conceptually halfway between individual contributions and
PACs. A conduit resembles a PAC in that it has an organizational sponsor,
usually a company, that sets up a separate bank account for each individual's
contributions. The accounts are generally funded through payroll deductions.
Each individual controls his or her own account, determines to whom contributions are made, and writes the checks.

As a way to promote and organize individual employee political giving,
conduits have few of the legal requirements imposed on PACs. However, the
sponsoring firm does not get the political benefits of delivering aggregated
contributions to candidates (although theoretically they could be bundled).
Some companies have gotten into trouble with the FEC for suggesting candidates to whom conduit participants might contribute.

In-Kind Contributions

PACs and individuals can contribute goods and services to federal candidates and committees. If in-kind contributions are made directly to federal
candidates, they must be paid for with hard dollars and be included in the
overall $5,000 limit. Even more useful are contributions of goods and services
to political campaigns in those states where corporations and unions can legally contribute directly to political candidates and party committees.

Labor unions in particular have honed this technique to a fine art, often by setting up PACs affiliated with their union locals. For example, telephones, computers, and other equipment can be leased to a favored political campaign at fair market value, often considerably less than the campaign would pay on the commercial market. The PAC must pay all costs in advance.

Another way of making an in-kind contribution is lending an executive or a political consultant to a campaign. Loaned executives provide an extra benefit since they establish relationships that can be very useful if the candidate wins. However, the PAC must pay all compensation costs, not just salary.

The services of public opinion research firms can also be provided on much the same basis. If a PAC takes a poll itself early in the campaign and waits a few weeks before giving it to the candidate, the reportable in-kind cost can be substantially depreciated.

An effective and inexpensive in-kind contribution is a letter urging the members of an association or other companies in a local business community to support a particular candidate. Media ads endorsing the candidate are more expensive, but they can help the candidate and enhance the PAC's visibility in the community.

An attorney knowledgeable about campaign finance law should be consulted about the details of such arrangements.

Independent Expenditures

In its 1976 *Buckley* decision, the Supreme Court upheld the right of any group to make unlimited political expenditures so long as they are not coordinated with the political parties or candidates they benefit. Although they must be paid for in hard dollars and reported to the FEC, there are no limits on the amounts that can be spent this way. Several conservative PACs that took advantage of the opportunity in 1980 to mount massive independent campaigns against a number of liberal Democratic U.S. Senators were credited with helping to defeat at least four of them.

In the years since, more and more interest groups have used independent expenditures to support or oppose particular candidates. These activities have not always been welcomed by the candidates who ostensibly benefit. Independent groups can siphon off contributions that might otherwise go directly into party or candidate coffers. Fund-raising is an expensive process, and the bulk of the money collected by such groups has sometimes paid for salaries and overhead, with a relatively small percentage actually being used for the purpose it was raised. In 1988, both the Bush and Dukakis presidential campaigns publicly requested certain groups to cease their independent activities in behalf of one or the other candidate.

Labor, environmental, and feminist groups used independent expenditures extensively in a January 1996 special Senate election in Oregon to pay for negative advertisements, telephone banks, precinct canvassing, and similar activities.

In June 1996, the application of independent expenditures was significantly expanded by the Supreme Court's decision in *Colorado Federal Campaign Committee v. FEC*. Political party committees had not been allowed to make independent expenditures because it was presumed that their outlays would be coordinated with those of candidates. The court said, however, that expenditures by political committees that are not coordinated with a candidate are independent and therefore not limited in the amounts that can be spent.

The effects of the *Colorado* decision were immediate. Several national political party committees, most notably the National Republican Senatorial Committee, established off-site independent units that undertook substantial (and generally negative) advertising campaigns that benefited various Republican Senate candidates. The presumably uncoordinated nature of these campaigns was illustrated by protests from several of the Senate candidates they were intended to aid who objected to the content and tone of some of the ads.

Although the decision does not directly affect interest groups, it has several important implications. First, over time it can reinvigorate the campaign role of political parties, which has been in decline for decades. Second, it will weaken candidates' own campaigns by diluting their control of campaign themes and messages. Third, the court explicitly left open for some later case the question of whether the First Amendment is violated by limits on *coordinated* party expenditures. Fourth, a dissenting opinion urged the court on First Amendment grounds to reverse its distinction, made in *Buckley*, between expenditures and contributions.

Notwithstanding the reservations of candidates, the likelihood is that the use of independent expenditures by both political parties and interest groups will be one of the great growth areas in future elections, second only to the expansion of issue advocacy. (This is discussed later.) For interest groups particularly, independent expenditures provide a means of stating *their* views on *their* issues, without regard to what candidates would like them to say.

Soft Money

Corporations have been barred from contributing directly in federal elections since 1907, and labor union contributions have been prohibited since 1943.

State regulation of corporate and union contributions is a mixed picture. Corporate contributions are permitted in thirty states and barred in the rest. Only ten states prohibit union contributions.

But even where they are permitted, direct corporate or union contributions can be made only to state and local campaigns, not to federal candidates. However, in these states, corporations and unions can contribute to state party committees that can use the money to free up hard dollars to give to federal candidates. State law governs the amounts that may be given to state committees and candidates. These direct union and corporate donations are called "soft money."

Moreover, corporate and union soft-money contributions can be given *in unlimited amounts* to national political party committees for a variety of party-building activities (such as overhead costs, voter registration and turnout drives, and certain national convention costs). Because the parties do not have to use hard dollars to finance such activities, money is freed up for contributions to their congressional candidates or for independent expenditures.

The national party committees all maintain special accounts to receive soft-money contributions within legal guidelines. The donors are not required to report them to the FEC; although the recipients must do so, they can maintain the confidentiality of the contributors. Soft-money contributions are not tax deductible.

The amount of soft money going to state and national political committees has been growing rapidly in recent years. Soft-dollar receipts by the national parties reported to the FEC reached over $270 million in 1996, plus an unknown but assuredly vast amount to state political parties.

Party committees sometimes use soft money to "buy" hard dollars from another committee, paying a premium that reflects the greater difficulty of raising hard money. For example, one state committee might pay $120,000 in soft money to its counterpart in another state for $100,000 in hard money.

Soft money became a major issue near the end of the 1996 campaign when journalists revealed that the Democratic National Committee had collected huge sums from Asian contributors, much of it from legally ineligible sources. So embarrassed was the DNC that it tried briefly to avoid filing a mandatory preelection report until after the election. Later, it was revealed that a number of generous soft-money contributors had been entertained in the White House and even invited to spend the night in the Lincoln Bedroom (leading some wags to rename the White House Motel 1600).

One of the reasons the use of soft money has been spreading is that the contribution ceilings on individuals and PACs have not been raised since the Federal Election Campaign Act took effect in 1972. This is another illustration of the principle of unintended consequences: The more one seeks to control political funds, the more likely new and unexpected outlets will be found. Political finance, like water, finds its own level.

Fund-Raising Events

Political dinners and similar events continue to be legitimate and effective, if tedious, staples of soft-money fund-raising. Inflation of campaign costs has overtaken the $100-a-plate dinner, which may now reach as high as $10,000 (or more) for the privilege of meeting and greeting the influential, dining on rubber steak, and being entertained by florid oratory. Cocktail parties, sports events, affairs hosted by show-business and other celebrities (especially at their homes), have all been used successfully.

Issue Advocacy

There is nothing new about issue advocacy. Interest groups have been using advocacy advertising to state their views on public issues ever since the Supreme Court's 1978 decision in *First National Bank of Boston v. Bellotti* gave First Amendment protection to corporate political speech and to the use of corporate dollars to pay for it.

What *is* new is the application of issue advocacy to political campaigns. A series of federal court rulings in recent years has interpreted language in the *Buckley* decision to mean that any political statement not expressly advocating the election or defeat of a particular candidate is protected by the First Amendment. The following examples of advocacy statements by different interest groups illustrate the point:

1. The Committee to Tax the Wealthy runs this advertisement: "Senator Alpha believes in tax fairness for the middle class and opposes special tax breaks for the rich. Write or call her office to congratulate her on her courageous position."

2. The XYZ Corporation sponsors a different ad: "Senator Alpha voted against a tax cut for all Americans. Call Senator Alpha and tell her that you're entitled to keep the money you earn, and that she should be ashamed of her vote."

3. The Anti-Tax Coalition has its own ad: "We need a senator who's against all tax increases. Senator Alpha isn't. Her thoughtful opponent, Billy Beta, promises to vote to repeal every single tax if he is elected. This November, vote for Billy Beta for the Senate."

4. The Sensible Tax Policy Council is also running an ad: "Americans need more people in the Senate like Billy Beta who opposes all taxes. What a terrific guy!"

Both the first and second ads state clear positions on the tax issue. One praises Alpha for her position and one criticizes her. One is paid for by an association, the other by a corporation. But neither one says anything about the election or expressly urges a vote for or against Alpha. Both ads are issue advocacy, both may be paid for out of the association or corporate treasury, and neither is reportable to anybody. They are political speech protected by the First Amendment.

The third ad also takes a clear position on the tax issue, but it expressly urges voters to vote for Alpha's opponent. It is an independent expenditure that must be paid for in hard dollars and reported to the FEC.

The fourth ad crowds the line somewhat by implying that Beta is a Senate candidate, but it stops short of saying so or expressly calling for his election. It *probably* is issue advocacy.

Labor unions and a variety of other liberal interest groups used issue-advocacy ads extensively in the 1996 campaign, primarily to criticize Republican congressional incumbents. A number of business associations gathered under the banner of "The Coalition" to raise and spend money to defend these same candidates. Because labor and business both used soft money for the purpose, they were limited only in the amounts they could raise.

There has not been a Supreme Court case testing the use of advocacy ads—naming candidates in the context of an issue but not expressly advocating their defeat or election. Both sides feel comfortable, though, that this kind of issue advocacy is protected by the First Amendment. Because such ads are considered to be free speech, there is probably little or nothing Congress, let alone the FEC, can do to regulate them.

Advocacy ads of this type are likely to proliferate in coming elections. Together with independent expenditures, it is probable that more money will soon be spent in this way during political campaigns by interest groups than by the candidates themselves.

PUBLIC FINANCING

Public funding of elections is a phenomenon that has grown in fits and starts. Presidential campaigns have been publicly financed since 1976, on a matching-funds basis prior to the presidential nominating conventions and exclusively in the general election. (Presidential candidates are not required to accept public funds, but those who choose to do so in the fall campaign may not accept hard money contributions from either individuals or PACs.)

Public campaign financing has been adopted in various forms by some states and localities, beginning in Iowa in 1973. Campaigns in New Jersey for governor, in Maine for all state offices, and in New York City for mayor are now publicly funded. Where public financing exists, funds go directly to candidates in some instances, to party committees in others. Some use a tax check-off procedure with no increase in personal tax liability (like the presidential check-off); others rely on a tax surcharge; and still others give citizens no option by appropriating the money from general revenue.

In its *Buckley* decision, the Supreme Court ruled that candidate expenditure limits are constitutional in federal elections only if the candidate agrees to accept public financing. Congress has never authorized public financing for Senate or House elections although both houses have tried to do so on different occasions.

Public funding of congressional campaigns has long been a heated issue. Supporters argue that it would stop incumbents' constant chase for money, put challengers on an equal footing, and prevent the use of political contributions to "buy" access. Opponents call it "welfare for politicians," and point out that the percentage of taxpayers who check "yes" on their federal tax returns has fallen year after year and has now fallen to about half what it was when the Presidential Campaign Fund was first instituted two decades ago. They also say that taxpayers should not be forced to subsidize candidates they oppose and that blocking the use of hard money in campaigns would only add to the pressures for independent or soft money expenditures to advance political causes and candidates.

A 1997 *Washington Post* poll found that public financing is supported by only 12 percent of the public and 26 percent of those who contribute to campaigns. These percentages rose to 52 percent and 49 percent, respectively, when the question was rephrased to couple public funding with strict limits on candidate spending.[5]

Many senators and representatives, who would have to vote to approve it, see little reason to provide taxpayer funds for their opponents when, as incumbents, they have ample public and private resources at hand to help them win reelection. Public funding for congressional campaigns will come, if it ever does, only when legislators' distaste for it is overcome by public outcry over some particularly egregious campaign finance scandal.

CAMPAIGN FINANCE LEGISLATION

Responding to complaints by reform-minded media editorials and interest groups (Common Cause, for example), members of Congress have been introducing bills for many years to amend the Federal Election Campaign Act. In 1994, the Senate and the House each passed a campaign finance bill but somehow never quite got around to reconciling the differences before Congress adjourned for that year's elections. Although President Clinton and some congressional leaders in both parties have paid lip service to campaign finance reforms, nothing has materialized—nor, despite the oratory, is it clear that anything significant is likely to be enacted in 1997 or 1998, except possibly soft-money restrictions. The political rhetoric on the subject is reminiscent of St. Augustine's prayer: "Oh Lord, make me chaste, but not yet."

The reform proposals call variously for abolition or restrictions on PACs, elimination of soft money ("sewer money," *The New York Times* dismissively terms it), curtailment of campaign expenditures by public financing incentives for congressional elections, modest increases in the ceilings on individual contributions, mandatory discounts in postal and television advertising rates for candidates, limitations on congressional fund-raising, curtailing issue advocacy and independent expenditures in campaigns, and so forth.

So blatantly unconstitutional are some of these ideas that alleged "reformers" have even proposed a constitutional amendment diluting and abridging the political rights protected by the First Amendment, thereby allowing Congress to enact legislation that the federal courts would almost certainly otherwise disallow. There is some superficial appeal to a constitutional amendment because it is the only way to change the *Buckley* decision and subsequent judicial rulings that flowed from it, unless the Supreme Court chooses to make its own changes in some future case.

After all, it was *Buckley* that said it is a violation of candidates' First Amendment rights to cap expenditures but perfectly permissible to limit the free speech of ordinary citizens with a ceiling on their personal political contributions, a distinction that defies common sense and that only a theologian could appreciate.

It was also *Buckley* that allows the wealthy to pay the entire cost of their personal political campaigns out of their own pockets while forcing their less well heeled opponents to raise money in small sums from many contributors—surely one of the most undemocratic edicts ever to emerge from the high court. The court justified this by saying that individuals cannot corrupt themselves, but it is surely a corruption of the political process when wealthy candidates can effectively buy seats in Congress.

Both the use of soft money by interest groups to fund issue advocacy and independent expenditures by political parties resulted from federal court decisions that flowed directly from the *Buckley* decision.

Absent a constitutional amendment, legislative remedies, which can only nibble around the edges of campaign finance as it is currently practiced, could lead to worse problems, as did the "reforms" of the 1970s.

The prospects for an amendment undermining the protections of the first article in the Bill of Rights are, fortunately, as unlikely as they are repugnant. The Senate defeated such an amendment in 1997. As Senator Daniel Patrick Moynihan has remarked, there are no problems of campaign finance so serious that they warrant tinkering with the First Amendment—forty-four words that define the basis of Americans' political freedoms.

A dilemma for "reformers" is that it is virtually impossible to stop one flow of political money without diverting it somewhere else. It is the principle of unintended consequences writ large. Think of campaign funding as a huge, high-pressure hydraulic system. If you dam or plug it in one place, a pipe will burst somewhere else, and create a new stream of money.

This is precisely what has happened in states that have tried to restrict campaign contributions and spending. After Oregon adopted a package of restrictions in 1994, campaign spending in 1996 dropped by more than 70 percent—but independent expenditures soared to more than $1 million, a sizable amount for a small state. Washington, Wisconsin, and other states had similar experiences.

When direct, hard-dollar contributions by PACs and individuals are restricted, the amount of soft money coming in increases. Restrict soft money at the federal level, and it flows to state parties. Limit soft money contributions altogether, and independent expenditures and issue advocacy increase.

Moreover, because the latter two cannot legally be coordinated with the candidates they are intended to benefit, these candidates lose control over their own campaigns—yet another unintended consequence with serious political implications.

A better approach would be to abandon the entire system of intricate and complex requirements and restrictions that now govern political finance. It creates a new problem for every one "solved"; it requires candidates to spend huge sums for lawyers and accountants to assure compliance; and it certainly has done nothing to enhance public confidence in politics and elections.

An alternative proposal would deregulate the entire ramshackle apparatus—replacing it with full, immediate, and effectively enforced electronic reporting and disclosure of campaign finances. Such reports of all contributions and expenditures would allow journalists, opposing candidates, and watchdog groups to monitor campaign activities and expose anything that seems improper or excessive. The voters could then decide whether a candidate's finances were innocent or egregious, mere peccadilloes or something that warrants defeat on Election Day. Enforcement of criminal bribery and corruption laws now in effect would continue to apply.

Most of the existing legal restrictions on contributions and spending would disappear under this new system, allowing individuals, business corporations, labor unions, and every other interest group to contribute directly to the parties and candidates they prefer. Direct corporate and union contributions are permitted now in most state elections, with no evidence that political campaigns in these states are any more corrupt than those for federal office. To encourage more individual political contributions, tax credits or deductions, repealed in 1986, could be reinstituted.

Disclosure and reporting are, after all, the means by which much of the economic marketplace is regulated today. Why not apply the same principles to campaigns, creating a deregulated "political marketplace" in which candidates can go back to basics, debating ideas and issues—which are what political campaigns are supposed to be all about.

POLITICAL PARTICIPATION

In *Animal Farm*, George Orwell's satire on socialism, a sign is posted at the gate of the animals' commune: "All pigs are equal." Soon someone scribbles a change. The sign now reads, "All pigs are equal but some pigs are more equal than others."

All citizens are equal under law, but in practice those who vote are more equal than others. And those who take part in the campaigns of winning candidates are the most equal of all.

Antedating the great surge in PACs was the development of programs to promote citizens' involvement in politics. Organized labor has had programs to involve its members in political activity since at least the founding of COPE in the 1940s. Business activity came later with the U.S. Chamber of Commerce "Action Course in Practical Politics," the founding of the Public Affairs Council (originally the Effective Citizens Organization), both in the 1950s, and the establishment of BIPAC in 1963.

The theory behind these efforts goes to the heart of what government relations is all about. What better way to influence public policy than to have a cadre of members or employees active in the political parties, where they can

- Be personally influential in the selection of candidates for offices at all levels
- Be personally involved in the campaigns of the political parties and help shape party platforms and candidates' positions on the issues
- Run for office themselves or become party leaders

In contrast to the activities of organized labor and the more recent efforts of environmentalists and feminists, business as a whole has had a spotty record

in actually getting executives and managers directly involved from the precinct up. This is partly because business executives generally find it easier to
give money than to contribute their time. Some executives also claim that corporate downsizing has increased managerial workloads, thereby reducing their
available discretionary time for politics and other outside activities.

More credible reasons are (1) a lack of knowledge of how politics is conducted and (2) personal hesitation, or even distaste, about consorting with
people whose ethics or conduct as a group have never enjoyed high repute. In
reality, as anyone who has ever actually participated in political activity knows,
the ethics of people in politics are at least as high as those in any other calling,
whether vocational or avocational.

Business has enjoyed considerably more success in building grassroots and
coalition programs than in fostering political participation, but even the best
of these programs can push unsympathetic legislators only so far. The best
way to take grassroots effectiveness to a higher plane is to add activities that
will involve business people and their local coalition allies in electing market-
oriented candidates to public office.

There are many steps individual companies can take to accomplish this,
including some newly sanctioned by the FEC.

- *Endorse candidates.* The FEC now permits corporations to expressly urge the election or defeat of federal candidates in brochures or other communications to managers, executives, and shareholders (though not to other employees) and to use
  corporate funds for this purpose. Announce the endorsement to the company's regular
  press list so that everyone in the community will learn of it. To keep the FEC
  happy, keep expenses minimal (how much can a press release cost?) and avoid any
  advance coordination with the candidate.

- *Hold meetings of shareholders, executives, and managers with the endorsed candidate.* Use phone banks to encourage them to register and vote for her or him; and
  provide them with transportation to the polls if necessary—again, all legally paid
  for with corporate funds. So long as the attendees are limited to the managerial
  class, you do not have to invite the preferred candidate's opponents to attend. Even
  if other employees will attend, opponents may be invited only if they ask.

- *Encourage the managerial class and shareholders to contribute personally to the
  candidate.* But avoid actually soliciting or collecting the money.

- *Sponsor nonpartisan voter registration and turnout drives, candidate visits, debates,
  and so on.* Any group of employees or the general public can be targeted, and as
  long as the event is nonpartisan, company funds can pay for it.

- *Integrate political action committee contributors with the grassroots program.* Encourage PAC contributors to participate in the grassroots program and grassroots
  network members to give to the PAC.

- *Expand grassroots training programs on government and politics to allow all managers, executives, shareholders, and spouses to participate.* Work with political
  party leaders to find opportunities for program graduates to become involved in
  local politics.

PACs and other vehicles for political contributions are important. Nevertheless, there simply is no substitute for direct personal involvement in partisan politics to establish and maintain a base for political—and ultimately, legislative—influence.

NOTES

1. "Survey of 414 individuals randomly selected from Federal Election Commission lists of contributors," *The Washington Post*, February 11, 1997, p. A–9.

2. Quoted in *The Washington Post*, January 29, 1997, p. A–12.

3. Business–Industry Political Action Committee, unpublished data from 87 PACs.

4. James E. Post and Jennifer J. Griffin, *The State of Corporate Public Affairs: 1996 Survey Results* (Washington, D.C.: Foundation for Public Affairs, 1997), Fig. 8.4.

5. *The Washington Post*, February 9, 1997, p. A–22.

Chapter 15

Communications and Technology

> Good government obtains when those who are near are made happy, and those who are far off are attracted.
>
> —Confucius

> Not every truth is the better for showing its face undisguised; and often silence is the wisest thing for a man to heed.
>
> —Pindar

Government relations is a communications process. In other chapters of this book, we have discussed the techniques of communicating issue positions to those who write and enforce laws and regulations and the use of other tactics and leverage to amplify the impact and effectiveness of the message.

Politics is also a communications process. Politics is a system of complex relationships, formal and informal, dependent on a vast array of communications for their establishment and maintenance.

Communications, in short, is the medium of politics and lobbying in all of their forms.

This chapter examines the different communications modes and target audiences discussed in earlier chapters and the application to them of new technologies.

The essence of education was once portrayed as a teacher sitting at one end of a log with the pupil at the other. In the same sense, it is the candidate and the voter who sit at opposite ends of the political log.

But lobbying communications are more complex. The process may start with the lobbyist and the lawmaker straddling the ends of the log, but soon the lobbyist gets up—possibly to be replaced by a constituent of the legislator, then by a campaign contributor, later perhaps by an ally with another interest group, and afterwards by another government official influential with the leg-islator. While they are talking, the lobbyist moves around discussing the issue with legislative staff aides and journalists. He may engage in political activity, either to reinforce the legislative relationship or possibly to replace the law-maker on the log with someone friendlier and more sympathetic. Finally the lobbyist comes back to the log and negotiates the best possible deal with the official sitting at the other end.

The whole time, communications have been taking place with those who make the decisions and with those who can help shape the forms the decision can take. Let's look first at those with whom the lobbyist has been talking and then examine the media used to talk with them.

TARGET AUDIENCES

As we have seen in previous chapters, there are various audiences with whom any interest group needs to consider communicating. For government relations purposes, the most important of these are the public officials who make and then administer the laws:

- Legislators
- Executive branch officials
- Regulators
- Key staff aides

Then, there are the intermediaries—constituents and others (family and friends) who can help carry the interest group's message to those officials.

Family
- Members (in the case of associations)
- Shareholders
- Executives and managers
- Other employees
- Retirees
- Spouses

Friends
- Trade associations and similar groups
- Suppliers of services as well as goods
- Customers and dealers
- Other elements of the interest group sector sharing a natural community of interest (e.g., other business organizations, other labor unions, other environmental or con-sumer groups, etc.)

Potential Allies

- Other interest group sectors
- Groups outside the natural community of interest who may be enlisted in coalitions on particular issues
- Local community officials and opinion leaders
- Intellectuals—academics and think tanks
- Political party committees and candidates
- The electorate—perhaps most important of all

The Media

- Newspapers and magazines
- Trade press
- Radio and television
- The Internet—increasingly utilized and important

COMMUNICATIONS STRATEGY AND TACTICS

A large array of communications can be used with these different audiences. Not all are appropriate to each, any more than the message should necessarily be identical. But each interest group should develop an overarching communications strategy and, within that comprehensive strategy, substrategies appropriate to each issue with which it deals.

Why an overall communications and outreach strategy? First, so that all those involved share a common understanding of the elements of message and tone to be conveyed. Second, to specify the image—the way people think of the company or group—that the organization wants to project to the world at large. (Actually, communications strategy should be a component of the organization's long-term mission and operating plan, but that is a subject for another discussion.)

Development of a communications strategy for a company or any other organization should deal with such questions as these:

- What its communications goals are—what essential corporate or organizational interests it wants to advance.
- What public image it desires and how that image should be fine-tuned among different target audiences. How to ensure that its actions and programs will receive understanding and approval among these audiences.
- When to speak out, to whom, and on what topics. Some companies, for example, may prefer to take a low public profile, speaking publicly on only one or two issues of the highest priority. In the name of labor solidarity, a union may have a policy of avoiding public comment on issues that put it at odds with another union.
- How to coordinate its public voice, a particular problem for multidivisional companies.

Audience research, including focus groups and market and public opinion surveys, is a valuable prelude to communications strategy development to determine how different audiences perceive the organization initially. Associations will find it helpful to know how the members perceive the group. Companies can obtain data about how managers, employees, and other internal constituencies view the firm, its management and policies, and its issue positions—important input before launching a PAC or grassroots program. Both kinds of organizations may want to probe the attitudes of opinion leaders and government officials before constructing a communications program to reach them.

As in every other aspect of government relations and public affairs, the support and involvement of the CEO and others in top management is critical in devising and executing communications strategies and programs. Not only is the chief executive's enthusiastic blessing essential to success in external (and indeed internal) communications, but top executives are now often their organizations' principal spokespeople and advocates on public issues.

Within the framework of the strategy and as appropriate to the issue and the audience, a number of basic communications mechanisms can be considered.

Newsletters

Newsletters are periodicals (that is, publications distributed with regular frequency), usually to an internal audience that may be either general or specialized. Examples of specialized internal audiences for government relations include grassroots program members and PAC contributors, among others. Newsletters can also be used with certain external audiences, such as coalition members.

The very word *newsletter* implies informative content. That certainly does not preclude statements of opinion, but people read newsletters for news and information. Newsletters can be used to motivate as much as to inform. While accuracy is vital, a dry recitation of dates and data is deadly. Like the content, the style and tone of a newsletter should reflect the interests of the audience. The same issue information may need to be interpreted differently to retirees than to active employees; franchisees and other small business owners tend to be more responsive to an emotional tone, even on economic issues, than corporate executives are. The purpose of the message is not only to convey facts but also to stimulate a sense of personal involvement in the issue on which action sooner or later will be requested.

Because computerization facilitates fine tuning of newsletter distribution, it is possible and sometimes useful to vary the content and style of the newsletter for different audiences. Different issues can be discussed with different recipients, according to their interests. Political topics, for example, can be discussed in depth with more sophisticated groups (such as executives, PAC supporters) or with retirees who have more leisure time.

Design and layout are important to stimulate newsletter interest. Logos, illustrations, and other graphics; attractive use of color, typefaces, and column layout—all enhance the readability of the newsletter. The writing may be positively scintillating, but if the design has a drab look, that deathless prose may never be read.

Personalized Communications

People do not always think about personal letters when considering potent communications media, but a carefully executed personalized letter can be powerful indeed. Even in an age of overflowing mailboxes, everyone likes to get personal mail, and many people read personal letters before they look at anything else. Personalized letters are useful in connection with grassroots programs, messages to allies and thought leaders, issue advocacy, PAC communications, and of course in communicating with public officials. Computer software facilitates a high degree of personalization so that letters, even more than newsletters, can be very finely tuned to the interests of the recipients.

To be credible, however, a letter should look and read like a letter and not the fancy product of a well-trained computer. Form and content should be guided by purpose: A letter appealing for legislative action needs to be constructed quite differently from one appealing for funds. Direct mail consultants can advise about such matters although it is important to be sure that the communications they produce reflect, in format, tone, and content, a message with which the signer of the letter is comfortable and that is appropriate to the intended recipients. Professional fund-raisers, for example, believe that multipage letters with copious enclosures produce more returns than a brief note; presumably they know what they are talking about.

On the other hand, letters to busy executives are likely to go unread if they exceed a single page. A good letter should state its purpose and a brief summary of its content in the first paragraph or two.

As noted in other chapters, a personalized letter should look *personal*, avoiding the use of envelope labels, computer codes, preprinted signatures, and other giveaways that this is a mass-produced communication. Other people screen the mail for top executives, and the more personal and important it appears, the more likely it is to reach the intended recipient.

Position Papers

Position papers are moderately detailed analyses of the issue, its pros and cons, and the rationale underlying the organization's position. Although they are primarily used by lobbyists, who leave them with legislators and staff, they can also be utilized as background information for the press or as attachments to a press release. They can also be used for internal or membership communications, such as grassroots education. *White papers* are a more comprehensive, research-oriented version of position papers, perhaps suitable for academics, legislative researchers, and other analysts who want in-depth material. At the other extreme are *issue fact sheets*—terser, more simplified versions used where a brief explanation is required, internally or externally.

Depending on their intended use, these three types of issue analyses can be prepared as unadorned documents or printed as brochures to present the organization's case in a visually attractive form, perhaps with graphics or other illustrations.

News Releases

Assuming the interest group wants to get press coverage about itself or its government relations activities, which is often but not invariably the case, the standard form to announce news is a press release. Announcements can be made to the press of candidate endorsements, organizational developments, special events, issue positions, issue-oriented research findings, and other news. Publication of a white paper might merit a news release, for instance, if it contains new information, such as results of an opinion survey or research project.

Apart from the subject of the announcement itself, the value of news releases is their promotion of media coverage that can not only make the organization better known to the public but also help influence its image—the way people think about the company or group. For this reason, there is enormous competition for good media coverage. No one can be sure the press will report the news as the organization wants, or even report it at all, but two techniques can help.

The first is cultivation of reporters and editors, in both the electronic and the print media. Public relations professionals develop relationships and reputations as helpful sources of accurate and reliable information, just as lobbyists do. Those relationships, built over time, can increase the likelihood of press coverage and fair reporting.

The second is the newsworthiness of the announcement and the professionalism of the release. Correct emphasis of the information presented is quite important. Some people write the way they tell a story, holding the punch line until the very end. But reporters (and readers) may never get past the first paragraph or two. For that reason, press releases, like news stories themselves, should always lead with the most important points, followed by identification of the announcer and then with appropriate amplification and documentation. Newspapers can print a press release verbatim, but they almost never do. Television and radio stations invariably condense a story, unless there is something in it that warrants feature coverage. Still, the release should quickly tell editors and reporters what the story is all about. Press releases can be delivered anywhere via fax or e-mail.

Press Conferences

Press conferences are meetings with reporters—national, regional, local, or trade, as appropriate—for important announcements. Because they provide opportunities for interviews with both print and electronic journalists, they can be a good way to stimulate news coverage if a story warrants. Press conferences need to be prepared with extra care since reporters will usually pose the most difficult questions they can, often in an aggressive manner intended to build a good story—good for the media, not necessarily for the organization. *Press kits* are often distributed; these might include a news release, issue brochures or fact sheets, background information on the organization, and the like.

Closed-circuit television and teleconferencing enable an interest group to hold press conferences with journalists anywhere.

Editorial Briefings

A supportive editorial in a local or national newspaper can often be very influential with legislators and officials on a current issue. Meetings with the paper's editorial board, usually preceded or accompanied by position papers, help explain the organization's views on the issue. Local television stations sometimes run editorials as well.

Third-Party Columns

A supportive column, a guest editorial, or an op-ed page article by a well-known expert or celebrity with no official connection with the interest group can be pure gold. So can an article by a coalition spokesperson, especially someone affiliated with a nonbusiness group (assuming the issue is an economic one). Almost as good is a similar piece under the by-line of a company or association officer. *Letters to the editor* may also generate attention. Like press releases, these materials can be sent by fax or e-mail.

Television and Radio Interviews

Television and radio interviews, including talk show appearances, are excellent (but also potentially dangerous) opportunities to explain the organization's issue positions. Thanks to communications satellites, the guest and the interviewer can be thousands of miles apart. Interviews are valuable because the spokesperson for the company or association can explain the group's position to a wide public audience without the problems of press interpretation. The hazard lies in the risk of a misstatement or poor answer to a tough question. Debates with issue opponents can be just as valuable and at least as hazardous (just as risky, of course, for the other side). *Actualities,* taped or telephoned issue statements provided to radio stations for use in newscasts, are useful and much safer, though less exciting.

Issue Advertising

Also called "advocacy advertising," this is the best way to assure that the interest group's message reaches the public unfiltered by the press. Developed originally by such companies as Mobil to enunciate issue positions and to build a positive corporate image, advocacy advertising is now widely used by companies, business associations, and a wide range of other groups. In labor disputes, for instance, management and unions have each placed ads to explain their side to the public. For similar reasons, many interest groups advertise their positions on legislative positions, even though few lawmakers admit to being influenced by them. Issue ads can also reinforce enthusiasm among coalition allies and grassroots participants.

It is difficult today to find an issue of a national newspaper or a magazine widely read by opinion leaders without seeing several advocacy ads, more often image ads than ads promoting an issue position. Archer Daniels Midland (ADM), the large agribusiness corporation, has sponsored such ads on all the Sunday morning public affairs talk shows for years; they undoubtedly helped sustain ADM's image during an embarrassing antitrust case. Defense contractors have also advertised frequently on these same shows, widely watched by opinion leaders and Washington policymakers.

Perhaps the best known issue ads were the "Harry and Louise" series sponsored by the Health Insurance Association during the 1993–1994 health care debate in Congress. Although Harry and Louise may not have influenced many members of Congress directly, they generated a substantial amount of congressional mail that *did* cut very deeply into public support for President Clinton's proposal and eventually helped defeat it.

The legitimacy of such ads was upheld by the U.S. Supreme Court, which ruled in its 1978 *Bellotti* decision that corporations have the same First Amendment rights as individuals. The court said that the plaintiff's ads were "the type of speech indispensable to decision-making in a democracy, and this is no less true because the speech comes from a corporation rather than an individual."

A series of subsequent rulings by various federal courts have broadened the rights of interest groups to engage in issue advertising. In 1996, advocacy ads were widely used by a variety of organizations to influence congressional elections. (See Chapter 14 for more on this subject.)

To be effective, an ad must be well written, readable, and interesting, with a clearly understandable message. The full-page ads of closely spaced small type often found in major newspapers—calling for the liberation of the Nagobichi Nine or the overthrow of the dictator of Tyrannistan—are usually a waste of money; few people will bother to plow though all that dense prose, let alone act on its message. An issue ad should appeal to readers' self-interest, sense of fairness or justice, or in some other way reach their emotions.

COMMUNICATIONS GUIDELINES

As organizations have sought to reach out to a widening circle of constituencies and allies in their search for support on public policy issues, the arts and expertise of public relations, advertising, and communications have become increasingly interrelated with those of government relations. In most large companies, public relations and government relations are now part of the corporate public affairs organization, and advertising often is as well.

The skills of public relations communicators are valuable in developing and deploying government relations materials for various target audiences. In some cases, it may be appropriate to utilize outside consultants, public relations firms, or advertising agencies—either to prepare materials or at least to provide an independent and objective evaluation for advertising, publications, or the press. Such an evaluation should include an appraisal of both text and the appropriateness of the intended medium, depending on the objective of the planned communication.

On the other hand, if materials are prepared on the outside, they should be carefully scrutinized to assure that the message has not strayed from plan and strategy. It is important not only to verify facts but also to be sure the tone is right and consistent; if the point is to convey the organization's concern and caring about a public problem, for instance, tough and aggressive language may be inappropriate; and vice versa.

For better or worse, there is no such thing as assured confidentiality in government relations or public affairs communications. In the words of the old public relations adage, "If you don't want to see it in *The New York Times* or on the evening news, don't say it at all." Truthfulness and credibility are therefore absolute imperatives.

The following checklist of generally accepted principles can help assure that the interest group's objectives and credibility are protected in all its public communications.

Public Involvement Issues should be framed to show how the public benefits from your side of the argument. Don't go public with a narrow, self-serving issue. If a moral principle is at stake (e.g., discrimination or injustice), lead with it. Citizens understand that if it can happen to you, it could happen to them.

Audience Targeting Identify the target audience before choosing the medium. That way, content can be specifically addressed to the particular group the organization wants to reach, and costs are held down.

Accuracy and Fairness If facts, data, and quotations are inaccurate or misleading, everything else the organization says will also be open to challenge. It may or may not be appropriate to include the other side's views (to arm

friends and advocates and provide rebuttal arguments), but they should be
reported fairly or not at all. Candor in stating how the issue will benefit your
side may take the wind out of attacks by the opposition if the information is
likely to come out anyhow.

Moderation and Balance Extreme statements, improbable predictions, and
heavy-handed language also endanger credibility. Statements likely to be met
with skeptical reactions should be documented. Threats are usually unwise
since they generate anger and risk retaliation; a threat (such as closing a plant
or facility if a certain bill passes) should not be expressed unless there is a
clear determination to carry it out. Political threats are always a mistake.

Simplicity and Clarity Language should be clear and grammatically correct, arguments and statements simple. Jargon should always be avoided. If
technical terms must be used, explain them. Don't over-inform; excessive details produce glazed eyes and tuned-out minds.

TECHNOLOGY AND COMMUNICATIONS

Technology continues to transform communications. Innovations are announced almost daily that utilize everything from personal computers and the
Internet to communications satellites. PCs today have many times the capabilities of the huge mainframes of only a few years ago. They not only can
generate all kinds of data and documents but, thanks to modems and the Internet,
can receive and send them anywhere in the world almost instantly.

All areas of government relations are being altered by the new technologies, but the greatest impacts are increased capabilities to identify, reach, and
motivate grassroots legislative communications. Technology cannot only get
more people involved, it can also get them more *intensely* involved. Sheer
numbers can be an overwhelming influence, as the senior citizens' lobby frequently demonstrates. But one needs look no further than the National Rifle
Association to see how intensity of member attitudes can transcend mere volume in grassroots effectiveness.

Communications technologies provide an enormous number and variety of
ways to reach highly specific population subgroups, including individual communities and neighborhoods. Many techniques are used now (or soon will be)
in government relations.

Cable television provides government relations professionals with a whole
new quiver of highly targetable communications arrows for influencing public opinion on their issues. With the proliferation and specialization of local
cable channels, relatively inexpensive advertising time can enable interest
groups to reach people in specific legislative districts or particular demographic
groups. This kind of capability will grow as more and more homes (not just
those in rural areas) acquire systems to let them access satellite feeds directly.

Communications satellites can be used for a variety of government relations purposes, ranging from teleconferencing to propagandizing. Satellite

technology is used to direct press releases, interviews, and features to local cable or broadcast television news departments anywhere. Satellite communications can be used to get any kind of message across to any group—to recruit, train, inform, motivate, propagandize, or fund-raise. *Teleconferencing* uses satellite transmissions to bring together people scattered across a number of locations in a single, live electronic meeting.

The *Internet* offers similar capabilities through the use of homepages and e-mail. Like teleconferencing (though without its visual element), the Internet can provide interactivity and two-way communications. The number of frequent Internet users is still modest, but it grows exponentially every year. Computers are becoming less expensive all the time, even as their capabilities multiply. Interactive integration of computers and home television is now in its infancy, but the day is probably not far off when people at home can send messages by satellite (perhaps using the Internet or cellular telephones as intermediaries) as easily as they now receive them. Candidates now use the Internet to reach voters. Internet fax is an emerging technology. The medium is also being used to conduct surveys. Internet advertisements can be purchased for issue advocacy purposes, and issue statements can also be included on homepages.

The implications of existing and emerging technologies for all kinds of government relations communications are enormous. The only limiting factor will be cost-effectiveness. Some communications techniques are more expensive than others, just as some tactics are more effective than others. For a number of interest groups, cost alone will be a limiting factor (although some technologies, like the Internet and local cable TV, can be relatively inexpensive). For others, the question will be not cost itself but cost-effectiveness. If the issue is important enough and the stakes large enough, both companies and membership organizations of all kinds will find a steadily widening array of communications media available with which to accomplish their legislative aims.

There will always be a need for direct lobbyists to close a deal, but it is in the area of grassroots communications that the future of government relations lies. There is always the risk that instant and universal communications will produce public policies based on the whim of the moment, without sufficient time for reflection and interest group interaction. Some interest groups will gain as a result and some will lose—but that has always been true. The more information the public can get from an increasing array of sources, the better the choices they and their elected representatives will be able to make. And that, surely, is no bad thing in a democracy.

Appendix

Sources and Resources

NATIONAL NEWSPAPERS

Several newspapers with national circulation are sources of information about national and international issues and regional developments.

The Atlanta Constitution
The Chicago Tribune
The Christian Science Monitor
The Los Angeles Times
The New York Times
The Wall Street Journal
The Washington Post

Note that *The Washington Post* publishes a national weekly edition, available by mail subscription, which covers political and governmental news stories and analyses nationwide. *The New York Times* publishes regional editions whose news content differs somewhat in various parts of the country.

FEDERAL ISSUES TRACKING AND INFORMATION

Periodicals on Federal Issues and Politics

Amid the slew of Washington information services, two are preeminent.

Congressional Quarterly Weekly Report CQ, as it is universally known, publishes a large number of Washington information sources. Its weekly magazine is a highly respected and authoritative guide to developments in Congress and politics, covering major legislation and congressional voting records. *CQ* also publishes a number of reference books (e.g., compendia of current and historical election statistics) and directories. Some of these are listed later. (Congressional Quarterly, Inc., 1414 22nd Street, NW, Washington, DC 20037)

National Journal This publication, also weekly, is the other indispensable guide to major federal policymaking. *National Journal* focuses more on developments in the executive and regulatory agencies than *CQ* does and is more analytical than descriptive. Emerging trends and issues are well covered. (National Journal, Inc., 1501 M Street, NW, Washington, DC 20005)

Several other publications cover government and politics in varying degrees of depth and quality.

Daily Report for Executives This voluminous newsletter provides authoritative coverage of legislative, executive, regulatory, and judicial developments on tax, business, and economic subjects, often including full texts of key documents and reports. Published in both print and electronic media. (Bureau of National Affairs, P.O. Box 40947, Washington, DC 20077–4928)

The Washington Times, a local newspaper, reports generally on national politics and legislation.

Two specialized newspapers report on congressional politics.

Roll Call: The Newspaper of Capitol Hill is published twice a week. (900 Second Street, NW, Washington, DC 20002)

The Hill This newspaper is published weekly. (733 15th Street, NW, Washington, DC 20005)

Newsletters and Other Political Publications

Washington floats on a sea of politics—partisan and personal, ideological, and institutional. Newsletters and other political publications abound. Many pontificate, a few are insightful and occasionally profound. All claim to offer an insider's analysis, and some do.

The American Political Report National and state political trends and developments. Kevin Phillips, editor. (American Political Research Corp., 4715 Cordell Avenue, Fifth Floor, Bethesda, MD 20814. Biweekly)

Business & Public Affairs Business and politics, social issues, lobbying, public opinion. Kevin Phillips, editor. (American Political Research Corp., 4715 Cordell Avenue, Fifth Floor, Bethesda, MD 20814. Biweekly)

Campaigns and Elections Magazine of news and analysis on management, techniques, and regulation of the political wars. (Campaigns and Elections, 1511 K Street, NW, Washington, DC 20005–1450. Quarterly)

Congress Daily Reports on the politics of legislation. Distributed by fax, e-mail, and (in Washington only) hand. (National Journal, Inc., 1501 M Street, NW, Washington, DC 20005)

CQ Monitor A daily schedule of hearings and other events on Capitol Hill. (Congressional Quarterly, Inc., 1414 22nd Street, NW, Washington, DC 20037)

The Cook Political Report Information on Senate and House election campaigns. Charles Cook, editor. (Government Research Corp., 1250 Connecticut Avenue, NW, Washington, DC 20036. Issued approximately every six weeks)

Corporate Public Issues Newsletter on issues management. (Issue Action Publications, 207 Loudoun Street, SE, Leesburg, VA 20175–3115. Semimonthly)

Elections InSight Comprehensive political analyses on congressional candidates and campaigns, political action committee operations, and the politics of major national issues. Bernadette A. Budde, editor. (Business–Industry Political Action Committee, 888 16th Street, NW, Washington, DC 20006. Monthly)

The Evans-Novak Political Report Commentary on politics by the syndicated columnists. (Eagle Publishing, Inc., 422 First Street, SE, Washington, DC 20003. Weekly)

Hotline: The Daily Briefing on American Politics Digest of news and commentary on politics from the national media. (The American Political Network, Inc., 3129 Mt. Vernon Avenue, Alexandria, VA 22305. Daily, distributed on line)

Impact Useful articles on government relations and public affairs. Wes Pedersen, editor. (Public Affairs Council, 2033 K Street, Suite 200, NW, Washington, DC 20006. Monthly)

The Rothenburg Political Report Analysis of national politics. Stuart Rothenburg, editor. (900 Second Street, NE, Suite 107, Washington, DC 20002)

The Southern Political Report Political trends, developments, and issues in the 12 states from Virginia to Texas. Hastings Wyman, Jr., editor. (P.O. Box 15507, Washington, DC 20003–5507. Biweekly)

Almanacs and Directories on the Federal Government

The number of directories listing people who make or influence policy in Washington seems almost limitless. Some, like the *Congressional Directory*, are published by the U.S. Government Printing Office whose catalogs are worth consulting. Most of the best ones are issued by commercial publishers. The following list notes many of the good ones, some of which can cost close to $300. Since there are often editions from competing publishers with varying ways of presenting the information, check them out in public and university libraries before buying to make sure you get what you need.

Leadership Directories, Inc. (104 Fifth Avenue, New York, NY 10011) publishes a number of directories called Yellow Books.

Associations Yellow Book Officers and staff of trade associations with budgets over $1 million. Semiannual

Congressional Yellow Book Members of Congress (including committee assignments) and key staff personnel. Quarterly

Federal Regional Yellow Book Over 30,000 officials in regional offices outside Washington. Semiannual

Federal Yellow Book Lists 38,000 officials of the executive branch, including regulatory agencies. Quarterly

Foreign Representatives in the U.S. Yellow Book Personnel of embassies, consulates, international organizations, plus U.S. representatives of foreign companies. Semiannual

Government Affairs Yellow Book Government relations professionals and outside lobbyists (federal and state) of companies and other organizations. Semiannual

Judicial Yellow Book All federal judges and staff. Semiannual

News Media Yellow Book Directory of journalists for national media. Quarterly

Columbia Books, Inc. (1212 New York Avenue, NW, Washington, DC 20005).

National Directory of Corporate Public Affairs Directory of 15,000 public and government affairs professionals in 2,000 corporations. Annual

National Trade and Professional Associations List of 7,500 associations and labor unions and key executives. Annual

Washington Representatives List of over 15,000 people in the Washington area representing companies and other organizations. Annual

Washington Lists 22,000 personnel with 4,400 Washington-based organizations in a variety of fields. Annual

Carroll Publishing (1058 Thomas Jefferson Street, NW, Washington, DC 20077–0007). CD-ROM versions are available free on request for purchasers of the print editions.

Federal Directory Lists 35,000 officials in the executive and legislative branches. Six times a year

Federal Regional Directory Lists 20,000 officials in federal field offices. Semiannual

Almanac Publishing Co. (P.O. Box 3785, Washington, DC 20007). CD-ROM versions are available.

The Almanac of the Executive Branch Profiles of 600 officials. Annual

The Almanac of the Unelected Biographies and responsibilities of 700 congressional staff members. Annual

The Washington Almanac of International Trade & Business Directory of 10,000 personnel with embassies, international organizations, media, lobbying firms, as well as federal officials concerned with foreign policy. Annual

Staff Directories, Ltd. (P.O. Box 62, Mt. Vernon, VA 22121).

Congressional Staff Directory Comprehensive reference to the legislative branch. Semiannual

Federal Staff Directory Directory of federal officials. Semiannual

Judicial Staff Directory Guide to the judicial branch. Annual

Other Reference Works

Federal Regulatory Directory Descriptions of regulatory agencies, the laws they enforce, and the officials who enforce them. (Congressional Quarterly, Inc., 1414 22nd Street, NW, Washington, DC 20037. Biannual)

Washington Information Directory Names, addresses, and telephone numbers for the federal government and private groups, by subject. (Congressional Quarterly, Inc., 1414 22nd Street, NW, Washington, DC 20037. Biannual)

Almanac of American Politics A wealth of political material including information on members of Congress and governors, with excellent profiles of their constituencies. By Michael Barone and Grant Ujifusa. (National Journal, Inc., 1501 M Street, NW, Washington, DC 20005. Biannual)

The Capital Source Directory of "the 7,000 most important people and organizations in Washington." (National Journal, Inc., 1501 M Street, NW, Washington, DC 20005. Semiannual)

Encyclopedia of Associations This is *the* compendium of interest groups of every shape and kind imaginable. A multivolume set that grows with each edition. (Gale Research Inc., 835 Penobscot Building, Detroit, MI 48226–4094. Annual)

Political Resource Directory A list of political consultants. (Political Resources, Inc., P.O. Box 3177, Burlington, VT 05401. Annual)

Politics in America In-depth profiles of each senator and representative. (Congressional Quarterly, Inc., 1414 22nd Street, NW, Washington, DC 20037. Biannual)

Public Interest Profiles Comprehensive descriptions of about 250 public interest and public policy groups from far right to far left and everything in between. Provides information on each organization relating to scope and interests, political orientation, funding sources, effectiveness, staff, budget, board of directors, etc. Compiled by the Foundation for Public Affairs. (Congressional Quarterly, Inc., 1414 22nd Street, NW, Washington, DC 20037. Biannual)

Federal Election Commission Publications

Campaign Guide for Corporations and Labor Unions Washington: 1996.

Campaign Guide for Nonconnected Committees Washington: 1996.

Combined Federal/State Disclosure Directory Washington: 1996.

Campaign Finance Law 96 Washington: 1996.

Federal Election Campaign Laws Washington: 1994.

Selected Court Case Abstracts Washington: 1997.

Supporting Federal Candidates: A Guide for Citizens Washington: 1996.

National Resource Organizations

Many national organizations, each with its own point of view, provide information on issues. Others are resources on governmental, political, or lobbying processes. Listed here are some of the more significant groups. (For others, see *Public Interest Profiles*, cited in the section on other reference works.) All those shown here issue newsletters or other publications that may or may not be restricted to members.

AFL–CIO Committee on Political Education (labor)
    815 Sixteenth Street, NW, Washington, DC 20006

American League of Lobbyists (lobbyists of all philosophic persuasions)
    P.O. Box 30005, Alexandria, VA 22310

American Society of Association Executives (associations' trade association)
    1575 Eye Street, NW, Washington, DC 20005–1168

Business–Industry Political Action Committee (leadership PAC for business)
888 16th Street, NW, Washington, DC 20006

Center for Responsive Politics (pro-reform analyses of campaign finance)
1320 19th Street, NW, Washington, DC 20036

Citizens Research Foundation (comprehensive studies on campaign finance)
3716 South Hope Street, Los Angeles, CA 90007

Chamber of Commerce of the United States (world's largest business association)
1615 H Street, NW, Washington, DC 20062

National Association of Business PACs (lobbying group)
901 North Stuart Street, Arlington, VA 22203

National Association of Manufacturers (one of the giants)
1331 Pennsylvania Avenue, NW, Washington, DC 20004

National Federation of Independent Business (major small business lobby)
600 Maryland Ave., SW, Washington, DC 20024

Public Affairs Council and Foundation for Public Affairs (association for business public affairs professionals)
2033 K Street, NW, Washington, DC 20006

U.S. Federal Election Commission (political regulator at the national level)
999 E Street, NW, Washington, DC 20463

STATE AND LOCAL ISSUES TRACKING AND INFORMATION

Periodicals

Newsletters on politics and legislation are published in many states and are listed in the *State Legislative Sourcebook* (see the section on state almanacs and directories).

Governing General issues in state and local government. (Congressional Quarterly, Inc., 2300 N Street, NW, Washington, DC 20037. Monthly)

Political Finance & Lobby Reporter Updates on developments. (Amward Publications, Inc., 2030 Clarendon Boulevard, Arlington, VA 22201. Biweekly)

State Government News Information on state policies and programs. (Council of State Governments, P.O. Box 11910, Lexington, KY 40578–1910. Monthly)

State Legislatures Topics of broad interest on state legislation and government. (National Conference of State Legislatures, Suite 700, 1560 Broadway, Denver, CO 80202. Monthly)

State Trends & Forecasts Studies on long-term changes in state government. (Council of State Governments, P.O. Box 11910, Lexington, KY 40578–1910)

State Almanacs and Directories

The following are general works covering the fifty states. If no address is shown, the publishing organization is listed under "Resource Groups."

The Almanac of State Legislatures Color maps and demographic data for legislative districts. By William Lilley III et al. (Congressional Quarterly, Inc., 1414 22nd Street, NW, Washington, DC 20037. 1994)

Book of the States An exhaustive and authoritative statistical compendium on numerous aspects of state government. (Council of State Governments. Biannual)

Campaign Finance, Ethics & Lobby Law Blue Book Summaries of laws and pertinent data for the states and the U.S. and Canadian federal governments. (Council of State Governments for an affiliate, the Council on Governmental Ethics Laws. Biannual)

Carroll's State Directory List of 37,000 executive and legislative officials. Print plus CD-ROM editions. (Carroll Publishing, 1058 Thomas Jefferson Street, NW, Washington, DC 20077–0007)

Carroll's Municipal Directory List of 35,000 municipal officials in 7,800 communities. Print plus CD-ROM editions. (Carroll Publishing, 1058 Thomas Jefferson Street, NW, Washington, DC 20077–0007)

Carroll's County Directory List of officials in counties. Print plus CD-ROM editions. (Carroll Publishing, 1058 Thomas Jefferson Street, NW, Washington, DC 20077–0007)

Compendium of State Lobbying Laws Information on state lobbying requirements, official interpretations, and sample registration forms. (State and Federal Communications, Inc., Suite 225, 1755 Merriman Road, Akron, OH 44313–5256. Semiannual)

Executive's Handbook on Political Contributions Summaries of campaign finance laws in each of the states, with calendars of reporting deadlines and elections, and lists of state compliance officers. (State and Federal Communications, Inc., Suite 225, 1755 Merriman Road, Akron, OH 44313–5256. Semiannual)

Lobbying, PACs and Campaign Finance 50 State Handbook Descriptions of each state's laws. (West Publishing Co., 610 Opperman Drive, Eagan, MN 55123. Biannual)

State Legislative Sourcebook By Lynn Hellebust. An indispensable resource guide to the legislative systems in each of the states. The book contains extensive information on legislators, lobbying, and legislative process and schedule, political newsletters, and much additional information. Telephone numbers for legislative status data and copies of bills are provided for every state. (Government Research Service, 214 SW Sixth Ave., Topeka, KS 66603. Annual)

State and Regional Associations of the U.S. Directory of 7,500 trade and professional associations. (Columbia Books, Inc., 1212 New York Avenue, NW, Washington, DC 20078–1744. Annual)

State Yellow Book Directory of executive and legislative officials in each state and of various intergovernmental organizations. (Leadership Directories, Inc., 104 Fifth Avenue, New York, NY 10011. Quarterly)

Resource Groups on State and Local Government

State and local lawmakers and officials are great joiners. There are associations of lieutenant governors and attorneys general, as well as the better known organizations of legislators and governors, among many others. These organizations exist to provide their members with opportunities to exchange information and ideas with peers from other states and localities concerning potential new policies, programs, and operations. If a state or local government develops new programs on AIDS, solid waste management, or budget controls, these organizations are the media by which counterparts across the country are kept posted, often through vast publication programs.

Many of these groups maintain corporate support programs and other channels to the private sector, as sources of both revenue and ideas. They are valuable resource groups because they provide opportunities both to influence public policy concepts on almost a wholesale level and also to develop contacts among state and local legislators and officials nationwide. The more significant associations are listed here.

American Legislative Exchange Council (conservative legislators)
    910 17th Street, NW, Washington, DC 20002

Council of State Governments
    P.O. Box 11910, Lexington, KY 40578–1910

Initiative Resource Center (information on initiatives and referenda)
    235 Douglass Street, San Francisco, CA 94114

International City County Management Association
    (professional municipal administrators)
    777 North Capitol Street, NE, Washington, DC 20002

National Association of Attorneys General
    750 First Street, NE, Washington, DC 20002

National Association of Counties
    440 First Street, NW, Washington, DC 20001

National Conference of State Legislators
    1050 17th Street, Denver, CO 80265
    also, 444 North Capitol Street, NW, Washington, DC 20001

National Governors Association
    444 North Capitol Street, NW, Washington, DC 20001

National League of Cities (most populous cities)
    1301 Pennsylvania Avenue, NW, Washington, DC 20004

U.S. Conference of Mayors (large and medium-sized cities)
    1620 Eye Street, NW, Washington, DC 20006

State Governmental Affairs Council (Private-sector association of over 100 companies
    and trade associations. It maintains liaison between its members and some of the
    state public-sector groups. Membership is open to organizations doing business
    in four or more states with full-time state government relations programs.)
    1255 23rd Street, NW, Washington, DC 20037

ELECTRONIC GOVERNMENT RELATIONS PROGRAMS
AND ISSUES TRACKING

Many management software programs and database libraries are available commercially to help government relations executives manage political action committees, grassroots programs, lobbying reports, redistricting, coalitions, media coverage, and the like. One firm, for instance, provides modular packages to manage federal and state PACs, grassroots, lobbying and lobbying tax reporting, media relations, and issues management. (Gnossos Software, 1625 K Street, NW, Washington, DC 20006–1604.) Because this is an industry in flux, contact the Public Affairs Council for an up-to-date list of providers and services.

Issues tracking is also highly computerized today. Several firms offer on-line federal legislative and regulatory tracking, plus some supplemental information. At the state level, direct access to the legislature's own tracking system is allowed in most states. Commercial services also cover about half the states, including all the larger ones. Both official and commercial services are updated in annual editions of *State Legislative Sourcebook*. Updated information on official state systems is also available from the National Conference of State Legislatures. The Public Affairs Council has information on commercial systems.

Legi-Slate On-line issues tracking in Congress and federal agencies, plus legislative database and voting records compiled by various groups. (Legi-Slate, 777 North Capitol Street, NW, Washington, DC 20002)

State Net Legislative and regulatory tracking, covering federal and state governments. (Information for Public Affairs, 1900 14th Street, Sacramento, CA 95814 and 1000 Potomac Street, Washington, DC 20007)

Washington Alert Service On-line congressional issues tracking. (Congressional Quarterly, Inc., 1414 22nd Street, NW, Washington, DC 20037)

Washington On-Line On-line congressional issues tracking. (Mead Data, 4200 Wilson Blvd., Arlington, VA 22203)

SELECTED WORLD WIDE WEB SITES

The number of web sites (a.k.a. "homepages") increases constantly, as does the scope of information contained in each. Quality of content varies considerably, but it is generally improving. Here are a few covering national government and politics. A more complete directory of political, federal, state, and interest group sites is found in *The Federal Internet Source*, published biannually by National Journal. (Parts of the sites for private organizations may be restricted to members and supporters. There may be a charge for accessing other sites. Government sites are free.)

http://www.senate.gov	U.S. Senate
http://www.house.gov	U.S. House of Representatives
http://www.thomas.loc.gov	Library of Congress. THOMAS covers legislation.
http://www.vote-smart.org	Project Vote Smart. State legislative tracking.
http:// www.fec.gov	Federal Election Commission information.
http://www.gpo.gov	U.S. Government publication catalogs and search engines.
http://www.bipac.org	BIPAC information on political developments.

http://www.europa.eu.int	Extensive information about the European Union.
http://www.pac.org	Public Affairs Council information on various public affairs topics, plus bulletin boards, software vendors, etc.
http://www.allpolitics.com	CNN/*Time* coverage of politics.
http://www.nytimes.com	*The New York Times* web site.
http://www.washingtonpost.com	*The Washington Post* web site.
http://www.wsj.com	*The Wall Street Journal* web site.
http://www.rollcall.com	*Roll Call* web site.

INTERNATIONAL ORGANIZATIONS

The following list notes major organizations affiliated with the United Nations. In addition, the United Nations itself comprises a large number of specialized subsidiaries. For further information, contact the U.N. Information Centers in New York or Washington.

Agency	Acronym	Headquarters
United Nations	UN	New York, Geneva, Vienna
Food and Agriculture Organization	FAO	Rome
International Atomic Energy Agency	IAEA	Vienna
International Civil Aviation Organization	ICAO	Montreal
International Fund for Agricultural Development	IFAD	Rome
International Labor Organization	ILO	Geneva
International Maritime Organization	IMO	London
International Monetary Fund	IMF	Washington
International Telecommunication Union	ITU	Geneva
United Nations Educational, Scientific and Cultural Organization	UNESCO	Paris
United Nations Industrial Development Organization	UNIDO	Vienna
Universal Postal Union	UPU	Berne
World Bank/International Finance Corporation	IFC	Washington
World Health Organization	WHO	Geneva
World Intellectual Property Organization	WIPO	Geneva
World Meteorological Organization	WMO	Geneva
World Tourism Organization	WToO	Madrid
World Trade Organization	WTO	Geneva

Selected Bibliography

The following publications deal with particular aspects of government relations for those interested in additional reading. Lists of periodicals, reference works, tracking services, resource groups, and related materials will be found in the appendix.

BOOKS

Alexander, Herbert E. *The Case for PACs*. Washington, D.C.: Public Affairs Council, 1983.

Alexander, Herbert E. *Financing Politics: Money, Elections, and Political Reform*. 4th ed. Washington, D.C.: CQ Press, 1992.

Alexander, Herbert E. *"Soft Money" and Campaign Financing*. Washington, D.C.: Public Affairs Council, 1986.

Alexander, Herbert E., and Rei Shiratori, eds. *Comparative Political Finance among the Democracies*. Boulder, Colo.: Westview Press, 1994.

Baran, Jan Witold. *The Election Law Primer for Corporations*. Chicago: American Bar Association, 1992.

Beck, Paul Allen, and Frank J. Sorauf. *Party Politics in America*. 7th ed. New York: HarperCollins, 1992.

Borchardt, Klaus-Dieter. *European Integration: The Origins and Growth of the European Union*. 4th ed. Luxembourg: Office for Official Publications of the European Communities, 1995.

Burson-Marsteller. *B-GRC Benchmark Study*. Washington, D.C.: Burson-Marsteller, 1994. (Survey of members of the Business–Government Relations Council, an organization of Washington corporate representatives.)

Business–Industry Political Action Committee. *Forward Thinking: What the Business Community Can Learn from the 1996 Elections to Protect Its Majority in Congress in 1998 and Beyond*. Washington, D.C.: The Committee, 1997.

Business–Industry Political Action Committee. *Reengineering Your PAC for the Next Century*. Washington, D.C.: The Committee, 1996.

Chase, W. Howard. *Issue Management: Origins of the Future*. Stamford, Conn.: Issue Action Publications, 1984.

Ciglar, Allan J., and Burdett A. Loomis, eds. *Interest Group Politics*. 4th ed. Washington, D.C.: Congressional Quarterly Press, 1995. (Each of the earlier editions contains different studies that are worth examining.)

Cowles, Maria Green. "The Politics of Big Business in the European Community: Setting the Agenda for a New Europe." Ph.D. dissertation. The American University, School of International Service, 1994. (A technical study of the role of three major European business associations.)

Delegation of the European Commission in the United States. *The European Union and the United States in the 1990s*. Washington, D.C.: The Delegation, 1996.

Dennis, Lloyd B., ed. *Practical Public Affairs in an Era of Change*. Lanham, Md.: University Press of America, 1996. (Chapters on various aspects of public affairs and government relations.)

Epstein, Edwin M. *The Corporation in American Politics*. Englewood Cliffs, N.J.: Prentice-Hall, 1969.

Ewing, Raymond P. *Managing the New Bottom Line: Issues Management for Senior Executives*. Homewood, Ill.: Dow Jones–Irwin, 1987.

Grefe, Edward A. *Fighting to Win: Business Political Power*. New York: Harcourt Brace Jovanovich, 1981.

Harris, Fred R., and Paul L. Hain. *America's Legislative Processes: Congress and the States*. Glenview, Ill.: Scott, Foresman & Co., 1983.

Hay Management Consultants. *1995–96 Washington Office Compensation Survey*. Washington, D.C.: Foundation for Public Affairs, 1995.

Hay Management Consultants. *1996–1997 Compensation Survey of Public Affairs Positions*. Washington, D.C.: Foundation for Public Affairs, 1996.

Heath, Robert L., and Associates. *Strategic Issues Management: How Organizations Influence and Respond to Public Interests and Policies*. San Francisco: Jossey-Bass, 1988.

Hrebenar, Ronald J., and Ruth K. Scott. *Interest Group Politics in America*. 2nd ed. Englewood Cliffs, N.J.: Prentice-Hall, 1990.

Hrebenar, Ronald J., and Clive S. Thomas, eds. *Interest Group Politics in the Midwestern States*. Ames: Iowa State University Press, 1993.

Hrebenar, Ronald J., and Clive S. Thomas, eds. *Interest Group Politics in the Southern States*. Tuscaloosa: University of Alabama Press, 1992.

Jewell, Malcolm E. *Representation in State Legislatures*. Lexington: University Press of Kentucky, 1982.

Jewell, Malcolm E., and Samuel C. Patterson. *The Legislative Process in the United States*. 4th ed. New York: Random House, 1985.

Key, V. O. *Politics, Parties, and Pressure Groups*. New York: Thomas Y. Crowell, 1964.

Kingdon, John W. *Agendas, Alternatives, and Public Policies*. 2nd ed. New York: HarperCollins, 1995.

Lowi, Theodore J. *The End of Liberalism*. 2nd ed. New York: Norton, 1979.

Mack, Charles S. *The Executive's Handbook of Trade and Business Associations*. Westport, Conn.: Quorum Books, 1991.

Magleby, David B. *Direct Legislation: Voting on Ballot Propositions in the United States*. Baltimore: Johns Hopkins University Press, 1984.

Mann, Thomas, and Norman J. Ornstein. *Congress, the Press and the Public*. Washington, D.C.: American Enterprise Institute and the Brookings Institution, 1994.

Mann, Thomas, and Norman J. Ornstein. *Intensive Care: How Congress Shapes Health Policy*. Washington, D.C.: American Enterprise Institute and the Brookings Institution, 1995.

Mater, Jean. *Public Hearings, Procedures and Strategies: A Guide to Influencing Public Decisions*. Englewood Cliffs, N.J.: Prentice-Hall, 1984.

McGuigan, Patrick B. *The Politics of Direct Democracy in the 1980s: Case Studies in Popular Decision Making*. Washington, D.C.: The Institute for Government and Politics of the Free Congress Research and Education Foundation, 1985.

Peirce, Neal R., and Jerry Hagstrom. *The Book of America: Inside 50 States Today*. New York: Norton, 1983.

Post, James E., and Jennifer J. Griffin, *The State of Corporate Public Affairs: 1996 Survey Results*. Washington, D.C.: Foundation for Public Affairs, 1997.

Rosenthal, Alan. *Legislative Life: People, Process, and Performance in the States*. New York: Harper & Row, 1981.

Rosenthal, Alan. *The Third House: Lobbyists and Lobbying in the States*. Washington, D.C.: CQ Press, 1993.

Sethi, S. Prakash. *Handbook of Advocacy Advertising: Concepts, Strategies and Applications*. Cambridge, Mass.: Ballinger, 1987.

Sorauf, Frank J. *Inside Campaign Finance: Myth and Realities*. New Haven: Yale University Press, 1992.

Sorauf, Frank J. *Money in American Elections*. Glenview, Ill.: Scott, Foresman and Company, 1988.

Stanbury, W. T. *Business–Government Relations in Canada: Grappling with Leviathan*. Toronto: Methuen, 1986.

Truman, David B. *The Governmental Process*. New York: Alfred A. Knopf, 1964.

ARTICLES AND ESSAYS

Achenbach, Joel. "The Staffers of Life." *The Washington Post*, January 6, 1997, p. C-1.

Bureau of National Affairs, Inc. "Lobbying in The European Union." *Daily Report for Executives*, July 28, 1994.

Coates, Dennis, and Michael Munger. "Legislative Voting and the Economic Theory of Politics." *Southern Economic Journal*, January 1995.

Cowles, Maria Green. "The EU Committee of AmCham: The Powerful Voice of American Firms in Brussels." *Journal of European Public Policy* 3 (3), 1996.

Cowles, Maria Green. "The European Round Table of Industrialists." In *European Casebook on Business Alliances*, edited by Justin Greenwood, Case 16. London: Prentice-Hall, 1995.

Edwards, Richard. "The Ethics of Lobbying." *Ethics: Easier Said Than Done*, Spring/Summer 1988, p. 106.

Faucheaux, Ron. "The Grassroots Explosion." *Campaigns & Elections*, December/January 1995.

Grier, Kevin B., and Michael C. Munger. "Committee Assignments, Constituent Preferences, and Campaign Contributions." *Economic Inquiry*, January 1991.

Jacobson, Louis. "Tanks on the Roll." *National Journal*, July 8, 1995.

Lanzalaco, Luca. "Constructing Political Unity by Combining Organizations: UNICE as a European Peak Association." In *European Casebook on Business Alliances*, edited by Justin Greenwood, Case 18. London: Prentice-Hall, 1995.

Meng, Max. "Early Identification Aids Issues Management." *Public Relations Journal*, March 1992.

Nord, Nancy A., and William H. Minor. "The New Lobbying Disclosure Act: What You Need to Know to Comply." *ACCA Docket*, July/August 1996. (Published by the American Corporate Counsel Association.)

Wheeler, Douglas P. "A Political Handbook for the Environmental Movement." *The Washington Post National Weekly Edition*, September 19–25, 1988.

Index

ABOUT THE AUTHOR

CHARLES S. MACK is President and CEO of the Business–Industry Political Action Committee in Washington, D.C., the "leadership PAC of the business Community." His career spans 35 years of corporate and association management and political involvement at national and state levels. Mack has been president of a trade association, a senior public affairs executive of a multinational food manufacturer, and a consultant to companies and associations. He also served on the staffs of the Republican National Committee and the U.S. Chamber of Commerce. Mack teaches government relations at George Washington University's Graduate School of Political Management. He is author of *The Executive's Handbook of Trade and Business Associations* (Quorum, 1990) and *Lobbying and Government Relations* (Quorum, 1989).